# EDUCATION, SOCIETY AND HUMAN NATURE

By the same author:

KARL POPPER

# EDUCATION, SOCIETY AND HUMAN NATURE
## An Introduction to the philosophy of education

ANTHONY O'HEAR
*Department of Philosophy*
*University of Surrey*

ROUTLEDGE & KEGAN PAUL LIMITED
London, Boston and Henley

First published in 1981
by Routledge & Kegan Paul Ltd,
39 Store Street,
London WC1E 7DD,
9 Park Street,
Boston, Mass. 02108, USA, and
Broadway House,
Newtown Road,
Henley-on-Thames, Oxon RG9 1EN
Printed in Great Britain by
Billing & Sons Limited
Guildford, London, Oxford and Worcester
© Anthony O'Hear 1981

British Library Cataloguing in Publication Data

O'Hear, Antony

Education, society and human nature.
1. Education - Philosophy
I. Title
370.1          80-41776

ISBN 0-7100-0747-7
ISBN 0-7100-0748-5 Pbk

To the memory of my parents

# CONTENTS

...for they were educated men, and education is in itself a *cordon sanitaire* for the individual against the mass in his own soul.

(Elias Canetti, 'Auto da Fé', p. 377)

# PREFACE

This book has grown out of lectures I gave at the University of Jos in Nigeria to students in the postgraduate summer schools in education in 1978 and 1979. I am grateful to the students I taught there for stimulating me in my thinking on the philosophy of education to the extent of making me want to write a book about it. Their backgrounds and concerns were naturally very different from my own, and they threw my presuppositions into sharp relief. The lively reactions of the Jos students undoubtedly helped me greatly in the formulation and development of my ideas.

I have tried to write an introduction to the philosophy of education. On the scope of such an introduction, I would make two points. First, although in the light of my philosophizing I make proposals about the overall goals of schooling and the curriculum, I make no attempt to spell out a curriculum in any detail. As I stress in the Introduction, the detailed application and development of such general aims as may be established philosophically must be left to curriculum experts, and I am certainly not trying to do their work in an inexpert way. Second, as I suggest in the Conclusion, an introduction to the philosophy of education can hardly avoid being at the same time an introduction to philosophy itself. Obviously, the philosophical issues raised in such an introduction cannot be exhaustively treated there. In order both to avoid giving any impression of completeness in what I have written, and to locate the philosophical concerns of this book in the mainstream of philosophy, I have from time to time related what I am saying to the work of major philosophical figures, such as Locke, Kant, Wittgenstein, Quine and Popper. In doing this, I have attempted not to give my readers anything approaching a complete understanding of the ideas of these figures, but rather to indicate to those who may be interested the source of some of the arguments I am considering, and to suggest the direction of further problems and complexities, which they might like to investigate for themselves.

Apart from the stimulation I received from the Jos students, I would like to acknowledge a considerable debt in writing this book to my colleague at Surrey, David E. Cooper. Not only did he read and comment on my manuscript as a whole, but he allowed me to draw freely in my chapters 1 and 6 on some of the arguments in his 'Illusions of Equality' (Routledge & Kegan Paul, 1980). It is worth adding here that although there are quite large disagreements between Mr Cooper and myself in some of our conclusions, this in no way lessens my debt to him or my gratitude. Finally, I should also like to thank Patricia Cooper, Ayo Adewole, Robin Haack and David Godwin, with whom I have discussed various matters connected with this book, and who have all helped me in various ways.

May 1980                                                              A.O'H.

# INTRODUCTION
# Philosophy and education

There are obviously general questions about the aims and purposes of education, which are broadly philosophical. Given that in educating we are trying to prepare our children for adult life, what we will want to achieve in educating will be determined by what we think desirable in adult human beings. Thus it would be quite possible for a man, because of his general values and beliefs, to want to educate his children differently from the way children are generally educated in his society. Of course it is true that in any society, education is an important means of socialization, but one of the things I will show in this book is that we can have educational ideals which can be distinguished from the actual functions a particular educational system might serve, and which a sociologist might study. In speaking of the philosophy of education, part of what is being spoken of is the systematic exposition and defence of the aims one thinks education ought to have, beyond any social functions it actually has or can be seen as having.

One's philosophy of education, then, will be distinct from a sociology of education; reflecting one's values and concept of what men ought to be, as opposed to what they might be in any particular society. It also, as I shall show, reflects one's ideals for society as a whole. In saying that a philosophy of education reflects one's concept of what men ought to be, it can be distinguished from a psychology of education. Human nature is not something that is just given. It is something we can make something of, in the light of how we conceive ourselves and others. Of course, there are many empirical or factual constraints on what can be done here; in education, there are constraints affecting a child's rate of development and capacity to learn, to assimilate and to live with others. All these are undoubtedly important matters in education, to be dealt with in the psychology of education. So also are questions relating to the efficacy of particular teaching methods, tests and so on. But what we are aiming at overall in education transcends the empirically given. It depends on our ideas as to how men should be and how they should live.

So a philosophy of education will attempt to specify a set of educational aims, justifying them in the light of our general ethical values. In the light of the aims fixed on, we will be able to give some general account of what it is we will want our children to have learned by the time their education is over. Not all education is formal education, but for the purposes of this book, and to keep things in manageable proportions, what I am primarily talking about here is formal education. However, in giving a general idea of what children ought to have mastered on leaving school, it is not for a philosopher to plan a curriculum in detail. This is for subject experts, curriculum planners and psychologists. However, fundamental decisions on what should be aimed at in the curriculum are matters of value, and should be discussed philosophically. There are also some very general things that can be said about the presuppositions of learning and understanding in any sense, which are philosophical in nature, and these too will be discussed in the course of this book. Something will also be said about the question of moral education, so far as what is at stake is theoretical rather than practical.

In stating boldly that the philosophy of education is concerned with educational aims, I am running counter to a tendency that has been present in much recent and worthwhile work in the area. This tendency has been to say that it is not for philosophers to lay down direct prescriptions to people working in various fields, but rather to adopt a second-order stance to human activities. What philosophers should do is accept what the experts are doing, and confine their attentions to examining the central concepts and presuppositions of the various activities. Only in this indirect way should philosophers seek to influence what is actually done in any field. In the philosophy of education, the following is a representative statement of the position:

> The philosopher's job is not to deduce purported educational implications from his general doctrines any more than it is to derive purported legal, historical or scientific implications....Education, in particular, must be taken as seriously in its own right as science is taken by the philosophy of science (Scheffler, 1973, p.19).

Similarly, R.S.Peters wrote at one time, with apparent approval, of philosophy having undergone a revolutionary change in the twentieth century. Peters saw the effect of this change being to rule out as illegitimate the attempts by earlier philosophers of education to lay down high-level educational directives, based on their conceptions of the good life and a good society (cf. Peters, 1966, pp.15-9 and 1973c, p.122). Conceptual analysis and the examination of presuppositions undoubtedly form part of the philosopher's task, but philosophers of education should surely not refrain from the discussion of goals and the laying down of educational directives, albeit at a high level. Despite what Scheffler says, it is not at all clear that education is something in its own right, in the way science may be. For the aims of science are clear and generally accepted by all scientists (they may perhaps be summarized as the explanation, prediction and manipulation of nature by means of general and quantifiable theories), but in education many disputes range around just what educational aims should be.

In other words, there is no general consensus as to what education is. Or, to put it yet another way, there may be many different concepts of education in different societies. So, even if we succeed in satisfactorily exploring the logical geography of the concept of education in one society or that favoured by one group of educators, we may still have done nothing towards deciding which concept of education is desirable and why, and this is surely a question of the utmost philosophical importance. But once we begin to deal with this question, we can hardly avoid laying down educational directives.

So one thing I am attempting here is to show how people's general systems of values and beliefs will affect what they think education should be. Thus in Chapter 1 I take a particular view of education, and show how it will be attacked from various ethical, religious and socio-political viewpoints. I then, in Chapter 2, outline and defend a scheme of education against the background of some general views and ideals for society, which I also attempt to defend. In Chapter 3, I say more about certain very basic tendencies in human nature which make mutual human understanding and learning possible. In Chapter 4 I consider some implications of the scheme of Chapter 2 for the curriculum, while in Chapter 5 I consider how moral education might be thought of, and what its aims might be. Finally, in Chapter 6, I deal with certain consequences of the view of education defended here for social policy as far as it has a bearing on educational matters.

# 1 OBJECTIONS TO LIBERAL EDUCATION

## LIBERAL EDUCATION

There is a standard view of education which is (or was until recently) enshrined in many of the educational practices and institutions of most western countries, as well as of countries influenced by the west. I do not wish to identify this view with any particular writer, because its assumptions are so widely held that many would take them almost for granted. Moreover, what I am interested in at this point is not elaborating a comprehensive theory of education so much as identifying a set of extremely influential assumptions. These assumptions have been attacked vehemently by their critics, while on the whole they have been unreflectively accepted by their supporters, so it is right to see how they might be defended against criticism. For the sake of brevity and simplicity, I shall refer to these assumptions under the title of liberal education, but nothing hangs on my use of this description, nor on whether other people think of liberal education in different ways.

Education, or the part of overall education which counts as liberal education, on the view being considered consists in initiating students into disciplines such as those of mathematics, science, history, literature and the arts. These disciplines exist in their own right, and there are people expert and authoritative in them. Students are to be taught by teachers who have some claim to authority in what they teach. All involved, students and teachers, are to be guided by the standards of excellence inherent in the disciplines concerned, wherever these standards might lead, even into conflict with church or state. It follows from this commitment to excellence that the disciplines are essentially open, and not to be closed to any competent voice by people either inside or outside the discipline. Students are to be assessed in the light of their achievements in reaching the standards involved. Some, it is to be expected, will be able, under encouragement, to achieve high degrees of excellence in what they study. Some of them will be able eventually to make contributions of their own to the disciplines, continuing and adding to the traditions. On the whole, the disciplines are taught and engaged in for their own sake, because they are recognized to be valuable in their own right and a part of any fully civilized existence. Liberal education, then, is not primarily vocational or practical.

Finally, it recognizes expertise, and works through the recognition of expertise and strives ultimately for work of exceptional quality in the subjects concerned, which by definition is not generally attainable.

The criticisms of liberal education which I wish to consider here fall into five main groups, although, as will be seen, there are connections between them. In the first place, I consider the idea that liberal education really only alienates man from his natural existence and thereby promotes unhappiness. What is taught in a liberal education is actually instrumental in taking people away from a genuinely good life. Then, second, there is the religious viewpoint which sees the proper role of education as being subservient to religion. The good life does not consist in studying things for their own sake, but only for the sake of the faith. Moreover a secular education, which a liberal education will be, may actually conflict with religious truth and values. Third, there is the idea that what I have described as liberal education would be inherently undemocratic and hence undesirable. Then, following on from this, there is the point made by a group of radical sociological writers who argue that liberal education is not only undemocratic and inegalitarian in itself, but that it is actually a direct reflection and reinforcement of western middle-class values, and thus an instrument of social and political control. Finally, there is the general objection to liberal education which is implicit in many of the other objections, that it is bound to fail because what is characteristically taught and learned in a liberal education is irrelevant to the lives of most of those being educated.

I do not claim that the objections I consider in this chapter are the only important attacks that can be made on the liberal concept of education. There is also, and above all, the idea that education and learning should serve particular socio-economic ends and be directed primarily at producing the producers (scientists and technicians) needed by society. I do not consider this position in detail in this chapter because much of the book is a criticism of this view and a defence of non-vocational elements in education. Also, in the next chapter I consider more directly what the proper role for vocational training in education might be. At this point it will be enough to say that advocacy of a purely vocational type of education presupposes that one believes that the lives and jobs that children are being prepared for by their education will be satisfactory for them, whereas I shall argue that one of the main functions of education is to help children extend the range and possibilities of their life choices, and that one of the main functions of learning is to enable people to get more insight into just what a satisfactory way of life might be. Purely vocational education and learning assumes that questions concerning choices of the ends of human activity and choices of role have been settled, and settled satisfactorily.

## LIBERAL EDUCATION IS UNNATURAL

One of the aims of this book is to show how what one thinks
about education cannot be separated from what one thinks about
life generally. What we will examine in this section is the
feeling that there is something unnatural, over-complicated and
unbalanced about the life of a man who has undergone a
liberal education, because the values of such an education
typically serve only to alienate men from each other and from
nature. The reflectiveness and commitment to lonely study
and to the critical attitude which characterize at least the
higher reaches of liberal education are seen in stark and
unfavourable contrast to the virtues typically (if ideally)
associated with a more natural or peasant-like life: simplicity,
fraternity, honour, hospitality, self-sufficiency, manual work,
closeness to nature. The liberal intellectual, because of the
way his mind has been developed, is cut off from the instinctive roots of his existence, and from the fundamental understanding of life and goodness which the peasant, for example,
naturally possesses. The intellectual is clever, but not wise.
Isolated as he is from the common people, he is a prey to
pride and arrogance. He is full of theories and pseudo-science,
but he understands nothing of importance about life. He lives
his life in self-serving groups of people like himself, and sees
himself (falsely) as a member of an elite, elevated above the
rest. But, in fact, the society in which he lives is decadent
and corrupt, politically, morally and culturally. Its decadence
is in part constituted by the flourishing within it of self-
seeking intellectuals and academics, while one of the chief
means by which it corrupts originally innocent children is its
system of education, through which the values and standards
of the intellectual are forced on their initially reluctant minds.

The picture of liberal education corrupting innocent children, and the associated preference for a simple country life
over a refined urban civilization, will be familiar to readers of
the writings of Rousseau and also of Tolstoy, who derived a
great deal in his views on education from his study of
Rousseau (cf. Berlin, 1978, p.240). According to Rousseau
(1762, p.16), in what I am calling a liberal education teachers
teach everything 'except self-knowledge and self-control, the
arts of life and happiness'. They do not attempt to prepare
children to live well, by remaining close to nature and by
building on their natural good instincts, which they would do
if they taught them how to live in harmony with nature by
bending their efforts to the necessities imposed on them by
nature. Instead, teachers, by their own elitism and contempt
for the unlearned, introduce children to the world of vanity,
in which men do not direct their lives towards providing the
necessities for themselves and their families, but more towards
gaining the esteem of others. The world of urban civilization
is in fact a world whose motive force is vanity, and, according

to Rousseau, the vain man can never be fully satisfied because he will always want more and more recognition from others. The simple peasant, on the other hand, can satisfy his material needs, and do so by his own efforts, without needing either to exploit the labour of others or to have the admiration of others. The peasant does not need the useless facts and dead knowledge of liberal education. Presumably only a sort of vanity and elitism could ever motivate a man to spend his life studying uselessly in libraries or laboratories.

Tolstoy, in similar vein, records in his 'A Confession' (1882) how in his youth he had believed in progress and how he had wanted to enlighten the ignorant. But he had not at that time known what to teach, believing as he did that 'the narrow circle of rich, learned and leisured people' (p.45) to which he belonged formed the whole of humanity. Only gradually had he come to see that it was precisely this parasitic, superfluous existence that was blocking for him the genuine understanding of life that simple people, in harmony with nature and its demands, possess instinctively. An education which enfeebles one's natural understanding of life and desire for virtue by inculcating the standards and vanity of a corrupt society should not, then, be imposed on others.

Rousseau's own educational prescriptions in 'Emile' (1762) very largely consist in outlining the sequence of what he calls 'negative education', in which a tutor will prevent a child from being corrupted by society and its ways by keeping him isolated from all undesirable influences, including, on the whole, other people. Education should not enfeeble a person's spirit by exciting unrealizable desires. In the sense advocated by Rousseau and Tolstoy, a natural life is an intellectually restricted one, and to that extent dull and mediocre. But this is not something Rousseau, at least, is afraid of. In fact, he explicitly advocates it: 'The world of reality has its bounds, the world of imagination is boundless; as we cannot enlarge the one, let us restrict the other' (1762, p.45). He also urges us to 'desire mediocrity in all things, even in beauty' (1762, p.372). So Rousseau is quite prepared to sacrifice excellence for a life that appears to him closer to our natural roots.

It is easy to criticize Rousseau and Tolstoy for their conception of natural innocence, for their idea that a pupil can develop free from social influence and for their idealization of the supposedly simple life of the country against that of the city. At the same time, they do raise a question which educators ought to consider seriously. Suppose it were the case that liberal education produced no appreciable gain in goodness or happiness on the part of those educated, or that it actually interfered with one's intuitive sense of goodness and rightness, as Rousseau and Tolstoy claim. Should it then be imposed (or inflicted on) children? We no longer share Socrates's confidence in the equation of virtue and knowledge. At the very least we have to face Mill's question as to the comparative

merits of the lives of a satisfied fool or pig and a dissatisfied
Socrates or man. But there is more to it than that. We are
also, in effect, being asked to provide a justification for
transforming traditional role-oriented peasant societies into open
societies based on liberal educational ideals, bearing in mind
that Tanzania, Libya, Iran, Algeria and China, among others,
may right now be opting against a western-style liberal education (and the advances in technology which may depend on
such an education) and in favour of an alternative closer to
the spirit of Rousseau - at least in an emphasis on fraternity
and simplicity as opposed to individual excellence, choice and
the free play of the mind. To this problem the standard counter
to Mill's question, that only a Socrates or man could be in a
position to answer the question, is obviously no rejoinder, as
we are now considering what is to be done for children, who,
as yet, are in neither the high nor the low category.

The challenge presented to the liberal educationalist is to
defend the pursuit of excellence in learning for its own sake,
against the view that learning is to be valued and pursued
only to the extent that is necessary to enable people to play
their part in the good and natural life. In the case of Rousseau
and Tolstoy, this challenge is posed in a particularly dramatic
way, because they both see the end to which learning should
be subject as the living of a simple, uncompetitive, peasant-
like existence. A natural reply to the challenge would be to
say that men are naturally competitive, and that even peasants
desire bigger farms. The fraternity and equality Rousseau
seeks can be achieved only by laws, probably repressive ones.
To this, Rousseau might reply that the laws would seem
repressive only to those who were used to a life of competition:
to those brought up in a different ideology, such laws might
well appear entirely just and natural.

To reply effectively to the challenge, I think we have to
look less at the uncompetitive nature of a society guided by
Rousseauian principles and more at the nature of learning
itself. Rousseau and Tolstoy place their faith in an understanding of life which they believe to be open to even the
simplest readers of the book of nature. While it is true that
unreflective goodness may be met with in simple, inarticulate
people, it is by no means clear that we can base any general
conception or understanding of the good life directly on such
examples, precisely because of the unreflectiveness of the
people involved (cf. Murdoch, 1970, p.53). Without some
more articulated view of human nature, and nature itself, we
are hardly in a position to say what is good or natural for man,
particularly (but not only) when we are, as now, in a period
of rapid social change and the disintegration of traditional
social structures. In other words, to criticize liberal education
as unnatural for man is to presuppose a correct understanding
of what is natural for him and what a good life would be. But
it is precisely here that knowledge is essential, in order to

avoid mistakes, illusions, false enlightenment and dangerous
oversimplification. Nietzsche's (1881, § 48) words are worth
pondering: ' "Know thyself" is the whole of science. Only when
a man shall have acquired a knowledge of all things will he be
able to know himself. For things are but the boundaries of man.'

To aim at that excellence in learning for which a liberal
education is a preparation is in part to aim at understanding
how things are with man and the world. To say, as the liberal
educationalist says, that learning is to be pursued for its own
sake is in part to say that what is studied cannot properly be
controlled or anticipated by outside influence. For the outside
influence to be justified in doing that it would have, itself,
to be in possession of the truth. We should certainly be sceptical of any claims on the part of political authorities to have
this knowledge, or to be able enthusiastically to articulate
people's unreflective sense of goodness, and wary of the
totalitarian and repressive implications of political attempts to
dissect or curtail learning, even in the name of ideals such as
fraternity or traditional goodness and stability. What Herzen
said over a century ago, on attempts to restrict or control
learning in favour of the utopian ideals of a society based on
peasant or folk virtues, remains valid as a defence of liberal
attitudes to knowledge, and his prophecies have turned out
only too true:

> One cannot stop intelligence because the majority lacks
> understanding, while the minority makes evil use of it...
> Wild cries to close books, abandon science and go to
> some senseless battle of destruction - that is the most
> violent and harmful kind of demagoguery. It will be
> followed by the eruption of the most savage passions
> (quoted in Berlin, 1978, p.299).

In other words, ignorance, especially enforced ignorance, is a
valuable ally to repression, while knowledge and learning and
the critical attitude that it is to be hoped a liberal education
will foster remain the best defences against false enlightenment.

So, even if intellectuals are not happier than others, and
even if as a class they are prone to the failings of silliness
and vanity, exposed so ruthlessly by Tolstoy and Rousseau,
there is a strong argument for saying that a society in which
intellectual life is flourishing and free, and in which its ideals
and discoveries are part of education generally, is likely to be
more desirable than an intellectually closed one, in which there
is a strong likelihood of false ideology and disastrous over-
simplifications being imposed on people, which can hardly lead
to happiness or natural goodness. The point to stress here is
that any present-day attempts to produce the sorts of society
approved of by Rousseau and Tolstoy must inevitably involve
enforced restriction of intellectual activity, and while this
could perhaps be tolerated during a state of emergency (as in
war-time Britain), it is unlikely to be acceptable as a basis for
social reconstruction. The innocence Tolstoy and Rousseau

value is past, if it ever existed. Modern attempts to revive it
would inevitably lose the very unreflectiveness and naivety
that is longed for, because they will involve the conscious
imposition on society of some radical blueprint and the suppression of contrary views. I shall explore this point further
later on, in the next chapter, but we will turn now to arguments directed against liberal education by adherents of dogmatic religions.

## LIBERAL EDUCATION IS IRRELIGIOUS

The claim by religious dogmatists that liberal education is ir-
religious is closely connected to the claim that it is unnatural.
Both claims presuppose that there is a correct understanding
of the nature of man and human life, an understanding which
should guide and dominate other human activities in general
and intellectual activities in particular. To an extent, the
rejoinder made to the arcadian romantic in the last section can
also be made to the dogmatic critic of liberal education, but
further light can be thrown on the undesirability of attempts
to suppress free enquiry and the education system that goes
with it by considering religious claims in their own right.
   For the religious dogmatist, thought and study which goes
beyond what is necessary for the practice of religion is
regarded as worldly and an irrelevant distraction, while cases
of conflict between religion and secular learning are regarded
as showing the evil nature of the unrestrained intelligence.
Children, whose minds are impressionable, should be shielded
from such examples of intellectual pride. In general, too, there
is the idea that education should take place in a religious
rather than a secular atmosphere, in which the prevailing
attitudes are in conformity with the spirit of religion.
   This attitude to education is by no means an irrational one,
given the original premises - that the world and its practices
are basically corrupt and that the truth about the world, man
and God has been revealed in religion. One can indeed sympathize with the attitude of religious-minded parents who wish
to shield their children from what they see as contamination by
a worldly education. In extreme cases, what may arise is a
conflict between two sets of rights, the rights of parents to
bring children up as they conscientiously see fit, and the
right of the children to a general education and educational
opportunities equal to those of their peers, a right defended on
their behalf by the state. This conflict is of its nature irre-
solvable by peaceful compromise when, as in the case of the
Protestant Amish sect in the United States, the demands of the
parents are extreme from an educational point of view.
   The Amish, whose forebears left Holland in the seventeenth
century in search of religious freedom, believe that separation
from the contemporary secular world is essential for salvation.

They live in communities of their own, life being regulated by
biblical and religious texts and local community rules. Some
communities even refrain from the use of modern technological
aids to work and life, such as electricity, cars and telephones.
They also avoid involving themselves with the machinery of the
state, refusing insurance, social benefits, military service and
even litigation. (The cases involving them have been brought
by others on their behalf.) At the same time, they are highly
efficient farmers, well able to support themselves and their
families. They are extremely law-abiding, except in the matter
of education. Here, though, they do come into conflict with
the state, for they believe that formal education for their
children should stop at the eighth grade (age thirteen to four-
teen). At this point, they believe that their children will have
mastered the basic skills of reading, writing and arithmetic
necessary to lead peaceful and fruitful lives in the community
as a whole. Education, as they see it, then begins to concentrate on 'worldly' subjects such as literature, art and music.
Such education is believed to militate against 'humility,
obedience to Christ, and submission to the will of God' (Prance,
1971, p.833). As a result of this, the stricter Amish communities have increasingly come into conflict with the state
authorities, as the latter begin to take a closer interest in
educational standards and practices even in private, rural
schools. Amish brethren have (on the whole unsuccessfully)
attempted to circumvent state insistence on public school education for their children (or education deemed to be equivalent
in standard) by setting up their own schools or simply leaving
one area for another. Some compromises have been reached with
more moderate Amish, but the stricter Amish, who will allow
no dilution of their practices, refuse to allow their children to
be educated as the state sees fit, and prosecutions and court
cases have resulted.

What is of interest to us here is not so much the details of
the cases, or the legal arguments, as the challenge to liberal
educational ideals which groups such as the Amish present.
Despite the fact that they and their children are law-abiding
and self-supporting (and hence obviously have enough education to know how to cope with life on a day-to-day level),
they refuse on religious grounds to allow their children even
to be instructed about the world that lies outside what they
take to be the context of divinely revealed truth. Obviously
they would also have no time for any pursuit of worldly
knowledge for its own sake. While it is possible to have some
sympathy for the attitude of the Amish parents, and to understand the reasons for their attitude, it does strike at the root
of liberal educational thought, which sees education as essentially self-regulating.

An apparently less extreme challenge to liberal thought is
also provided by tendencies within some major religions which,
unlike the Amish, do have high traditions of learning and

culture of their own. While one could think in this context of Catholicism and its emphasis on church schools, Islam is an equally interesting case. In traditional Islam, as in the medieval period in Christianity, theology, law and exegesis were the basic disciplines in education, despite there also being a strong mathematical tradition. Natural science, however, had little place in traditional Islam, perhaps because although critical enquiry was encouraged up to a point, in all areas it was always 'limited by authority and by an overriding concern not to disturb the delicate balance of truth resting on divine revelation' (Brown and Hiskett, 1975, p.95). This remains a crucial aspect of contemporary Islamic attitudes to learning, together with an insistence that education does not upset the traditional values and life-style of the faithful community. Indeed, the scholar is seen as a man and as a member of the religious community before he is a scholar. 'A person has one face and the stuff of his scholarship is but the stuff of which the lives of the members of his community is made', to quote from a speech made in 1971 by an Islamic leader, the Waziri of Sokoto, on behalf of graduates of Ahmadu Bello University in Zaria, Nigeria. The Waziri also made the point that knowledge, although timeless and universal, has a purpose and 'a commitment to a particular world view' (cf. Brown and Hiskett, 1975, pp.467-71). The apparent contradiction involved here can be dissolved by taking the commitment and purpose of knowledge to be the commitment and purpose of those pursuing knowledge. Clearly some scholars may have as the goal of their scholarship the furtherance of Islam, or of Marxism, or of Christianity, or of knowledge itself, and the nature of these goals may lead to differing attitudes to one's research and its limits. (Discussion of the cultural relativist thesis that truth itself is subject to cultural variations is postponed until we look at radical sociological attacks on liberal education later in this chapter; clearly a believer in revealed truth, such as the Waziri, cannot be a cultural relativist.)

So the attitude of traditional Muslim teachers would be that respect for divine authority, rather than independent critical objectivity, is the prime virtue to be cultivated by scholars and educators. The aim of education must be first and foremost to preserve and foster the traditional faith and its practices, and to create a divinely ordered community on earth. There is clearly an opposition between this aim and that of liberal educational thought. This aim is, of course, not peculiar to traditional Islam. Many Catholic educationalists would subscribe to something similar, and so, interestingly and significantly, would educators in the USSR, where the ruling faith is Marxism and the divinely ordered community the classless society. I shall have more to say later in this chapter on the specifically Marxist claim that liberal education is really itself an ideologically closed system, but here it is worth noting that in practice in the Soviet educational system, as Edmund J. King

(1962, p.239) points out,

every item of instruction (every definition in every book) is under the strictest scrutiny: every alien intrusion of non-communist interpretation is also carefully guarded against. If any such intrusion takes place, it is 'contained' and corrected. This ideological safeguarding is far from being merely negative. It acts as an internal leavening or stiffening throughout all subjects and extra-curricular activity.

King goes on to say that the 'spirit of communism' enthuses and vivifies Soviet schools just like a 'good Catholic atmosphere' in Catholic schools, and that Soviet children do indeed 'live and work and think and speak like communists', as they are exhorted to. He also says that people are, on the whole, unwilling to prejudice what they believe to be the gains the system has brought them by reacting against any of this, and while, knowing what we know, we may be somewhat sceptical that this is the real or only reason for acquiescence in the system, one cannot help being struck by the parallel between the line of thought King is drawing attention to and the religious idea that paradise is worth any sacrifice, intellectual or otherwise.

Naturally, not all religious thinkers would insist that the primary aim of education was to support religious practice, nor would they agree with the Amish that study should be confined within limits set narrowly by religious dogma. In Islam, for example, members of Mu'tazilite tradition argued, like St Thomas Aquinas in Catholicism, that men had a religious duty to use their reason to assess the claims of revelation. Both Mu'tazilites and Thomists attempted a synthesis of theology and classical Greek thought, and both were convinced of the ultimate harmony of secular learning and religious revelation. Such religious believers will presumably not be opposed to the intellectual freedom striven for in a liberal education, even while admitting that it may not always be clear in particular cases how reason and revelation are to be reconciled. It is rather the religious fundamentalist, who sees religious truth as opposed to the ways of the world and who sees the claims and discoveries of worldly knowledge as a potential temptation to faith, who will wish to restrict and confine learning and study, and to whom the defender of liberal values in education must provide an answer.

To an extent, what one says about the fundamentalist challenge to liberal thought will depend on what one thinks of the truth-claims of the religion in question, and I am not over-optimistic about convincing a man who believes that he is in full possession of the only way of avoiding eternal damnation that he should allow his children to be exposed to the possibility of turning away from the faith. Nevertheless, it is possible to make the following points. Religions, particularly religions such as Christianity and Islam which are based on revealed books, claim to give the truth about man and the

world. Claims to truth should be able to withstand criticism
and scrutiny if they are not to lose their status as truth-
claims. In the case of religion, however, there is no general
consensus or agreement throughout the world about the status
of the claims of any particular religion, or of religion in
general, nor is there any generally accepted method for the
evaluation of such claims. It is indeed this fact which raises
in a pre-eminent way the possibility of a conflict between faith
and reason. In the light of this, even sincerely convinced
religious people should be prepared to concede, at least as a
theoretical possibility, that the claims they make for their particular revelation might actually be false. Certainly they should
admit that acceptance of them is or ought to be a question of
judgment, on which there can be honest and sincere differences
of opinion. In these circumstances, can it be right for people
to prejudge the truth of these matters in general (by denying
the right of learning and research about man and the world to
flourish freely in the light of critical objectivity), or to pre-
empt such decisions for their children (by shielding them from
the effects of secular thought)? The point is that religious
claims are essentially contestable (something that is implicit in
the very contrast between faith and reason). To refuse to
allow what ought to be a matter of judgment to be tested, or
to foreclose such tests on behalf of others, is to run a severe
risk of being deceived oneself or of being instrumental in the
deception of others. The view attributed to Pascal, according
to which one should believe in Christianity, even though one
is less than fully certain of its truth, because of the mag-
nitude of the loss if one disbelieves and is wrong, surely loses
its force when you consider that there are many competitors to
Christianity, all equally promising terrible consequences to
infidels. You clearly cannot believe them all, which immediately
raises the issue of judgment between them and rational assessment of religious claims.

In fact, many religious people would themselves be unhappy
about the stultifying and possibly self-defeating effects of a
closed religious upbringing, especially in a world which is both
pluralist and changing. Too uncritical and strict an adherence
to old ways makes change, when forced on one from outside by
general changes, painful and difficult. Uncritical teaching of
religion can lead to total loss of faith at the first whiff of doubt.
New problems are best coped with generally by those who have
some practice in independent thought. But these are pragmatic
considerations, and do not provide a full enough answer to the
fundamentalist insistence that reason must be treated as subservient to faith. The considerations about truth and false
enlightenment, which I have developed in the previous paragraph and at the end of the last section, would apply even
where society was stable and a particular religion generally not
criticized in that society. From the point of view of its truth
and acceptability, it is hard to see how any religion essentially

differs from other claims to truth about the overall nature and
purpose of human life. The only way to avoid illusion and
deception here is to allow for full and free examination of the
claims. The alternative strategy runs the risk not only of
massive deception, but also paves the way for repression and
dictatorship. Even if we ourselves decide, as a matter of
rational choice, to abandon reason, have we the right to bring
up our children in such a way that we hope that they will not
be in a position to use their reason to assess and possibly to
modify or abandon the faiths their parents have regarded as
desirable? Indeed, as I shall argue further in Chapter 2, there
is a strong argument to show that even if a religious faith (or
some other overriding social ideology such as Marxism or
Rousseauian romanticism) were true, its full meaning and implications would emerge only when confronted with contrary
opinions. Heresy and secular thought have been instrumental
and vital to the development and understanding of Christian
dogma itself (especially in the patristic period) and of the
significance of Biblical texts (for example, in the Victorian
worry about evolution). Where there is no opposition to a
ruling ideology, stagnation of thought is inevitable, and there
are surely strong grounds for objecting to this, even if one is
convinced of the truth of a religious faith or some other ideology. Perhaps the defender of liberal intellectual ideals can
derive a guarded optimism from the fact that even the most
ideologically repressive religions and regimes appear to be
unable to stifle all vestiges of intellectual dissent from within.
Whether this is so or not, I hope in this section to have illustrated the nature of the conflict between liberal education and
religious fundamentalism, and to have provided some answer on
behalf of liberal education.

## LIBERAL EDUCATION IS UNDEMOCRATIC

The attacks on liberal education which have been considered in
the last two sections arise from a conflict between, on the one
hand, doctrinaire claims about the overriding purpose of human
life and the nature of human happiness, and, on the other,
openness and independence of liberal education and its disciplines. An initial defence of liberal attitudes (to be developed
further in the next chapter) was given on the grounds that
such claims must be open to full and free examination and
criticism, if they are to be distinguished from indefensible and
potentially harmful dogmas. The attacks on liberal education
which will be considered in the next two sections come from a
somewhat different angle. They are based on objections to its
insistence on expertise and excellence, and involve ultimately
an attack on the very idea of authorities in areas of knowledge.
While they object to claims of expertise on behalf of liberal
teachers and academics, the notion of such authority is not in

itself something which religious fundamentalists or even writers such as Rousseau and Tolstoy would necessarily reject, for both these groups of opponents of liberal education appear to agree to setting limits to free enquiry in the name of an authoritatively accepted and imposed blueprint for the direction of human life. The objections to liberal education which we are going to consider next share with the earlier objections the idea that learning must be made to subserve ends outside itself, but the way the end is conceived now involves a deep hostility to the very idea of an expert or an authority on anything.

What I am calling the democratic attack on liberal education amounts in effect to an assertion of an extreme populism: the idea is that only those things which can be fully communicated to everyone, and on which everyone has a view, are really worth teaching. Many readers would no doubt feel that no one could really hold such an extreme view, but as I will show, such a view is implicit in some contemporary writing on education, and it was pretty explicitly advanced by Dewey. Some would no doubt object to this view being tagged 'democratic', but, while I would sympathize with this feeling, there is a certain naturalness about the use of 'democratic' here if only because in the educational sphere Dewey has irrevocably attached this sense to it. (Indeed, this section should serve as a warning against the incautious use of a term whose meaning tends to shift with the political ideology of the person using it.)

Dewey's educational populism interestingly derives from some quite defensible views about the nature of meaning and language, but the derivation itself is highly suspect. According to Dewey (1916, p.16), words and things 'gain meaning by being used in a shared experience or joint action'. Thus I understand the word 'helmet' by becoming aware of the use of helmets in social and public life, by doing which I enter into a partnership with helmet users. What Dewey says here is very reasonable: someone who knew only that the word 'helmet' referred to objects of such and such a shape and size, without realizing the use to which men put such objects, would have a very impoverished understanding of both the word and the thing. Equally, one could hardly be said to understand concepts such as the number 3 or the neutrino in abstraction from the role they play in mathematics or physics, and mathematics and physics are public activities, developed through the co-operation of many people.

In addition to showing that the significance of things for us are, at least in many cases, dependent on the existence of shared activities, Dewey also characterizes human beings as being basically interested in social activity. He points out that communities would be impossible if many of our interests were not social: thus, in addition to the co-operation involved in the satisfaction of basic needs, many of our activities, such as game-playing, theatre-going, love-making or educating, would be impossible for isolated individuals. This is also true and

important, but the 'democratic' conclusions now drawn by Dewey
from our natural interest in social activity and from the derivation of meaning from shared activity simply do not follow.
Having said that all meaning is based in shared activities, he
concludes in effect that the richest meaning is to be found in
activities shared by all. The way in which Dewey comes to
this position seems to be through thinking of societies in
addition to individuals as being enriched by taking part in
shared activities. But he confuses an activity which is shared
with one which is sharable by anyone, and so the ideal of a
society with the greatest possible number of shared activities
is transformed into the ideal of a society all of whose activities
are shared by the greatest possible number. He says that we
can measure the 'worth of a form of social life' by the extent
to which 'the interests of a group are shared by all its members and the fullness and freedom with which it interacts with
other groups' (1916, p.99). The proposition that all meaningful
activities are shared activities is thus misread as implying that
fully meaningful activities are fully shared or sharable by all.
This being so, mediocrity necessarily follows as an ideal,
because excellence in any activity is by definition beyond what
is generally attainable or even appreciable at any given time.
It is highly unlikely that any but the most basic and least
involved activities will be completely sharable by everyone,
even though, as I shall argue in Chapter 6, the attempt to give
everyone some share in the various activities of high culture is
highly desirable.

That I am not misreading Dewey is clear from what he says
about the cultures of democratic and non-democratic societies.
He speaks of a class-divided society as being one in which the
culture of the upper classes is sterile and turned back on itself, their art being showy and artificial and their knowledge
overspecialized, and of 'spiritual' culture and the development
of the inner personality as being futile and rotten precisely
because it cannot be freely and fully communicated (cf. 1916,
pp.84,122). Although there is indeed something unhappy, even
tragic, about people who are unable to share their feelings and
experiences for whatever reason, and however undesirable
class-divided societies are in many ways, there seems no reason
why cultural sharing has to involve everyone for a strong culture to flourish. The briefest survey of world history leads
one immediately to the conclusion that Dewey's view about culture is manifestly false. If one were to compare Periclean
Athens with Harold Wilson's England, Renaissance Florence with
the output of Soviet socialist realism one might be tempted, let
us hope mistakenly, to conclude precisely the opposite. At any
rate, it makes one wonder how a thinker of the reputation of
Dewey could have been so blinded to the facts by his own
prejudices. Equally, as the example of classical Athens again
shows, it is the sheerest sentimental trash to want to believe
that any society which values a plumber less than a philosopher

will produce neither philosophy nor pipes that hold water
(Babs Fafunwa, 1967, p.56). In democracy on the other hand,
according to Dewey (1916, p.87), we have at least the possibility of 'associated living' and of 'conjoint communicated
experience'. Indeed democracy is ideally for Dewey a form of
life, rather than a mode of government. It should be the
society with the greatest number of points of contact between
individuals, and the greatest number of viewpoints being
brought to bear on any given subject. No doubt it is true that
in many areas (such as science) the more distinct and worthwhile opinions that can be assembled the better, but it is hard
not to conclude that Dewey does not see the greatest number
of viewpoints in purely numerical terms, convinced as he is
both of the 'intrinsic significance of every growing experience'
(1916, p.109) and that the more numerous the ties that bind a
group, and the more who participate in those ties, the better
the quality of life of the group as a whole. He goes so far as
to say that a curriculum must be selected with a view to
emphasizing what concerns the experiences shared by the
widest group, what connects with the common interests of men
as men and what is relevant to the problems of living together
(cf. 1916, pp.191-2).

So, from some apparently abstract ideas on the nature of
meaning, Dewey develops a view of society and education
involving an extreme populism. It is interesting and significant
that a similar progression of thought to Dewey's can be found
in Marxism. Thus Marx and Engels (1845, p.78) claim that
'only in community with others has each individual the means
of cultivating his gifts in all directions', which would be
plausible if it meant that most meaningful activities and subjects
are publicly developed and shared, but implausible, to say the
least, if it is taken, as it is by Mao, to be an attack on private
activity and independent thought - for him, liberalism of this
sort is 'a corrosive which eats away unity, undermines cohesion,
causes apathy and creates dissension'. A true communist should
be 'more concerned about the party and the masses than about
any private person' and 'subordinate his personal interests to
those of the revolution' (Mao Tse-Tung, 1937, p. 33). So anything that is private, personal and not universally communicable
is worthless and the fruit of undesirable social division. Educators, in Dewey's (1938, p.85) view, should seek to make
schools themselves into micro-democracies (in Dewey's sense of
democracy), in which all individuals can contribute some viewpoint, in which teachers are seen as only the leaders of group
activities or intellectual companions of their pupils, rather than
authorities, and in which 'the teacher's suggestion is not a
mould for a cast-iron result but is a starting point to be
developed into a plan through contributions from the experience
of all engaged in the learning process.'

Similar conclusions to those of Dewey, though divorced from
the reflections of meaning that underlie his, can be found in

more recent writers on education. Thus Rosen and Rosen (1973, p.38), in their study of the language of primary school children, speak of teachers and pupils joining in shared investigations rather than the teacher 'holding the centre of the stage' and 'indulging in histrionic performances and feats of skill with the chalk on the blackboard'. They also speak of good schools as being those that use 'real language' for 'real purposes' and which aim to turn 'the increasing flow of experience into connected usable sense' (1973, p.255). A similar view of the classroom as a context for negotiations between all participants, teachers included, is held by Everett Reimer (1971, p.90), who asserts in support of this that a philosophy of freedom must begin by denying the right of any man to impose truth on another.

What all this democratization of the classroom amounts to is a repudiation of the teacher as an authority on what he is teaching, and a claim that pupils have as much to contribute to any worthwhile study as the teacher himself. For the time being, we can simply assert against this position that nothing that has so far been said has demonstrated the falsity of the common-sense view that in many subjects the truth is nothing if not cast-iron, and is in any case unlikely to be open to discovery by children, unless the teacher is exercising his authority surreptitiously by dishonestly controlling the outcome. Equally, Dewey has not shown that all worthwhile knowledge arises from 'real-life' problems, nor do his reflections on meaning do anything to justify his advocacy of cultural mediocrity and endless group discussion of all decisions and discoveries. To find a more thoroughgoing repudiation of the teacher's authority, and defence of the idea that all currently accepted propositions should be regarded as open to question and discussion by pupils, we must turn to the next group of opponents of liberal education, who see the claims of liberal educationalists to be transmitting objective knowledge as spurious and, covertly, politically motivated.

## LIBERAL EDUCATION INVOLVES CLASS CONDITIONING

An influential group of writers from broadly left-wing sociological backgrounds have recently made pleas for radical reforms in education, or even the abandonment of schooling altogether (e.g. Young, 1971 and 1977; Reimer, 1971; Illich, 1971; Freire, 1972; Postman and Weingartner, 1971). The starting point for these analyses is often the fact that even where education has been free and open to all for some time, the actual achievement of pupils has still by and large reflected class differences. In England, for example, middle-class children still achieve far more in terms of examination results, university places and so on (to say nothing of the social advantages associated with these) than their working-class contemporaries. The levelling effect of mass education, which many people hoped for, has just not come about. The inference which has been drawn is that what goes on in traditional schools with liberal conceptions of education, in terms of their structures and assessments, of the content of what is taught and of the language in which it is taught, is itself a reflection of the values of the ruling class. Hardly surprising, then, that members of the oppressed class find greater difficulty with schooling than those born and brought up in an environment in which these values are accepted and propagated. Most schools, to put it bluntly, teach middle-class knowledge, in middle-class language with middle-class methods (teachers as author-ities and assessors), thus reinforcing existing social divisions and inequalities. Working-class children exposed to such schools and assessments will naturally tend to do badly, because what is taught has very little relevance to their lives or ways of thinking.

In place of traditional schooling, the writers being considered recommend, like Dewey, that schools (if they exist at all) should concentrate on co-operative and non-authoritarian investigations into real-life problems. Where the sociologists go beyond what Dewey says is in their identification of the criticized aspects of liberal education with the machinations of an oppressive dominant class. It is this aspect of the sociological criticism of liberal education and the relativism that underlies it that I will be con-cerned with here. (I shall have more to say on the extent to which education can or should be aimed at social levelling in Chapter 6.) The class domination thesis is usually combined with a claim to the effect that truth and reason (or, more prop-erly, what are called truth and reason) are no more than arbitrary conventions and constructs which liberal educational theorists and practitioners mistakenly erect into absolute norms, thus oppressing the unfortunate pupil who deviates from them, who might in fact be doing so because he is constructing for himself an equally valid view of the world. The way in which these various themes are connected is well brought out in the following representative passage by Michael F. D. Young (1971, pp.5-6):

> If logic, 'good' reasoning, asking questions, and all
> the various sets of activities prescribed for the
> learner, are conceived of from one perspective as sets
> of social conventions which have meanings common to
> the prescribers, then the failure to comply with the
> prescriptions can be conceived, not as in the everyday
> world of the teacher as 'wrong', 'bad spelling or
> grammar' or 'poorly argued and expressed', but as
> forms of deviance. This does not imply anything about
> the absolute 'rightness' or 'wrongness' of the teachers'
> or pupils' statements, but does suggest that the inter-
> action involved is in part a product of the dominant
> defining categories which are taken for granted by the

teacher. Thus the direction of research for a sociology
of educational knowledge becomes to explore how and
why certain dominant categories persist and the nature
of their possible links to sets of interests or activities
such as occupational groupings.

According to Reimer (1971, p.92), part of the answer to the
implied question of the last sentence would be that schools are
'obviously as much designed to keep children from knowing
what really intrigues them as to teach them what they ought to
know', and he sees this as part of the great process of secrecy,
mystification and inoculation against real learning by which we
are all prevented from knowing how our lives are actually controlled by military establishments, multi-national companies and
ruling classes generally. For Althusser (1971, pp.145-9), too,
education, like other apparatuses of ideology, is seen as controlled by the dominant force in society, here capitalism, and
used by capitalism as the primary means of enforcing and
reproducing its ideology. Illich is even more specific, seeing
the education system, with its bureaucracy of degrees and
examinations and its packaging of knowledge into subjects, as a
prime way of indoctrinating future consumers with the values
of consumerism and institutionalized life in general (Illich, 1971,
esp. Ch.3).

The division of the curriculum into subjects is itself an
integral part of the controlling mechanism. In the first place,
such divisions give the impression that there is a set order to
knowledge, and that in each of its branches there is a pyra-
midal power structure with experts at the top and ignorant
objects at the bottom, who need to be filled up with deposits
of knowledge (Freire, 1972, pp.45-6). Those who do not comply
with the curricular divisions, or who cannot see the point of
them, will make no progress up the pyramids, while those who
do progress will tend to be docile and accepting of authority
and the status quo. Middle-class children, being far more used
to rigid divisions and categories and abstract concepts, thus
have a hidden subsidy before schooling starts; while those
whose lives are dominated by the fluid and common-sense attitudes of folk knowledge are at a definite disadvantage. (I shall
have more to say on this point in discussing the views of
G.H.Bantock in Chapter 6.) Moreover, as Bernstein (1971, p.56)
puts it, disciplines organized hierarchically make of the knowledge involved 'private property with its own power structure
and market situation . . . (in which) children are encouraged
to work as isolated individuals with their arms around their
work' - again something favouring the solitary bourgeois child
over the communally minded slum dweller. Assessments, too,
are objectionable, because behaviour is only categorized as able
or stupid in the light of the social-class judgments or other
expectations of those who are doing the categorizing (cf. Keddie,
1971, p.155; Postman and Weingartner, 1971, p.97) - who are
naturally middle-class educational bureaucrats. Even if the

bureaucrats were not middle-class, and the categories were re-
thought, assessment would still involve labelling, snubbing and
excluding - and hence, at least to Sarup (1978, pp.79-80),
would remain objectionable. Of course, it may be objected here
that some pupils actually do know more than others and that
they just are better informed than others. Similarly, teachers
are in an authoritative position relative to their pupils, and
they have a duty not to relinquish their authority. To this the
standard reply is that all human beings are meaning makers,
students as much as teachers, and that there is no absolute
truth to which anyone has direct access; once this is understood, it is hard to say whose meanings are most valuable.
Anything else smacks of an objectionable epistemological
positivism.

   According to Esland (1971), an epistemology which holds
that there are truths about reality which we can sometimes
grasp is fundamentally dehumanizing, because it presents as
given (or legitimizes) a world which in fact is and has to be
continually interpreted by human agents. Esland appeals to
Wright Mills (e.g. 1939) at this point, who was fond of asserting that standards of truth and falsity and of logical validity have changed from society to society. Clearly, though,
more than actual variation in standards of acceptability is
needed to show that any perception of the world is due to the
activity of the perceivers in question and can make no claim to
absolute truth. Unfortunately, actual argument and example are
rather thin on the ground here. Three strands can, however,
be recognized. First, it is said that perception itself depends
on the activity of perceivers, their expectations, points of view
and so on. No doubt this is true, and it has in a sense been
shown by psychological experiments. But it does not follow from
this that we cannot distinguish between better and worse perceptions, between those that pragmatically, at least, are more
useful for our future conduct. Indeed, it seems obvious that
we can do this, and hence give some content to the distinction
between true and false perceptions. Second, it is said that the
categories and concepts we use to divide the world depend on
our interests, theories and expectations. Much play is made
here of cultural diversity in schemes of categorization. Again,
the point is quite correct and needs to be made to correct a
naive form of realism about our view of the world (the world to
a dog or a Martian doubtless looks quite different). But again,
we must guard against too hastily concluding too much,
because from what has so far been said it does not follow that
really there is no table on which I am writing. Even if we
create concepts, we do not create the objects they refer to,
and we are sometimes able to discover (as in the case of
phlogiston) that there are in fact no such objects. We impose
our concepts and theories on nature, but nature kicks back,
as Popper has put it. So it is sometimes possible to distinguish
truth from falsity within a system of concepts (in the case of

my example, the system of physical-object concepts). Also, nothing has been said so far to show that it might not be possible to judge between theoretical systems. I shall have more to say about the basis on which such comparisons might be made in Chapter 3, but for now it is enough to make the obvious point that the conceptual scheme of an uneducated child is hardly likely to be as successful in the prediction and manipulation of nature as that of Einstein. Equally, while a conceptual scheme could be imposed on nature that divides animals into those that run, those that fly and those that crawl, and then subdivides each group into travellers by day and travellers by night (and the Navaho Indians do have such a scheme, cf. Lévi-Strauss, 1966, p.39), it would be idle to pretend that such a scheme was as useful in the explanation and prediction of natural phenomena as that of modern zoology. So conceptual schemes can sometimes be judged in terms of their success and failure in the tasks they are addressed to.

Third and finally, Young (1977, pp.236-52) in particular has appealed, at least in a qualified way, to the idea that mathematics is a human construction, rather than a set of facts independent of human activity. The point of doing this in this context is presumably that mathematics is often taken as a model of certainty and security in reasoning, in contrast to the rather uncertain status of much of our physics, for example. Constructivism in mathematics is a theory designed to show that mathematics does not tell us facts about an ideal, Platonic world of unchanging, perfect, impermeable mathematical objects, but rather works out the implications of certain human constructions (such as numbers or geometrical shapes) and our decisions about how they are to be manipulated.

However, against Young's appeal to this view of mathematics, it must be stressed that constructivism does not sanction the view that there are no experts in mathematics, nor would it lead us to conclude that the criteria for success in mathematical reasoning were determined in any way by power structures, either inside or outside mathematics. (Young, 1971, pp.6,8, appears to hold that such criteria are related in a significant way to characteristics of the socio-economic order.) There would, in fact, be nothing inconsistent in holding, on the one hand, that all mathematical theorems were the results of human decisions and inventions, and, on the other, in introducing people to these results in a highly authoritarian manner, any more than there would be anything inconsistent in teaching the grammar of a language in an authoritarian way. It just does not follow from the fact that a practice is based in human conventions, or that there is no transcendent or divine criterion of truth in it, that there cannot be expertise in it, or that it is open to any unqualified beginner to change the practice with impunity as and when he pleases. There would be something mildly pathetic about an uneducated child who refused to use plural verbs with plural nouns or to work with Euclidean axioms on the grounds that he was objecting to the conventional nature of the dominant defining categories and their links to sets of interests or occupational groupings. I shall have more to say shortly about the role of authorities and hierarchies within subjects. For now it is necessary to state only that it remains obscure just how any links to extra-curricular interests might lead mathematicians (as opposed, perhaps, to sociologists of mathematics) to accept as valid any particular pattern of mathematical reasoning, or to incline to one theory or another of the nature of mathematics. The reason for this obscurity is fundamentally that mathematicians in their mathematical work will as a rule see success in terms of mathematical problems and results, a point of view which leaves no room for the incursion of political or class prejudices. Indeed, in the absence of detailed examples to show how particular calculations and criteria for mathematical validity are related to characteristics of the socio-economic order, one may wonder just what the claim that they do would amount to, or whether it actually has any intelligibility at all.

More generally, it is worth remarking here that logical and mathematical deviance among logicians and mathematicians is neither so widespread nor so extensive as Esland and Wright Mills suggest. In logic, for example, no contradiction in standard classical logic becomes a theorem of any deviant logic. Deviant logics tend to be more restrictive than classical logic as to what inferences are permitted. Moreover, the amount of logical deviance empirically discoverable among foreign tribes must, at the pain of unintelligibility of native idioms, be strictly limited. If, for example, we translated a certain native word as 'and' and then we found that the natives consistently refused to assent individually to each of the sentences p, q and r, although they assented to p, q and r when they were conjoined by this word, we should have to question whether the word was really to be translated by the English 'and' or in some other way. Taking the latter alternative would, of course, show a difference in the native language (no word exactly equivalent to 'and') rather than in what reasonings they accept as valid. The latter alternative is surely preferable to the former, for if we took the former we would be making the behaviour of the natives - in refusing to assent to p, q and r when taken individually, and yet accepting the conjunction of sentences when joined by what we are translating as 'and' - so bizarre as to be incomprehensible. As I shall suggest in considering relativism again, from a slightly different point of view, in Chapter 3, a main function of translation is to make the behaviour of those whose language we are translating intelligible. The point being made here is that a translation of a native language that made native reasoning appear too divergent from our own would fail in this function, and hence be unacceptable as a translation.

We can accept that much of our picture of the world is based on particular ways of looking at it, on the adoption of schemes of classification which might in other circumstances be different, and on theories which are not simply read off from the facts but which are the product of the imagination of those who propose them. But the fact that one scheme of classification could conceivably be replaced by another does not mean that the statements we make when we use it are thereby arbitrary or untrue, nor does the work of scientific theorizing stop with the imagination of scientists. There is also the work of testing and evaluating the theory, and, in due course, of rejecting it if it turns out to be untenable in the face of the facts. (The admission of a degree of slack in determining just when a theory has become untenable does not mean that there are not points when it is impossible to deny that one theory is definitely better than another, or that a particular theory is just too problematic to be maintained in its current form.) So, against Esland and those who write like him, it is quite possible to hold both that the world is interpreted by human agents and that we can judge that some of our interpretations are better than others. In other words, epistemology can fully admit the activity of human beings in interpreting and theorizing about the world without lapsing into subjectivism or relativism. The possibility of improving and testing our theories, the fact that some bridges work while others collapse and that we can some-times explain why this is so, show that relativism can be avoided and that our modes of thinking are not unbreakable cages. It is, of course, true that at any given moment we are making certain assumptions about truth and reasoning, and idle to think that we can ever think or reason at all without some presuppositions, but this in itself is quite harmless for the objectivist so long as he is able at the next moment to defend or criticize these assumptions, or some of them, should they come under attack or appear to be impeding progress.

So the epistemological considerations adduced by Young and his colleagues do not support the view that criteria of truth are arbitrary or determined by purely sociological consider-ations. What they say does not undermine in any radical way the assumptions that there can be genuine expertise in various fields and that teachers ought to be authorities or experts. In fact, even if relativism were correct, there would still be some-thing disingenuous in thinking that universally recognized cultural achievements such as Euclidean geometry, Newtonian physics, Marxist economics or even how to make a pot could effectively be taught in a totally non-authoritarian manner, or that untaught beginners could usefully criticize them. But clearly, once a degree of truth and openness is admitted in the various areas of knowledge, a line of authority from experts down to beginners is necessary so that beginners can gain from the fruits of the search for truth at the outside edge of a discipline.

Sociological critics of liberal education would be on firmer ground than in basing what they say on a generalized relativism if they were to point out that in non-scientific subjects at least there is a constant likelihood of syllabuses and curricula centring on topics which are of interest to (if not in the interest of – there is a constant confusion between the two) those who are teaching, rather than those who are taught. What I have in mind here is the sort of case in which there is a well-developed indigenous tradition in the subject in question, and foreign standards and texts are imposed as paradigms from outside. An example would be Northern Nigeria, where English rather than Islamic literature became the main focus of humanities teaching, and it could be claimed with some justice that one culture was trampling on another even though that other was more firmly based in the lives of the people. Equally, one could object to concentrating on English political history in African village schools.

While fully allowing that examples such as these are of insensitive behaviour, they do not seem to me to strike at the roots of the liberal concept of education. They seem rather to point to defects in the sensibilities and knowledge of particular educators. Liberal education strives for excellence and openness in all its disciplines. Even at the lower levels of a discipline there is ideally a knock-on effect from the spirit and discoveries made by those at the higher levels. What counts as excellent in a particular area is, or ought to be, determined by standards internal to the subject in question. A study of history that takes political history as the sole or main area to be studied is, by virtue of that fact alone, an inadequate history, an inadequate reading of the past. So there are good reasons in the subject itself for not concentrating on English political history, and presumably, in a similar way, literary critics could give literary reasons for valuing Islamic texts. The point, then, is that the disciplines forming a liberal education can be seen as having standards of excellence internal to them, which might be perverted by practitioners because of sociological or historical factors, but which transcend particular places and times.

Some people will, of course, deny this last point, but care is needed to see just how the social influence is supposed to work. It is particularly hard to see in the case of mathematics and the natural sciences, whose problems and theories are largely generated by the state of the subject at the time, and where the answers are controlled by nature or by the rigours of deductive argument. What the sociological determinist will have to do is show in some detail how particular episodes in the history of science, such as the pre-Einsteinian controversy on the ether, are explicable in economic or political terms, rather than in terms of the problems the scientists were facing. For one of the most notable things about science is the way in which people from quite opposed political and social backgrounds can agree on what is scientifically valuable or relevant. Cases

where extra-scientific considerations have interfered with the
course of science, such as the Galileo case or the Lysenko
affair, stand out in scientific history as exceptional and universally condemned by scientists; which is not surprising, as
it is hard to see how any successfully developing study of
nature, confronted as it is with natural facts, could for long be
moved rather than impeded by political or social considerations.

It may be true that there is a socio-history of science to be
written, showing, as Kuhn (1962) has suggested, that science
is typically dominated by cliques and authorities within the
scientific community who prevent, actively or passively, the
emergence of views contrary to current orthodoxy. Even if this
were so, however, it would still have to be shown that the
scientific orthodoxy somehow reflected prevailing orthodoxies
outside science (that American scientists were currently bourgeois capitalist in their science and Russians Marxist-Leninist
or state capitalist in theirs). But against Kuhn and those who
think like him, it is highly questionable that any purely sociological account of science, which took no account of the
scientific problems and the responses of nature to them, could
provide insight into the behaviour of scientists. This is because this behaviour is largely a response to those problems.
On the other hand, a grasp of the methods and problems of
the subject without any sociological or psychological knowledge
of the scientists involved, communally or individually, will allow
one to construct a coherent account of much of the scientific
behaviour of particular scientists, even though from this perspective some episodes might appear inexplicable. These will be
the episodes like that of Michelson sticking to his ether hypothesis until the 1930s, or where the behaviour of an individual or
group is not what would be expected from a scientist concerned
solely and rationally with scientific problems, and where explanations of an external sort would have to be sought, for example
that the scientist was out to defeat a rival or acting under
political pressure. So it is only where scientists deviate from
strictly scientific standards that psychological or sociological
explanations of their behaviour become relevant to explaining it.

What this shows is that science and the study of nature have
their own standards and yardsticks, to which the diversely
motivated and committed individual scientists have to conform if
they are to make a mark as scientists. The fact that science
throws up its own problems and solutions, and new problems in
the wake of these solutions, also suggests that what scientists
(as opposed to technologists) are interested in cannot be fully
or adequately explained in terms of extra-scientific or practical
interests, such as developing a bomb or curing a disease. Not
only is the history of theoretical physics quite remote from the
practical applications of the subject, but research directed to
narrow practical aims often ends up being less influential in
practical terms than pure research aimed at a deep understanding
of some aspect of matter. The limitations, even from a practical

point of view, of purely practical research without a strong
underlying theory are in fact generally admitted by scientists,
who realize that it is more profitable all round to be interested
in producing explanatory theories, and to be guided in research
by the problems that arise from this rather than by specific
practical interests.

Something of the sort might also be true in the arts and the
humanities, although artistic expression and literary and historical analyses are more obviously open to influences from
outside the subjects, as the control of unideological nature is
not so obviously effective. Nevertheless, there is such a thing
as the objective problem situation confronting a historian, or
even an artist or composer, and to which he is responding,
even though part of what he considers relevant or wants to
express may be a direct reflection of his socio-historical circumstances. Thus Schoenberg responded to what he considered
the breakdown of tonality - a problem intelligible as such only
in musical terms and to which he developed a musical solution -
in terms of what he described as the logic of human thought.
This case is particularly interesting because, although Schoenberg was consciously influenced by a general cultural movement
for clarity of thought and expression which can plausibly be
seen as having its roots in the social circumstances of the time,
what he actually had to do in order to achieve his goal was
produce a musical solution to a musical problem. In other words,
even in the case of art, general ideological ideals have to be
translated into artistic problems and solutions, and ultimately
judged as such. In any case, one of the most important aspects
of the liberal concept of excellence in the disciplines is that
they should be fundamentally open, that they should not be
dominated or controlled by extra-disciplinary considerations
(such as a church or artistic commissar) and that anyone may
contribute his ideas to the discipline, whatever his personal,
political or social motivations. Thus even if Marxists had
originally been in the forefront of developing economic history,
this is now an accepted and essential element in history, because economic historians have been able to show the explanatory power of economical analyses. Even if Prokoviev, writing
a work like 'Alexander Nevsky', was attempting to respond to
a demand to produce music available to large masses (as he
put it himself in 'Pravda' in December 1937), the result is to
be judged (and probably in this case ultimately rejected) in
terms of its musical content and value. There are also cases in
subjects such as psychology and sociology where practitioners
are very quick to respond to general cultural climates (such
as the scientistic idea that the intelligible is the quantifiable or
its supposed reverse, a mish-mash of humanism and Marxism),
and where there is indeed something like a gap between one
incommensurable paradigm and another, but this sort of thing
is not characteristic of developed disciplines in which there is
a clear sense of aims, methods and achievements. Once again,

what one has to say is that the response to them will have to be judged in terms of the light they throw in explaining and predicting significant tracts of human behaviour.

Having, then, suggested in some detail that liberal education can be defended by appeal to its ideal of openness against the charges of relativism and bias made by Young and his colleagues, this section can be concluded by a brief look at some of the more specific criticisms they make of liberal educational practices. First of all it is unclear that any sort of education can avoid assessment (or labelling) of students in some way or other. This would seem to be so whatever one might say of the inadequacies of actual examination systems, or the abuse of academic qualifications as job-securing certificates. For education, of whatever sort, involves developing some abilities or skills or knowledge of pupils, so it is surely integral to this process that success should be evaluated in order to know how best to proceed (cf. Barrow, 1978, p.119). Education without evaluation of some sort obviously runs the risk of being hopelessly out of step with the needs and achievements of the individuals being educated. Then again, it is hard to see how, as a matter of convenience at least, a general education could be handled without some curricular divisions, though (as I shall suggest further in Chapter 4) there need be nothing sacrosanct about actual sets of subject divisions, nor, indeed, need what I have been calling separate disciplines be regarded as completely self-enclosed and discontinuous with each other. Finally, against a possible implication of what we saw Bernstein saying (p. 21), it by no means follows that a holistic attitude to knowledge - that all subjects are ultimately interconnected - rules out the possibility of experts and authorities in particular areas. The two points are just not dependent on each other in this way.

## LIBERAL EDUCATION IS IRRELEVANT

I want, finally, to turn to a very general point made frequently by Rousseau, Dewey, Reimer and the Rosens (taking a few examples from those we have looked at), and implicit in much current educational thought. This is the idea that a fruitful education must be based on objects and concepts which are within the real life (i.e. extra-curricular experience) of the children. The sociological twist to this seems to be that working-class children should be given a working-class rather that a middle-class education. (It may not be idle to mention here that this is a rather peculiar response to the fact of class divisions on the part of those who disapprove of them, for it will serve only to intensify them.) Liberal education, of course, is an effective rejection of the demand to take the real life of pupils as a criterion of what should be taught, because it sees subject areas as having their own problems and content which develop at least in part because of the nature of the subject, and hence independently of the individual concerns and backgrounds of those engaged in them.

Now, it may well be, especially at primary level, that the most effective way of introducing topics to children is through their own lived experience, though the current popularity of war comics and space sagas might make one sceptical of too literalistic an adherence to this. Also, it is very unclear in what sense much of the content of 'middle-class' education (Shakespeare, Latin, physics), which middle-class children are supposedly able to absorb because of their home environment, is itself part of that environment. However, the main point that needs to be made here is the extremely restrictive nature of an education which confines itself to children's 'real-life' experience and their own interests and daily problems (unless this is taken in a truistic sense, according to which anything someone is interested in becomes a real-life problem for him). Not only would this mean that most of science, history and art would be closed off from most pupils, but it would also be an effective denial of the idea that education is to be a breaking of barriers and a widening of horizons, intellectual and social. It would in fact be a way of keeping people in the state in which they had been brought up. Of course, it might be that, as with Rousseau, this is what is really wanted, in which case the response made to Rousseau will be appropriate here, but I suspect that with the sociological writers at least it is rather an unintended consequence of the attempt to derive prescriptions from sociological doctrines of the class basis of liberal education.

In the next chapter I elaborate and defend a scheme of education deliberately intended to expand the horizons of pupils beyond those implicit in their day-to-day lives. At this point I will simply reproduce a passage from Thomas Mann's 'Doctor Faustus' which is certainly a useful corrective to the notion that education can or should proceed only by means of the 'relevant'. Mann's narrator is describing the lectures on music given by the eccentric stammerer Wendel Kretschmar that he and his friend, the future composer Adrian Leverkuhn, went to as teenagers in their small home town:

> The lecturer was talking about matters and things in
> the world of art, situations that had never come within
> our horizon and only appeared now on its margin in
> shadowy wise through the always compromised medium
> of his speech. We were unable to check up on it except
> through his own explanatory performances on the
> cottage piano, and we listened to it all with the dimly
> excited fantasy of children hearing a fairy-story they
> do not understand, while their tender minds are none
> the less in a strange, dreamy, intuitive way enriched
> and advantaged. Fugue, counterpoint, 'Eroica', 'con-
> fusion in consequence of too strongly coloured modulations',

'strict style' - all that was just magic spells to us,
but we heard it as greedily, as large-eyed, as children
always hear what they do not understand or what is
even entirely unsuitable - indeed, with far more
pleasure than the familiar, fitting and adequate can give
them. Is it believable that this is the most intensive,
splendid, perhaps the very most productive way of
learning: the anticipatory way, learning that spans wide
stretches of ignorance? As a pedagogue, I suppose I
should not speak in its behalf; but I do know that it
profits youth extraordinarily. And I believe that the
sketches jumped over fill in of themselves in time
(Mann, 1974, pp.58-9).

Mann's irony is obviously directed at the scruples of his narrator over the use of the anticipatory way of learning. It is
indeed a shame that a genuine appreciation on the part of many
teachers of the worth of children's lives and experiences often
seems ultimately to produce a doctrinaire pedantry that would
exclude from the curriculum all that is not 'relevant' to the
immediate social circumstances of the pupils.


CONCLUSION

In this chapter, I have examined five lines of criticism against
what I have called liberal education. I have tried to show how
those who claim that education should be subservient to some
overall view of life are to be answered. What I said about
avoiding possibly false enlightenment, in the case of the thought
of Rousseau and religious fundamentalist thinkers, can also be
applied to those who would see education and learning as subservient to nationalistic or political ideologies. I then showed
what is involved in the rejection of the liberal ideals of expertise and excellence, and how in Dewey's case, at least, this
rejection is based on a fallacy. Then I showed how the radical
sociological attack and its underlying cultural relativism might
be answered, above all by stressing the essential openness of
the methods and aims of liberal education. What I said there
could also be applied to claims that liberal education is racially,
as opposed to socially, biased. My answer to the radical sociologists of education means that we do not have to consider
alternatives to education (such as abolishing schools altogether)
in order to respond to what they see as problems, because the
'problems' are either not really problems at all, or can be dealt
with within the liberal educational framework. Finally, I suggested that not all learning should be directly relevant to
problems of everyday life. But although I have shown how
these criticisms of liberal education might be answered, I have
not provided a full justification of it nor have I defended the
liberal concept against a purely vocational one. This will be
attempted in the next chapter, in which I outline and justify a

concept of education somewhat broader than what I have been calling liberal education, although it includes liberal education as a central component and its ideals as paramount.

# 2 A MODERN EDUCATION AND ITS JUSTIFICATION

## INTRODUCTION

What I aim to do in this chapter is develop a concept of education that is appropriate to life in the type of pluralist and developing society that is characteristic of much of the world today. This type of society throws up particular problems and stresses of its own, which anyone living in it should be prepared for. In one sense, then, there is a certain relativity about my proposals, and I can readily concede that other types of education may be more likely to prepare people for lives of nomadic pastoralism, Spartan militarism or Cuban collectivism to take three examples of forms of life significantly different from that of the contemporary west. Nor am I concerned to argue whether a bush nomad, in the absence of any formal schooling, receives an upbringing rather than an education, for nothing of any importance hangs on verbal disputes of this sort. The important thing to decide is the type of upbringing appropriate for our children. Whether this counts as 'education' or not according to anyone's concept of education is larely immaterial, if only because, as has already emerged from Chapter 1, people's concepts of education and its aims are never independent of their general social and ethical ideals. A plurality of aims is also significant; many discussions of education falter because they assume that any system of education must have one overriding aim, whereas I shall argue that a decent upbringing for children will have a number of aims, from a number of different points of view.

In Chapter 1, I considered what I called the liberal concept of education. The concept to be developed here includes the liberal concept as its core, but this would be too narrow to satisfy all our educational aims, as I hope to show in considering some influential writings of R.S.Peters, in which he attempts to outline and justify by appeal to facts about human rationality something very like my liberal concept of education. I then consider whether some overall end such as happiness or self-fulfilment can satisfactorily be regarded as the sole aim of education, before attempting to outline the type of education appropriate to actual life in contemporary pluralist society. I close the chapter with an attempt to justify open, pluralistic societies against closed societies. In other words, I think that all human beings would be better off living in pluralistic societies and having an education appropriate to this type of

life; so that what I say is an implicit criticism of those systems
of education to be found in closed societies, and a limitation of
the extent to which I am prepared to be relativistic about either
education or society itself.

## R.S.PETERS'S CONCEPT OF EDUCATION AS INITIATION

In his earlier writings on education, R.S.Peters expounded and
attempted to defend a view of education not at all unlike that
of the liberal education discussed in Chapter 1, combined with
some degree of moral education (cf. Peters, 1966, 1973b, 1973a
and elsewhere). It should be mentioned that Peters has subse-
quently modified his view of education, widening its scope and
altering some of the earlier emphases, so as to take account of
at least some of the criticisms which I am about to make of the
earlier view (cf. Peters, 1979). None the less the earlier view
is, in the main, clear, challenging and influential, and worth
discussing in its own right.

Underlying Peters's analysis of education is a view that
philosophy should begin from the analysis of concepts, rather
than with attempts to pronounce on substantive questions of
value and fact. He therefore initially derives his conclusions
about education by analysing the concept of education, although
he does in the end admit that what he is analysing is not free
of cultural and evaluative overtones; in fact, he says that it
is based on the ideal that emerged in the nineteenth century
of an educated person as being someone developed morally,
intellectually and spiritually (Peters, 1973b, p.54). Hence the
possibility that other cultures and times might have had other
senses of 'education', and hence the need to go beyond conceptual analysis to the work of justification, for it will still be
possible for someone to accept Peters's analysis, as far as it
goes, as a correct account of the current meaning of 'education',
and to say that therefore he does not approve of people being
educated (in Peters's sense). However, this need is somewhat
obscured in some of what Peters says because of the opening
moves in the analysis, which seems at first sight to suggest
that it follows from the very meaning of the word 'education'
that everyone must be in favour of education.

According to Peters, education is by definition a process in
which something of value is passed on from teacher to pupil.
As a result of this, desirable states of mind are developed in
the pupil. In saying this, he distinguishes education from
teaching activities in which something harmful is transmitted,
such as methods of torture. The desirable states of mind which
education produces involve the development of intellect and
character, although, especially in his early discussions of the
concept, Peters tends to stress the cognitive aspect of such
development.

As education involves the acquisition of something desirable

in itself, Peters concludes that it is wrong to think of it as a
means to an end. The means-end distinction is understood in
terms of examples like catching a bus to listen to a concert,
where the means (the bus journey) is taken not for its own
sake, but only in view of the valued end (the concert). Of
course, not everything in a genuinely educational process must
be valuable in itself, but it must be seen as contributing to
the acquisition of a state which is desirable in itself. Thus
pupils might be expected to learn French irregular verbs, but
this would still be genuinely educational so long as the reason
for making them do this was that they would later get a grasp
of French literature and culture, which is a worthwhile end.
On the other hand, if the learning of French verbs was done
for purely mercenary reasons (say so one could transact business better in the EEC), it is doubtful whether Peters would
consider the process as genuinely educational, although arguably
the businessman might develop an awareness of a new culture
by learning French, which Peters would probably consider
something worthwhile in itself. What is clear, though, is that
Peters considers it to be a crucial misunderstanding of education (which inculcates states of mind desirable in themselves)
to think of it as a means to an end, even though extrinsic
goals such as getting better jobs or socialization in some general sense might be achieved through the process of education.
In fact, he rejects as improper all questions of the type 'What
is education for?' or 'What is the use of education?' He says
that because by definition education produces desirable states
of mind, these questions make no more sense than asking the
point of reforming people, because to reform people just is to
make them better. Of course, questions could be asked about
the point of trying to reform people, when the methods involved are costly and uncertain and may deform rather than
reform, but there does seem to be something odd about asking
the point of a successful and genuine reform.

    Saying that education is an end in itself leads Peters to
reject any instrumental or vocational account of education. He
would have little time for the politician who looked at the education system in terms of its ability to provide clerks or com-
puter programmers, or to create a national consciousness or
spirit of urgency. To look at it in these ways is to misunderstand the nature of the concept, by assessing what is supposed
to be worthwhile in itself in terms of purely secondary side-
effects. It is also to imply that education is a task that can be
regarded as completed once the way is prepared for whatever
its goal is. Peters, like Dewey, regards education as something
life-long and essentially uncompletable. Even though I shall
argue that Peters's rejection of any instrumental thinking in
connection with education is too austere a view of a rather
broad concept which can accommodate various aims and goals,
Peters does raise pertinent questions about the need for further justification of ends, such as the increase of productivity,

which are frequently and typically cited as educational aims in
public and political discussions of the subject. Once we get
beyond the satisfaction of basic needs, it is necessary to
develop ideas as to the nature and style of living that the
increased productivity is to enable us to bring about. A purely
instrumental attitude to education would mean that pupils would
be taught to think of social goals as given, where it is surely
one function of schools and universities to lead people to
question existing goals and to develop new ones. On the other
hand, it smacks of merely verbal point-making to say that an
underdeveloped country's attempts to modernize itself by educating its people is a misunderstanding of the concept of education. Moreover, Peters's presupposition that what is regarded
good in itself cannot also be regarded as a means is dubious.
I can play a game of tennis both because I enjoy it for itself
and as a means of exercise and social contact. Equally, as I
shall stress later, academic education can be valued both for
the desirable states of mind of the individuals who profit from
it (as an end in itself) and for the various desirable effects in
society of the presence of such individuals (as a means to some
social goals). These two attitudes to education are not necessarily in conflict, even though they would be if the means-end
distinction was regarded (as it appears to be by Peters and
many others) as a matter of an exclusive either-or. Also questionable is Peters's attempt to rule out thinking of the aim of
education as being self-realization on the grounds that this is
to look at education in an instrumental way. There are doubts
to be raised about thinking of education as aiming at self-
realization, but this is surely not one of them, for the defender
of self-realization here would simply deny that any activity was
valuable except in so far as it brought people to self-realization,
or in other words assert that no activities are valuable purely in
themselves.

For Peters, characterizing education as the development of
desirable states of mind in people does not imply that any particular activities, such as lecturing or tutoring or essay writing,
are to be gone in for. As he says, the concept of education
marks out any process of training by which someone's intellect
or character are to be formed. As such,

> I take the concept of 'education' to be almost as
> unspecific in terms of content as something like 'good'
> or 'worthwhile' with the notion of 'transmission of' or
> 'initiation into' prefixed to it. It is slightly more
> specific than 'good' because of the cognitive criteria
> to do with depth and breadth of understanding and
> awareness [that go with it] (Peters, 1973b, p.43).

For Peters, the cognitive aspect of education is highly important.
For him, an educated man must possess a body of knowledge
and a conceptual scheme to organize it, as well as some understanding of the reasons and principles underlying what he knows.
So someone who had mastered only pot-making or ancient history

and not much else could not be regarded as educated, even though what he had mastered might be highly valuable. Equally, activities such as billiards or bingo, which lead to no general improvement in intellect or character, cannot be regarded as educative. So Peters sees a genuine education as involving more than ability in particular areas. The educated man can connect what he knows in such a way that his overall outlook on life is transformed and improved.

Finally, given that education leads to a general improvement and transformation of the educated man, by initiating him into subjects and activities which are valuable in themselves, we will expect an educated person to care about those things that form the basis of his education. For him, Mill's question about the relative merits of poetry or push-pin is necessarily answered in favour of poetry, because someone who really cares about poetry will realize its superiority over push-pin. Peters (cf. 1973b, p. 47) has no hesitation in saying that someone who in later life appeared to be influenced in no way by the worthwhile pursuits of his educative years would, by virtue of that, be properly described as uneducated (presumably despite his schooling). Equally, someone who was a rogue or a snob (and whose character had been unimproved or even made worse by his knowledge) would be educated only in an 'inverted commas' sense (1973b, p. 41). Both these points are questionable. It seems far-fetched to think of Tolstoy, who professedly turned his back in later life on his knowledge and learning for the sake of the peasant life and virtues, as being no longer educated, and even more far-fetched to think of Nietzsche's contempt for the 'common herd' as making him educated only in an inverted commas sense. However, apart from quibbles about the correctness of Peters's linguistic analysis, there are some rather more fundamental points to be made about both his method and his conclusions.

In one of his writings on the concept of education, Peters (1973a, p. 88) admits that someone could quite consistently agree with his analysis of the concept (as initiation into worthwhile activities) and yet assert that he wished to give himself or his children a vocational training rather than an education. Conceptual analysis, Peters says, cannot on its own settle substantive moral problems, and the question of whether to educate someone or merely train him for a role or a job in society is a moral one. Further justification, both of the decision to educate rather than train and of education itself, are required. Yet this is rather curious if, as Peters has said elsewhere, 'education' is like 'reform' in marking out states of mind or character which are desirable in themselves. How, leaving aside practical problems of attainment, could someone not desire something like education, which is or leads to what is desirable in itself? In other words, it is hard to see how someone, given a situation in which both courses were open to him, could opt for a vocational training to the exclusion of an education. And yet there does seem to be something right about Peters's admission that moral issues cannot be settled by conceptual analysis alone.

What I think may have happened is this. In some of his thinking, Peters is taking education to be an entirely unspecific term, like good. 'How could a man not desire the good?', when 'good' is not taken in a merely conventional sense to refer to what is valued by some group or groups, does seem to be a genuinely problematic question. On the other hand, 'good' also has a specific, conventional, culture-relative sense referring to what some people value, in which we can easily imagine people rejecting the good. If this is true of 'good', it is even more true of 'education', which is generally used to refer to the sort of organized activity which goes on in schools and universities, the study of natural science, languages, literature etc., games-playing, religious services and so on. We could easily imagine someone opting against education in this specific, time-relative sense. No doubt, some of the defenders of education in this sense will claim that the states of mind and character produced by it are good in themselves, and Peters may well be right in that people will generally speak of education only in the context of activities which are at least generally regarded in some society or other as good in themselves, but that the activities involved in a particular system of education, such as liberal education, are good in themselves is just what the critic of that system will want to deny, and why a justification of this claim is required. Such a justification is what Peters attempts (1966, pp. 160-61 and 1973c) when he claims to show why having a body of knowledge, an articulated conceptual scheme and some commitment to rational enquiry - what might be regarded as the outcome of a successful liberal education - are desirable in themselves. What Peters is now doing is defending a specific concept of education, the one he is interested in when he takes a broad cognitive perspective to be an essential component of education.

Obviously Peters cannot give an instrumental justification of a liberal education, in terms of the benefits that might accrue to a society composed of liberally educated people, for example. What he needs to do is to show that the states of mind and character in question are, like happiness, ends in themselves and constitutive of any full human life. Part of his objection to talk of self-realization as an educational aim is that not all that a man might consider to count as the fulfilment of his self is in fact desirable, if, say, sadism was one of the man's character traits. The concept of self-realization needs to be spelled out so as to admit only what are really desirable traits. Implicit in Peters's argument is the contention that the development of one's knowledge and rationality is part of any full human life; he is fond of quoting Socrates's assertion (Plato, 'Apology', 38a) that a day spent without discussing goodness and all the other topics he is interested in is a wasted day and that an unexamined life is not worth living. Peters also points out that knowledge and understanding are enjoyable and absorbing, reflecting our love of order and system. But he needs to show that these are not merely preferences on his part and Socrates's, and to show that they reflect something basic and integral to human life.

The answer is to point to the place reason plays in life: 'human life is a context in which the demands of reason are inescapable' (Peters, 1973c, p. 253). This is because in everything we do, practical and theoretical, we are assessing beliefs and expectations, evaluating goals and courses of action, judging conduct and ideas. This puts us, whether we like it or not, whether we admit it or not, under the demands of reason to justify and assess whatever comes before us. The activites of which liberal education consists ('of which the curriculum of a university is largely constituted'; Peters, 1966, p. 162) are simply the systematic workings out of these demands. Their pursuit is rationally justified just because they are the activities involved in any process of justification. So you cannot consistently be making rational assessments in any area of life and believe that these (university) activities are not justified, or refuse to admit that they are worth pursuing. To do this would be to want rational justifications and assessments of some of your activities at the same time as refusing to accept what is ultimately involved in making any such assessments. Even in asking whether educational activity is justified one is asking for a rational assessment or justification. It would, in short, be contradictory or 'irrational for a person who seriously asks himself [this] question... to close his mind arbitrarily to any form of inquiry which might throw light on the question which he is asking' (Peters, 1966, pp. 162-3).

One of the problems in coming to grips with this argument is its high level of generality. When its bones are fleshed out, however, it begins to seem rather unconvincing. What Peters seems to be arguing is that because we use our reason in assessing our day-to-day beliefs and activities we are therefore committed to the desirability of the pure seeking-after-truth that is supposed to go on in universities. Leaving aside doubts about the extent to which most of the university curriculum is concerned with questions of ultimate justification or truth, we must ask in what sense human beings are 'under the demands of reason' (Peters, 1973c, p. 254) in everyday life. It is true that we have and use the ability to reason in order to decide on beliefs about where food is or how it might best be obtained or what sort of food is most nutritious, and so on. Reasoning ability is obviously a powerful instrument for the satisfaction of goals we set ourselves, and in the evaluation of competing goals in the light of our ultimate goals. But it does not follow from our being under the demands of reason in this instrumental sense that we are thereby committed to any non-instrumental use of our reason, to find out truth absolutely or to find some transcendent justification for our ultimate goals. Peters wants to

argue that a man who accepted the benefits of the instrument of
reason but who eschewed any questions about ultimate truth or
ends would be, by that fact, inconsistent. It is difficult to see
why this should be so: one is not, in general, inconsistent in
refusing to develop a tool as an end in itself. Peters would
probably reply that reason is not just a tool, and that the sense
in which reason is embedded in human life is indeed in the
ultimate justification-asking sense. Not only is it doubtful whether
this is generally true (many people never ask ultimate questions
about truth or life, preferring to accept life as it is), but even
if it were I am not sure that the conclusion Peters wants would
follow.

If being rational means engaging in truth-seeking and value-
assessing for its own sake, then there is obviously a sense in
which a man who abandoned such questioning or who refused
to accord it any value would be being irrational. But Peters's
argument is intended to show not only that he would be irrational
in that sense, but that he would be actually inconsistent in
having used reason up to a point and then abandoned it. But,
against Peters, he may have abandoned the pursuit of further
rational enquiry and justification for good reasons. He may have
arguments, of a sceptical sort, to show that ultimate truth is
unattainable, at least by purely rational or speculative means,
and then combine them with ethical or religious considerations
about the purpose of human life and the belief that human happiness consists in a quiescent acceptance of life as it is, without
ultimate justifications, or only as it is revealed through a
religion. He may combine this line of thinking with biological
arguments about human rationality having survival value so
long as it is kept in its place, but being a nuisance if it comes
to dominate a man's life. Or he may accept a broadly pragmatist
view about truth (or the nearest we can get to it) consisting in
usefulness and workability, and so reject the pursuit of any
research or line of questioning which had no practical import, at
least in the long term. For such a man the worth of any line of
research or questioning would be decided only through its
practical results, even if he was prepared to give a certain
amount of leeway to researchers before they came up with any
results. (This sort of thinking is prevalent in 'technological'
universities.) All these people would certainly have examined
their lives (and would therefore escape Socrates's scorn), but
they would have come to the conclusion that learning for its
own sake is not a particularly worthwhile activity.

While disagreeing with this conclusion, unlike Peters I cannot
see that this is an implicitly contradictory position to be in, if
only because the question raised by Rousseau, Tolstoy, religious
fundamentalists and technologically oriented people about the
ultimate value of learning in the context of human life in general
remains a real one. For all of them, reason is and should remain
fundamentally a tool to be controlled by other ends. My arguments against this position do not stem from considerations, such

as those adduced by Peters, about reason taken in isolation from
more general features of human life and society. Peters's argument from rationality seems to me to leave the question of the
value of pure research open. My defence of learning is based on
an attempt to show that a society in which learning is not valued
for its own sake is likely to be a less desirable society generally.
Before exploring the implications of this further, in developing
a concept of education rather wider than that of Peters in its
inclusion of vocational elements, we will turn to an examination
of whether education can be justified by appeal to the notions of
personal happiness and self-fulfilment.

## HAPPINESS AND SELF-FULFILMENT

The main thing I want to argue in this section is that happiness
and self-fulfilment are not, logically, the sort of things that one
can aim at directly. You cannot aim at something which is necessarily a by-product of something else, and both happiness and
self-fulfilment are essentially by-products in this way, a fact
which is reflected in their entirely unspecific nature. Thus we
can be told that someone is happy or fulfilled and understand
what is meant, without having any clear idea of the details or
nature of his life or achievements. A man can be happy or fulfilled only in or through being or doing something else, such
as writing a symphony, being a parent, meditating or smoking
dope. Happiness and fulfilment are necessarily the results of
being in other states or doing other things. It is true that you
can attempt to bring about happiness or self-fulfilment by
getting yourself into one of those other states, and in that sense
aim at them indirectly. You can aim at these other things for
the sake of the happiness or fulfilment you might get from them,
but when one speaks of the goal of a particular activity or process such as education as being the happiness or fulfilment of
those being educated, you will also have to spell out the direct
means by which you hope or believe happiness or fulfilment are
to be brought about, before anyone will understand just what it
is that you are aiming to do in your education. A crucial point
here is that the type of happiness or fulfilment achieved at any
point will be determined by the activity or state which brings
them about. The sense of fulfilment one has from writing a book
is quite different from that which one might have from climbing
a mountain or raising a family. This is largely because the
states of happiness or fulfilment one might have in the long term
are connected with the way one sees one's life and activity. It is
because happiness and fulfilment are unspecific concepts, referring essentially to states that are dependent on other states, or
achievements, and the way one sees those states, that different
people can have such different ideas about what exactly is
entailed in seeking happiness or fulfilment, and speak of them
as existing on so many different levels. Fulfilment, indeed, is

even less specific than happiness, which does entail a degree of
contentedness with one's existence, but fulfilment can manifestly
be found in all conditions and spheres of life, and be either
short term or long term. A man's idea of a fulfilled life is, as I
shall suggest later, inextricably tied up with his general ideas
about life and value.

So there are logical reasons why it is unsatisfactory to say
without further specification that one's aim in educating people
is to bring about their happiness. Then, as we shall see, there
are further reasons, to do with both psychological and general
factual considerations, why it may be unsatisfactory to educate
even for the sake of happiness. Finally, Iris Murdoch is probably
right in speaking in one of her novels of happiness as a flimsy
thing, and a consideration which other more substantial educational goals may be allowed to override. These points must now
be examined.

There is an important distinction to be made between being
happy and feeling happy. As I have already hinted in speaking
of happiness in the long term as being related to the way one
sees what one is doing, being happy is, as Dearden (1972, p. 98)
points out, a state of mind which requires an object, something
one is happy with. Thus a man can be happy with his job, his
marriage, his children or even his life, and he can be happy
with some parts of his life and unhappy with others. Feeling
happy, on the other hand, is a state one can be in even in the
midst of all sorts of disasters and worries. You need only to
uncork the bottle. People are fond of imagining futuristic
societies which are controlled by the widespread use of happiness-
inducing pills, and the exaggerated horror that is normally
evinced in right-thinking people by such fantasies argues some
ambivalence in attitudes towards them. Indeed the very same
people who throw their hands up at the thought of our future
life being run along these lines tend to look much more favour-
ably on tales of primitive tribes spending their days in states
of intoxication induced by plants. Euphoria of this sort, though,
tends to be short-lived and unreliable (we have not yet per-
fected ways of achieving it). It is even more unpredictable when
it is a by-product not of chemistry but of such things as walking
on hills or listening to music. While such feelings may be an
integral and central part of someone's concept of the good life,
the distinction between happiness as a feeling and happiness as
a state of mind remains, because such a person will be happy
(state of mind) only if his life consists of actually achieving the
desired feelings of happiness - that is, only if he is able to
conceive his life as being as he wants it.

Because being happy is a state of mind requiring something
one is happy with, its fulfilment requires a match of some sort
between reality and desire. This match is a necessary rather
than a sufficient condition of happiness, because it is a common
experience that one's desires can be fulfilled without bringing
about the expected and hoped-for happiness. On the other hand,

it is hard to see how a man could be happy in some respect were
at least some of his desires not being satisfied in that respect. I
prefer to speak of happiness in terms of a match between reality
and desire than in terms of a man's enmeshment or involvement
in some task or state (cf. Barrow, 1975, p. 62), because people
can obviously be fully enmeshed in some activity or circumstances
(such as a tedious mechanical job or a bad marriage) without
being happy, and also it is quite possible to think of examples
of people being happy in circumstances in which they or their
powers are not fully involved (such as in their nightly bingo
session, during which they also dream about the Spanish hol-
iday they are hoping to win). It is partly because of the com-
plications involved in the match between desire and reality that
the connection between education and happiness must be problematic. On the one hand, a man may be quite content with his
life without any formal education, while, on the other, an
educated person may be faced with all sorts of problems he
has no control over and which make his life hard and difficult.
Further, as Peters (1979, p. 467) puts it,

It might be said that a man who is made redundant through
no fault of his own, loses his wife, or has a heart attack
should be able to cope better with such adversity if he is
educated than if he is not. This may be so, but it is a
speculative suggestion. For how a man copes with such
adversity is a very individual matter depending as much
on his temperament as on the quality of his awareness.

It is hardly possible (or clearly desirable if it were possible) to
change a man's temperament by educational means. Even if it
were, it could hardly be done to the extent of making someone
happy with a major disaster in his life or work.

What education can do, however, is affect a man's desires and
his concept of what counts as a good or happy life, and bring
about the reality-desire match by working on his desires rather
than by helping him to produce appropriate changes in reality.
This, in effect, is the aim of education in Plato's 'Republic', at
least for the workers and the auxiliers. Plato's ideal state is
divided into three classes, the rulers (guardians), the soldiers
(the auxiliaries) and the workers (including farmers). These
divisions are supposed to correspond to various divisions in
human individuals between mental and animal functions; indeed
the well-run state and the well-functioning individual person
are seen as images of each other. Rational reflection is the
prerogative of the rulers, while the auxiliaries and the workers,
being incapable of it, are only to be educated through music
and art (carefully censored to make morality attractive) and
through gymnastics (to build up bodily strength). Only the rulers
are to be educated in rational and reflective study. Not only is
this education aimed at fitting people to perform their roles in
the state, but it is organized so as to keep their desires and
knowledge within that appropriate to a particular station. Above
all, all citizens are to be indoctrinated with a noble lie

(or magnificent myth, according to some translations, but the
translation hardly affects the sense of what is going on);
according to this, each child is fashioned by a god from a mixture of earth and metal – copper or iron in the case of the
workers, silver for the auxiliaries, gold for the guardians – and
there is a prophecy to the effect that a state will be ruined when
its actual rulers are made of copper or iron. Plato represents
Socrates as being asked if there is any way of making people
believe such a story, and commenting in reply that it will be
difficult in the first generation, but that even so, it should
serve to increase the loyalty of the citizen to the state and each
other ('Republic', 415a–d).

There is certainly something tantalizing in Plato's vision of
an organic state whose members are happy because they are
contentedly filling the roles that are appropriate to their abilities
and needs, and who are kept from mental disturbance or intellectual unrest by a system of censorship and repressive education. It is also true that people's happiness with their lives
is closely related to the ways in which they conceive their lives,
their horizons and expectations, and that the lower these are
the more likely they are to be satisfied. Expectations can be manipulated or affected in ways that are less conscious or premed-
itated than those advocated by Plato; for example, by instilling
in people the idea that they are going to do certain types of
work, or that they are members of certain social or racial groups
and will therefore occupy certain predetermined social positions.
It may be true, as Barrow (1975, p. 79) suggests in his defence
of Platonic education, that the completely happy man is the one
who is able to do all that he wants to do; it is further true that
someone's education can so mould his desires that he is easily
satisfied with a particular, pre-assigned role. (The tradition-
alistic objection of Islamic teachers to western education is based
on just this point.) But one wonders whether educators can be
satisfied with fitting people for roles in this way. This is not
merely because of the gross and repressive implications of
deciding at an early stage that a particular individual is copper
or silver rather than gold, and as a result giving him a second-
or third-rate education. It is also because there are many other
values relevant to education, such as respect for truth, respect
for the integrity of others and desire for excellence, which
would come into direct conflict with an education which saw its
role in terms of deliberately restricting the intellectual and
moral horizons of numbers of children. To say at this point that
one should not expand people's horizons in their education,
because this may lead to later frustration with the jobs they
actually manage to get, may appear to be motivated by a genuine
concern for people's welfare and satisfaction. In fact, when one
reflects on the fact that such concern will actually lead to
supposedly enlightened people deciding that others should not
be enlightened for their own good, it becomes evident that the
concern is nothing more than a more or less cynical acquiescence

in a situation in which the majority of people's lives are impoverished in terms of their work, their culture and their enter-
tainment. (The view that a large number of people should not be
educated fully because they are incapable of it will be considered
in Chapter 6.)

The flimsiness of happiness arises from the fact that it can
easily coexist with, or even, as Plato so vividly illustrated, be
actually dependent on, an acceptance of the second rate for
oneself or (worse) for others. Is what Plato proposes in part
a reflection of the easy way happiness is content to coexist with
illusion? For if happiness is a contentedness with one's life or
work, it is hard to see how a man who understands anything of
the nature of himself or others or his society, or what he is
working at, or who sees how life itself is so tenuous, can easily
achieve happiness, except perhaps as the sort of mystical
indifference to fate that Wittgenstein speaks of - the world of
the happy man being the same as that of the unhappy man, only
waxing rather than waning. A happiness that rests on illusion
concerning any of the unhappy facts about life and the world is
flimsy in another way too, because such illusions are bound
eventually to be shattered. Even a religion that is optimistic in
the long term about human life has to come to terms with the
actual pain of suffering and the loss involved in death, if it is
not to seem facile and superficial to people when they are confronted with crises in their lives. Nietzsche's 'The Birth of
Tragedy' is a profound work of moral philosophy (if not of
scholarship) because of the way in which he connects the Greek
'cheerfulness', so esteemed by Winckelmann and Goethe, with a
strain of terrible pessimism in Greek culture. (Sappho: 'If the
gods so love death, why do they not die themselves?') Any
happiness that is lasting has to come to terms with truth, although
of course coming to terms with truth will not necessarily result
in happiness. On the other hand, illusion and barbarism go hand
in hand, and educators should not put themselves at the service
of any barbarism, however 'noble' or 'magnificent' its preten-
sions or appearance.

It is perhaps because of the way happiness is quite consonant
with mediocrity that some educational theorists have preferred
to speak of education as aiming at the fulfilment of an individual's
potentialities, or his free growth (e.g. Dewey, 1916, pp. 100-1).
Beethoven might thus be described as fulfilled, although he was
in any uncontroversial sense of the word unhappy throughout
most of the later years of his life. However, there are problems
with speaking of education in terms of growth or fulfilment
which arise from the unspecific nature of these concepts, and
which suggest that these ways of speaking are quite vacuous.
In the first place, an individual may have potentialities that it
would be better not to fulfil or allow to grow. For example, a
child might have dishonest or cruel tendencies. Dewey (cf. 1938,
pp. 28-9) actually discusses the case of burglary, and tries to
defend his claim that education should aim at growth on the

grounds that growth as a burglar should be ruled out as it would stunt further growth by curtailing one's openness to experience. It is hard to see why this should be so. After all, Wagner certainly got money under false pretences from the unfortunate Ludwig II of Bavaria. In any case, a professional burglar might, during the course of his career, develop all manner of new plans and techniques of some high intellectual complexity, to say nothing of taking an interest in the lives and experiences of many other people from diverse backgrounds, all of which Dewey would presumably approve of.

Even of those potentialities we think worth developing it still has to be decided whether they should be developed in schools, or the extent to which their development should be an educational aim. For example, someone might be excellent at a game such as football, but even if we give sport a place on the curriculum, it is unclear that schools should be doing the work of junior professional football teams. The problem with all talk of fulfilment in an educational context is that once it is seen that no unqualified notion of fulfilment can really give any practical guidance, what is needed is a sense of what powers and abilities are to be developed, and this requires a set of general attitudes to individuals and society. I shall attempt to give some account of what might be needed in the contemporary world in the next section.

Before leaving the general topic of happiness, however, a point made by both Rousseau and Dewey is worth bringing out. Dewey (1916, p. 109) says that 'no alleged study or discipline is educative unless it is worthwhile in its own immediate having'. This obviously connects with his insistence that all genuine learning involves a real discovery on the part of the learner, but his objection to seeing what goes on in school as a preparation for something else is shared by Rousseau. In 'Emile', Rousseau rather dramatically says that if the time of education is regarded as a preparation for the future and treated accordingly, and a pupil then dies aged twelve, his life and efforts will have been largely wasted, whereas if his education had concentrated on letting him live as a child, even an early death will follow a full life. Herzen's words are entirely in the spirit of Rousseau:

> We think that the purpose of the child is to grow up,
> because it does grow up. But its purpose is to play,
> to enjoy itself, to be a child. If we merely look to the
> end of the process, the purpose of all life is death
> (quoted in Berlin, 1978, p. 196).

Rousseau and Dewey obviously exaggerate here, as so often. Some things, such as the learning of grammar or of tables of elements, have to be undertaken not because of any intrinsic interest, but because they are necessary steps to something worthwhile. In the case of many subjects, the significance of what has to be absorbed with effort and difficulty in the early stages emerges only later. Also there is value in the habits of

self-discipline and concentration which are learned only through
the doing of unwelcome tasks.

On the other hand, Rousseau and Dewey are right in suggesting that children should be treated as children, and not cut off
from childish life in a grotesque effort to turn them straight
away into small adults. Even from a pedagogical point of view
there is an obvious advantage in teachers understanding the
nature and development of children. But more than this, schools
should be happy places in which there is a sense that much of
what is going on is being enjoyed and valued for what it is at
the time. The problem is to find material that is both attractive
and at the same time really fulfilling for the pupils, so that we
are not just patronizing them by indulging what we take to be
their fancies and tastes; but the cost of failure is that we are
adding to the heartache expressed in so many 'Bildungsromanen':

> How much of all the things we spend our whole time in
> school doing is really going to get anyone anywhere?
> What do we get anything out of? I mean for ourselves –
> you see what I mean? In the evening you know you've
> lived another day, you've learned this and that, you've
> kept up with the timetable, but still, you're empty –
> inwardly I mean. Right inside, you're still hungry, so
> to speak (Robert Musil, 'Young Törless', pp. 31-2).

## A MODERN EDUCATION

Questions about types of education can hardly be answered
independently of the social background in question. This goes for
educational proposals as well as for analyses. To an extent the
views of Rousseau and Tolstoy, on the one hand, and of Peters,
on the other, cannot answer many of the problems arising from
the social reality confronting educators of the late twentieth
century. Like it or not, we have gone beyond the stage of
simple, enclosed tribal or village life. Even in the most backward
villages of Africa you can find radios. The drift to the towns
goes on. Urban life has an immense attraction for village children. The fact that many urban people feel the opposite is
irrelevant, because what we are faced with is the spread of ideas,
the suggestion that modes of life exist and are available which
are different to traditional ways. Only a conscious, centralized
and (as I shall argue further in the next section) unacceptable
imposition of censorship can even attempt to stop the influence
of these ideas.

Peters (in his earlier writings) takes a view of education which
to some extent comes to terms with modern life but which fails to
answer the crucial question, which is not about the meaning of
'education' but about what we should do to bring up our children now. He says that 'teaching science with limited (i.e.
economic and technological) ends in view should be distinguished
from educating people' (1973b, p. 57), and that Spartans and

primitive peoples had no education, because what they did in
bringing up their young did not conform to his sense of education. To this, Spartans, primitives and people interested in
technological education would presumably reply that their
primary interest is not in knowing what 'education' means, but
in producing the skills, knowledge and habits of mind and
character that are necessary and valuable to young people
entering the world. So, in distinction to Peters, Rousseau and
Tolstoy, the question I will now address myself to is not, 'What
does "education" mean?' or, 'Is a primitive village society
better than modern civilization?' but, 'What would we want our
children to learn in school?'

On the assumption that any adult person in a modern non-
totalitarian society is not automatically going to fill some traditional or assigned social role, and that his manner of life,
including his political and religious beliefs, is not simply going
to be laid down for him, I suggest that the following abilities
will be necessary:

1    ability to support him or herself;
2    ability to make informed choices about life, including
     career, religion, politics, life-style and general attitudes;
3    ability to decide what is and what is not morally accept-
     able.

Corresponding to each of these abilities, we will expect a person's
education to provide him with the necessary basis, i.e.

1    sufficient skills to obtain work;
2    a general education giving a reasonable understanding of
     the nature of man and the world;
3    an education in morality.

Even where someone does opt for traditional roles and beliefs, it
is important to realize that he or she is now to a greater or less
extent making a set of choices in a way that was not the case in
traditional societies, so the sort of education I am proposing
will have served its purpose for that person too.

What my proposals here rest on is the contemporary historical
fact that traditional societies, in which there was no question of
people making personal decisions about their lives and beliefs,
have by and large broken down. The presence of alternatives
is continually presented to people everywhere by the increase
of mass communication, universal primary education and the
growth of towns, new roles and so on. Questions about one's way
of life are inevitably raised by all this, and the unquestioning
frame of mind central to traditional ways, which made them so
secure, is immediately broken. This situation can lead to two
alternative strategies. The fact of personal autonomy can be
accepted for what it is, and people encouraged to make their own
choices by giving them both opportunity and necessary information,
largely through an open system of education. Or it can be
deplored and legislated against, in the name of some ideal of
fraternity, national or social. This would imply a restricted and
closed attitude to education. I shall argue against the latter

course of action in the next section, and assume here that we
are considering education in a free society, though the bluff
reflection on human nature of a former colonial Governor of
Nigeria is worth recalling now in passing:

If there is one lesson which the writer has learnt
thoroughly in the course of thirty five years spent in
trying to manage other people's affairs for them, it is
that on the whole they prefer to manage them themselves
(Bourdillon, 1945, p. 56).

So education is to fit people to manage their affairs for themselves, and to do this by enabling them to make their own
choices on as wide and informed a basis as possible. The first
and most obvious prerequisite is the ability to make a living for
oneself. This requires at least basic literacy and numeracy,
together with whatever else is needed to start on more specific
training for particular jobs. There would be a danger, however,
were schools themselves to take on training of too narrow or
specific a sort, and this is similar to the danger of giving
working-class children a working-class curriculum. The danger
is that, far from extending the range of a child's choice, such
an education would tend to filter people into specific areas of
employment and social niches, thus reinforcing class divisions
and limiting rather than widening areas of effective choice.
There is also the added danger that in a time of rapid technological change such training could quickly become out-dated.
On the other hand, there is no reason why general technical
abilities, such as a little computing skill or basic engineering
and mechanical principles, should not be taught in schools,
particularly if society has a need for such abilities and this need
is reflected in job opportunities. The implication of this point is
that schools should be sensitive to social needs. This is not
because society (or the state) is in all probability paying for
education, nor is it to assert any priority in education of social
over individual interests. It is rather because people do not
make choices in a social vacuum, and what schools must aim to
do here is give people the chance to make a living in the society
they will actually enter. This has an interesting implication
where, as in many developing countries, particular social needs
are pressing and identified as such by the state. In such a
situation, there will presumably be many more jobs available in
these than in other areas, and it would be absurd for schools
not to reflect these needs in their curricula, as far as these
relate to the fitting of pupils for self-sufficiency. Because the
jobs will be where the state has decided they should be, in
giving pupils the basis required for training in these areas
schools will at the same time be answering the explicit needs of
society and providing their pupils with a realistic framework for
a choice of occupation.

To talk of schools fitting pupils for self-sufficient lives is not
simply to think of them providing pupils with some vocational
training. A certain amount of general knowledge of a practical

sort, from first aid to the running of household accounts, is presupposed by any reasonably competent person, and much of it could easily and economically be imparted in formal lessons. Where this is so, only an unreasonable bias in favour of academic education could exclude a small but significant amount of school time being spent on such lessons, particularly where there is little evidence that parents do or can impart this knowledge to their children. Time in school is, of course, limited, and it will be said that general practical knowledge and vocational training will involve too great an expenditure of time. The reply to this is that I have only so far said that pupils are to be given the basic and general training employers would expect people to have before embarking on more specific training or apprenticeships. At the same time, it is unrealistic to expect schools to turn out individual pupils each having all the requirements for starting courses in nursing, civil engineering, computing, personnel management, journalism, architecture, car mechanics, farming, printing, photography and so on. The obvious suggestion here, which is actually incorporated into the Soviet system of education, is that pupils should in the later stages of schooling be offered as options a range of training courses, each option preparing them for some more specific course or group of courses. The range of options offered should as far as possible be both wide and responsive to social circumstances, and the guiding spirit behind what is done should be to ensure that all pupils leaving school have some basis for seeking jobs. Even if they do not actually capitalize on this basis, having it will extend their ability to fend for themselves and to choose what they do. Even from a strictly academic point of view much of what is learned in vocationally orientated courses will be worthwhile, because of the interrelationships between technological and academic knowledge.

Academic study should form the core of education, because it is here that pupils will be given the general understanding of man and the world, to enable them to make important life choices in an informed and responsible way. Because the aim of such study will be the transmission and acquisition of truth, the values and methods will be those of what I called liberal education in Chapter 1; that is, an emphasis on open, self-regulating studies undertaken for their own sake and in the light of their own criteria of excellence. Speaking of them being undertaken for their own sake does not, of course, entail that they are undertaken out of sheer indulgence, nor that there is anything anti-social about them. What it means is that workers in these fields are not guided by extra-disciplinary principles or ideologies.

Any truly democratic society should naturally want its autonomous members to be in the best possible position to make reasonable judgments about life and society without being open to manipulation or an easy prey to obscurantism; hence the need for independence in study. We still have to say something, however, about what precise areas of study should be pursued and taught in a society that wants to see its members in a position to make informed choices on important matters, both public and private. In what follows, I am not of course proposing that pupils in schools will themselves pursue studies in any area so as to push back the boundaries of the subject. What I am assuming is that through university-educated specialist teachers there will be a continuity between subjects as taught in schools and as pursued in universities, so that in schools there will be an awareness of what advances are being made in any discipline and its current directions. In this way, pupils will get a sense of current thinking in any area as well as past achievements, and in this way be able to bring the best available knowledge about man and the world to bear on their own attitudes to work, religion, politics and life generally.

The first area which affects a person's ideas about himself and the world is his conception of the physical world. This is the area covered by the natural sciences. The natural sciences do not only give us information about the nature of matter and our environment. Men are part of the material world and occupy an evolutionary niche. So our conceptions of the universe, of matter, of biology, of the animal kingdom and of physiology will all have profound implications for the way we think about ourselves, even though much of what is discussed in science may appear to be very remote from daily life. Such steps in science as the removal of final causes from physics and Darwin's theory of evolution obviously had a fairly direct bearing on ideas about men and their environment, but they in turn depended on much more remote-seeming discoveries, and their implications may take us far into the realms of astronomy and subatomic physics.

So apart from any technological by-products, scientific research performs an essential role in forming, modifying and correcting our conceptions of ourselves and our lives. No serious education can be considered adequate which does not attempt to acquaint pupils with leading theories and speculations about matter and nature. Science education should not consist simply in allowing pupils to perform simple experiments with everyday substances, and inducing low-level laws about chemical composition or heat-expansion from them. To restrict it to what pupils might be able to 'discover' for themselves would be to remove from it what justifies its inclusion in the academic curriculum, as well as to deprive pupils of the stimulus of being introduced to insights of profound imagination and beauty. It should emphasize the speculative and explanatory aspects of science, and the way in which these are controlled by observation and experiment. In this way, pupils will be led to grasp something of the nature and limits of scientific thought; they will not only grasp the scientific picture of the world, they will also come to understand something of the place science has in our picture of the world. All this is, of course, quite independent of any technological applications of science. The teaching of technology or applied science certainly has a place in school as part of vocational training, but it would be missing the main point of the teaching of science to confuse the two. In addition, both scientific discoveries and the applications are unpredictable, so to pursue science only in so far as it has obvious technological applications would be restricting from the point of view of technology.

Mathematics is clearly an integral part of modern science, and its study is certainly justified because of this. That it should be regarded as an independent discipline to be studied for its own sake may perhaps be less clear, until one reflects on the way that its concepts and rules are independent of any particular applications. The clue to its pervasive usefulness lies precisely in its abstractness and generality. Equally, unless its techniques and conclusions are followed wherever they might lead, possible applications and uses might be missed, for, as in the recent example of castastrophe theory, the actual applications of mathematical techniques and their power in illuminating other areas often becomes clear only after the mathematics involved has been fully explored for itself. So this would be a powerful argument against confining mathematical teaching to a child's concrete perception of quantities, or giving the impression that mathematics is too closely tied to the physical world. (Another argument to the same effect – from mathematics itself – is that number theory, which is a tool of unbelievably widespread application in the physical world, cannot be satisfactorily based on a combination of logic and any simplistic notion of a class or set of objects, as Russell's paradox of classes demonstrates.) If mathematics had no applications to other areas of knowledge, its study would not be more justified than that of chess or the glass-bead game. Given that modern knowledge is inconceivable apart from mathematics, and given that its future applications and usefulness are unpredictable without knowing how both it and science generally are to develop (and the two are inextricably linked), its pursuit as a glass-bead game (i.e. for its own sake) is both desirable and fully justified.

A study of history, geography and social and behavioural science, including anthropology, is also necessary to any informed sense of the nature of society and our current problems. Again, we can hardly foresee what areas of history or anthropology might throw light on our current situation, or correct or refine our ideas about ourselves and mankind, until they are undertaken. Uncriticized and absurd myths about one's own social or racial group, stereotyped ideas of what other groups are like, shallow and implausible nationalisms, religious bigotry and class prejudice are, of course, major causes of discord in the world. It is to be hoped that social, behavioural and historical studies would be a corrective to much of this, but one thing that history has to teach us is that there are no simple lessons or conclusions to be drawn from history, and that clean hands and 'pure right' facing 'absolute wrong' are rarities in

human experience. Rather, a study of history and human
behaviour might have as its fruit a great deal of insight into the
complexity of most situations and the multifarious causes of most
actions, as well as of the diversity of life-styles and attitudes.
Anthropology is not simply a matter of gathering quaint tales
about the behaviour of others; by giving us an insight into the
mixture of strangeness and familiarity in the behaviour of people
leading very different lives from our own, it can lead us to perceive, in a way that would not otherwise be possible, the nature
of our own presuppositions, as well as previously unnoticed
elements in our own lives of bizarreness, artificiality and conven-
tionality. In other words, the study of other peoples and times,
apart from its intrinsic interest, is, by the contrasts it presents,
an essential means to understanding one's own life and society,
which is in turn necessary if one's decisions are to be informed.

The study of at least some foreign language is a useful, if not
essential, adjunct to the understanding of other cultures. It is
also of great importance to the study of literature (and the
feebleness of the English about foreign languages becomes more
marked the more one travels). A study of literature and the arts,
on the other hand, has a vital place on the curriculum, because
they represent the way people have attempted to come to terms
in imaginative ways with their lives and problems and to express
their sense of significance of life and its goals. This point
will be developed further in our consideration of the so-called
'two cultures' debate in Chapter 4 and in the chapter on moral
education, but it is worth adding here that it is perhaps by
artistic means most of all that people's hopes, desires and
ambitions can be transformed and widened. Because of the possibilities here, a narrow concentration on what is 'relevant' is
most depressing. There are many ways of capturing children's
interest in artistic expression, and one of them may be by
showing what writers and other artists have made of experiences
similar to their own, but to confine the study of literature and
the arts to works of this sort, as would be required if working-
class children were to be given a working-class education, argues
a high degree of dogmatism and patronizing parochialism on the
part of teachers, where what is required is breadth of vision,
imagination and enthusiasm. To deprive children of truly
imaginative encounters with the works of Dostoevksy, Shakespeare, Dickens, Beethoven, Turner and so on, either because
of timid parochialism or by a pedantic attitude to the letter rather
than the spirit of texts, is to remove from the study of the arts
its aim and justification. Even more misguided would be an
attempt to justify enforced cultural deprivation on the grounds
that factory work hardly requires any appreciation of the arts,
and that to implant it in future factory workers is only going
to make them unhappy with their personal prospects. The answer
to this would be to point out that perhaps they should be unhappy with them - and that it is not the job of teachers to make
people accept the unacceptable.

Of course, it may be that in practice, for all sorts of social and cultural reasons, some pupils reject all that they are given in their education, but to suggest that teachers should acquiesce passively in this state of affairs and give up all attempts to fire the imaginations of their pupils is tantamount to arguing against the value of education at all.

It will naturally be asked whether religion has any place in what I am calling general education. As the overall aim of this part of education is to enable people to make informed choices about their lives, the answer must be that some grounding in the main religious traditions ought to be given, as these are major and serious attempts to answer the ultimate questions of life and death and to come to terms with experiences of an unworldly sort. To an extent, information relevant to religion will be presented in the scientific, historical-behavioural and artistic parts of the curriculum, but there is clearly a case for a systematic presentation of the main religious alternatives. What schools should not do is either attempt to teach one specific religion, as if it were not a matter of individual judgment and choice, or water the teaching of religion down into a mixture of civics and bland humanitarianism. To do either of these things would be to deprive pupils of the basis they need to make choices where choice is of the essence. It is interesting that my proposals here actually suggest that there should be more teaching of religion than is common in sectarian schools, which characteristically preach (rather than teach) only one religion, presenting only the sketchiest accounts of other religions. The social and mental constriction involved here is to be deplored, especially when combined with the feeling that doubt is somehow immoral and wrong. To teach about several religions in itself emphasizes the choice element and the idea that what is at issue is faith rather than knowledge, and so avoids any suggestion of unwarranted indoctrination.

The final area in which education is required is in the area of morality. As I shall argue further in Chapter 5, morality is not a specific subject but is involved in various ways in all human activity, so it will not make further demands on an already full curriculum (except ideally for some small consideration of moral philosophy at the highest level of schooling). How morality might be taught, and what to teach it might consist in, will be considered in detail in Chapter 5. Although there the model of morality as involving free decision-making by fully autonomous and purely rational agents will be criticized, it remains true that a society in which people are to be regarded as autonomous is also a society in which individuals will have to make moral decisions, and the basis for making such decisions should therefore be included as a part of education. Even in a rigid theocratic society some internalizing of values is desirable, because, as Peters points out (1979), people cannot be policed all the time. People also need practical education in how to live together in such a way as not to interfere with each others' rights, and schools have an important role here too. Of course, moral education, like any other branch of education, may fail: a young person may leave school with very little respect for others, just as people may leave school with virtually no skills or knowledge. But if school is to prepare individuals for life outside school, it would be failing even in its duty to pupils themselves if it did not introduce them to the considerations on which concepts of human good and evil have been based, and in the light of which it is to be hoped a good life can be led. Individuals may reject the considerations, but to leave pupils without any insight into them is to deprive them of the best chance they have of leading a life that makes sense humanly, personally and socially. From a social point of view, of course, individuals with a firm grasp of the commitment to good moral values are the best defence against corruption and totalitarianism.

What I hope has become clear in this section is that, in an education preparing people for life in an open society, individual and social goals will tend to converge. An open society needs well-informed people, qualified to work for a living, with a firm understanding of morality. An individual in such a society will be the better off if he is able to fend for himself, and to understand enough about life and the world to make his own moral, personal and political choices in an informed way. I have argued in considering general education that the sort of knowledge required to satisfy these ends cannot be restricted to 'real' answers to 'real-life' problems, but that it must necessarily involve broadening a person's horizons far beyond his own experience. It will probably be objected that what I am proposing is far too ambitious in terms of time available and of children's abilities. On the first point, I have some scepticism. Immense amounts of time are wasted in schools, and, as I shall suggest in Chapter 4, children are sometimes forced to do things in schools which ought to be a matter of their choice, and so what makes a broad general education seem impossible may be the presence of curricular demands that in fact ought not to be made. But it may be that the general education I am advocating can be brought about only at the expense of early specialization in school. I can see no great loss in postponing specialization until university. Peters is quite right to stress the need for a broad cognitive perspective in education. On children's abilities, these naturally vary. Perhaps only the best will get all that I want them to out of schooling, however long it lasts. I shall have more to say on this in the final chapter. However, deliberately to aim at less than a broad general education and some vocational training as the outcome of the 15,000 hours children spend in schools would seem to be an implicit admission, on the part of educators, that de-schoolers are correct when they identify the main functions of school as child-minding and slotting them into pre-assigned social roles. I hope that educators will agree that an education along the lines I have suggested will fit pupils in an open society to perform their part well in life both towards others and towards

themselves (as Mill puts it). The educational demands made by a
genuinely open society on its citizens are (or ought to be) far
higher than those of a closed society, in which individual freedom
of thought and choice is not highly valued and little attention is
paid to preparing people for the exercise of such freedom. What
we need to do now is to examine some of the arguments in favour
of open societies.

## THE OPEN SOCIETY

I prefer to talk about the open society rather than democracy,
because not all democracies are open societies, although in
admitting the right of all citizens to choose and criticize policies
an open society must be democratic in some sense. A democracy,
like Dewey's for example, in which activities which were not
fully communicable were discouraged would place restrictions on
freedom of thought and activity that would not be acceptable in
an open society; nor would a democracy in which the will of the
majority or of a particular class was allowed to curb freedom of
thought, and freedom to pursue activities which harmed no one
be an open society, even if the motive behind the curbs was to
increase social equality. The open society is fundamentally a
pluralist society, one which respects as far as possible the freedom of individuals to think and act as they choose. Its govern-
mental policies will be open to criticism and discussion from any
quarter, while its government will be open to replacement by
peaceful means. So it will be a society with a legal and institutional framework allowing for peaceful change and aiming to
safeguard the liberties of thought and association of its citizens.
An open society will not impose social blueprints on individuals
or on society as a whole without giving and continuing to give
its members the chance to criticize and modify its policies, nor
will it legislate so as to make some particular government un-
removable by constitutional means. It is obvious that democracies,
even with genuine majorities in favour, could fail to be open in
this sense, by voting for repression. The open society is
obviously an ideal to which actual societies in their institutions
come closer or depart further. But there is more to an open
society than good institutions; these institutions have to be
operated by people committed to openness. An open society
requires an educated population: an educated population, vigilant
and capable of thinking for themselves, is the best means to
maintain an open society and to increase its openness. What I
have to say about the open society in this section is heavily
dependent on writings of J. S. Mill ('On Liberty') and Sir Karl
Popper (especially 'The Open Society and Its Enemies'). Before
going on to outline a defence of the open society, largely drawn
from Mill and Popper, I will consider an argument in favour of
autonomy in thought and behaviour which does not seem to me
to be successful.

Dearden (1968, p. 46) argues that even to ask whether it is a good thing for me to make my own choices (and hence to value my autonomy, and presumably, in consistency, that of others too) is to decide in favour of autonomy, because whatever I decide about this issue, even if I decide to put myself under the authority of someone else, will be my own decision. Hence, according to Dearden, there is some inconsistency in autonomously rejecting autonomy. This argument is rather similar to Peters's justification of education, and is open to a similar type of objection. Just as there seems to be nothing inconsistent in a man's using reason up to a point and then deciding to abandon rational enquiry, so there is nothing inconsistent in a man autonomously deciding that he will in future submit to some authority or closed institution, because, say, he values the security it gives him above the exercise of choice. Indeed, in a genuinely open society there should be nothing to stop individuals opting for such an alternative. Isaiah Berlin (1969, p. 131) has eloquently expressed the feeling that personal autonomy is a supreme value:

I wish my life and decisions to depend on myself, not on external forces of whatever kind. I wish to be the instrument of my own, not other men's acts of will. I wish to be a subject, not an object; to be moved by reasons, by conspicuous purposes, which are my own, not by causes which affect me, as it were from outside. I wish to be somebody, not nobody; a doer-deciding, not being decided for, self directed and not acted upon by external nature or by other men. . . . This is at least part of what I mean when I say that I am rational, and that it is my reason that distinguishes me as a human being from the rest of the world.

Berlin's sentiments will no doubt seem admirable to those of a liberal persuasion. But, as the example of those who freely enter religious orders shows (to say nothing of armies and political parties), whether one values freedom of choice for oneself in any particular area is a matter of personal preference. One is hardly contradicting oneself by putting oneself under the authority of another. A powerful case could indeed be made out for saying that in fairness and consistency, I should not restrict the choices of others against their will, and that such interference would amount to an assault on their integrity and authenticity. True as this is, however, what I now want to argue is that there are powerful reasons of a social and utilitarian sort for advocating a society in which there is freedom of thought and action, and that these reasons would be cogent even to a man who freely rejected freedom for himself in his own future life.

On freedom of thought and discussion, Mill argues that attempts to restrict opinions on any matter which are contrary to one's own imply that one is convinced that one's own opinions are correct. 'All silencing of discussion is an assumption of infallibility' (1859, p. 143). In saying this, Mill unfortunately overlooked the possibility of a merely cynical suppression of

opposing trends of thought. Aside from this, though, it is highly
unlikely that anyone is entitled to an assumption of infallibility.
Even in logic and mathematics, where proof procedures are well
established, no one has a monopoly of truth or is immune to
error. In natural science, there are always doubts about even
the best-established theories, while matters of religion, social
policy and ethical belief are highly contentious and much dis-
puted. But Mill argues convincingly that even if an opinion is
in fact true, suppression of opposition is likely to do harm,
because the strength, complexity and full implications of a theory
emerge only through its defence against criticism. When an
opinion becomes an orthodoxy, it loses much of its vitality and
its defenders cease to realize its value. This point is, of course,
well illustrated in the history of a religion like Christianity. The
meaning and significance of its claims became clear even to
believers only in the early Councils, which were called to define
the true faith in distinction to competing heresies. However, one
must concede, on probabilistic grounds at least, that one's own
opinion on most matters will not be the whole truth, if it is not
actually false. In such cases, suppression of opposition may well
involve suppressing what is at least part of the truth: 'It is
only by the collision of adverse opinions that the remainder of
the truth has any chance of being supplied' (Mill, 1859, p. 180).
To this could be added Popper's view that it is primarily in being
confronted with criticism that a theory reveals its weaknesses
and strengths. Thus restricting freedom of thought and discussion is a poor way not only of advancing knowledge, but also
of treating one's own favoured theories.

Mill bases his defence of freedom of action largely on the
debilitating effects of custom, especially where this is enforced.
He points out that there is less readiness to admit that we should
act on our desires and impulses than that we should be free to
form our own opinions. Against this, he argues that strong
desires are the result of an energetic character, and that it is
always the mentally energetic who have made original discoveries
in life-style as well as in the growth of knowledge. Without
people deviating from old practices 'human life would become a
stagnant pool' (1859, p. 193), and genius requires an atmosphere
of freedom in which to flourish. The somewhat ambivalent outcome of the presence of Goethe's free-acting genius on those
surrounding him, and the fact that Goethe himself insisted on
strictly conventional attitudes from others, is intriguingly analysed in Thomas Mann's 'Lotte in Weimar'. Nevertheless, Mill is
right to draw attention to the stuffiness and, I would add,
hypocrisy that is inevitably present in a society where custom
reigns supreme. Moreover, the effects of a life of rigid adherence
to customary ways can be devastating to people who find that
social change and development are rendering customary solutions
to contemporary problems inapplicable.

Mill's view that freedom of action is to be allowed so long as the
actions involved affect only the agent has been criticized on the

grounds that there are hardly any such actions, Certainly , it is
hard to draw a line between public and private conduct, and hard
to defend the view that the state should never attempt to enforce
laws relating only to the welfare of agents themselves (for example, on the compulsory wearing of crash helmets by motor
cyclists). But the discussion of freedom of action in 'On Liberty'
is still valuable because of the way it suggests that there is no
clear division between freedom of thought and freedom of action.
An atmosphere in which conduct is strictly regulated is unlikely
to be favourable to criticisms of the laws, and the suppression
of criticism is, of course, a restriction on freedom of discussion.
Any such restriction is unlikely to be self-contained for, as we
have already shown, views about human life and conduct are
affected by theories and ideas from all areas of knowledge, so
that a rigid, monolithic and intolerant society is unlikely to be
favourable to free discussion in any area. Nor is an atmosphere
in which originality in practice is frowned upon likely to be conducive to the challenging of authorities, which originality of
thought also implies. Certainly science and literature have not
on the whole flourished happily in societies without a degree of
social and intellectual openness. In modern times, scientists and
writers have continually clashed with totalitarian regimes, in a
way which hardly seems accidental.

So Mill's arguments in defence of an open society are largely
aimed at bringing out the intellectually and socially stultifying
effects of a closed society, and pointing to the consequences of
this for truth and originality. A defender of a closed society
may not be completely convinced by this, because he might claim
to value security and stability above truth and originality, and
he might even accept a degree of repression and universal
illusion as consequences. But as I argued in Chapter 1, we
should not be too sanguine about the likelihood of human happiness being produced generally on the basis of uncriticized false
ideas about man and the world. Apart from this, Popper's 'The
Open Society and Its Enemies' is an impassioned analysis of the
effect on a society of the 'degree of repression' required to
close social policy off from open discussion and criticism.

Popper is interested in two main forms of the closed society:
ancient tribalism and modern totalitarianism. Ancient tribal
society is characterized by its domination by uncriticized custom
and taboo. The laws of society are not regarded as essentially
different from the laws of nature; they are seen as sacrosanct
and unchangeable. The tribal society itself, in its simplest form,
is like a biological organism in which the individual members are
held together by semi-biological ties such as kinship, communal
living and effort, and whose identities are defined largely in
terms of the position they have within the group. In open
societies, on the other hand, organicity and the irrational
respect accorded to law and custom are largely absent. Laws may
be changed and criticized. Individuals have a degree of social
mobility and are not defined purely in terms of their initial role

within the group. Indeed, the links binding members of the open
society tend to be far more abstract and impersonal than the
essentially biological ties binding a tribe together.

Tribalism is by now largely destroyed. The reasons for this
are many and varied. They include the growth of commerce and
communication, with consequent new classes engaging in commerce
and so not fulfilling traditional organic roles within the group,
and contact from new ideas challenging the sanctity and natur-
alism of tribal customs. The result of this is the end of the belief
that the tribe is all and the individual nothing. Individual
initiative and self-assertion is a fact, and so is interest in the
individual for himself. There is both gain and loss in the ending
of tribalism. The gains include an increased respect for the
individual, and the possibilities of learning the truth about men
and the world that are opened up by the waning of the influence
of received tribal beliefs. Losses include the loss of security
accorded by tribal identity and membership, the struggle of
individuals and classes who now must find their own positions in
society, and the strain of having to make one's own decisions -
in short, all that goes to make up what Popper calls the strain
of civilization. One response to the strain is a yearning for the
irresponsibility and warmth of tribalism, which Popper sees as
the basis of much of the contemporary craving for revolutionary
and totalitarian solutions to modern problems. Indeed totalitarian
ideologies which think of the state as greater than the sum of its
members can usefully be seen as latter-day attempts to reinstate
the closed tribal society. But even though primitive tribal
societies may have provided a happy life for most of their members, this is unlikely to be the case with modern attempts to
return to the tribal virtues by turning our backs on the practice
of free discussion and criticism of social policies.

The modern utopian (whose prototype is Plato) believes that he
has a blueprint for a better society than the present post tribal
one. In his Utopia the strain of civilization will no longer be
felt. If he did not believe in his blueprint, he would hardly be
in a position to argue that he has an alternative to the open
society, in which individual rights and freedoms are respected,
and in which criticism and discussion were admitted. What Popper
does is argue that imposing a utopian blueprint, even in the name
of ideals such as harmony, equality or fraternity, will inevitably
lead to tyranny, and hence is to be rejected as a course of
action. (I take it that there is no need to argue that an open
society is better than an arbitrary tyranny, in which people and
their lives are subject to the whims of the tyrant. What the open
society has to be defended against is the attempt to show that a
benevolently motivated closed society might be a happier and
better society to live in than an open society.) It is clear, in the
first place, that no one can be absolutely sure that his blueprint
for society is completely correct. There is no intuition which can
give us such knowledge. In effect, however, the utopian defender of the closed society is claiming access to such intuition; if

he is willing to admit rational criticism and consequent modification of his utopian plan, he ceases to be advocating a closed society. However, the attempt to run society on closed lines, even in the name of a utopian ideal, is going to result in unacceptable tyranny. In other words, a closed society in contemporary circumstances, even when it is guided by utopian ideals, is bound to be an unhappy one. So we should not abandon to openness of free discussion and criticism of social policies, even if we are convinced that we have a good model of a better society.

The reason for this is that all social actions tend to have consequences unwelcome to and unforeseen by their agents. An example of an unwelcome consequence of a social action is the man who enters the market for a house and automatically pushes the price of houses up. An example of an unwelcome and unforeseen consequence of a social policy is given by the various acts controlling the renting of property in Britain, as a result of which the property available for renting has become scarcer and more expensive. We are very far from being able to predict the consequences of social policies (if we were, we could presumably act in advance to prevent unwelcome ones). The utopian planner in a closed society is most vulnerable to the adverse effect of unwelcome results of his policies. This is both because his blueprint will tend to be one for society as a whole, and hence have far greater and more widespread consequences than a small-scale piece of social engineering, but also because he will not be able to collect and consider criticisms of his planning from those affected by them. As an authoritarian, running a closed society, he will necessarily discourage criticism. As a result of this he will have little chance to hear about and correct the effects of his policies. He will not even know if his policies are leading towards or away from his original aim. There is the further point to be considered that if a utopian authoritarian government comes to power as the result of a revolution, the experience of the effects of the policies may well lead to the revolutionaries' (or some of them) changing their ideals. But this will be to admit the falsity of the original blueprint, which in turn removes any justification for the original imposition of a closed society. In fact, anyone who does not take up a totally dogmatic and inflexible attitude to his plans is in practice admitting that they are less than certain, which admission would appear to deprive of its main putative justification any attempt the planner makes to suppress all unwelcome criticisms. What Popper does is to emphasize the human cost involved in the imposition of an uncriticizable blueprint. For the material on which the blueprint is imposed consists of the lives of human beings. Unlike primitive tribal societies, there is nothing really natural about a utopian blueprint. At most, it may correspond to someone's idea of nature. But the attempt to impose it will involve the destruction of whatever open institutions already exist, or the prevention of any from developing, even though with the ending of tribalism many people will be wishing for such institutions, and this will involve the suppression of opposition – lying, the corruption of truth, imprisonment, banishment, executions. So a closed society in the modern world, even if it is based on the best of ideals, will naturally gravitate towards deceit and tyranny. The implication is that a better society than the present one is likely to emerge only by the adoption of open institutions, in which attempts at reform and improvement are regarded as modifiable and criticizable.

Popper's own presentation of his arguments tends to emphasize the dangerous implications of imposing wholesale changes on society and what he sees as the desirability of developing social institutions through piecemeal reforms (because these are easier to control and criticize). I shall have some critical things to say on his advocacy of social engineering in Chapter 4, but a major element in his attack on utopianism is the demonstration that imposing a utopian blueprint leads to tyranny. I have argued, from a slightly different angle, that a closed society will be justifiable only to the extent that its defenders believe they have a correct blueprint for a good society. But the upshot of this will be that the blueprint is treated as uncriticizable. Even if it does not have to be imposed by sweeping away all existing institutions, as happens in the cases Popper considers where revolutionaries impose totally new solutions on society, but builds on or preserves existing institutions, I have argued that the freezing of all criticism and discussion that is implied by the refusal to admit opposition is likely to lead in the end to tyranny just the same. My conclusion is the same as Popper's (1945, vol. 1, p. 200):

> Arresting political change ·is not the remedy [to the strain of civilization]: it cannot bring happiness. We can never return to the alleged innocence and beauty of the closed society. Our dream of heaven cannot be realized on earth. Once we begin to rely upon our reason, and to use our powers of criticism . . . we cannot return to a state of implicit submission to tribal magic. . . . The more we try to return to the heroic age of tribalism, the more surely do we arrive at the Inquisition, at the Secret Police, and at a romanticized gangsterism. Beginning with the suppression of reason and truth, we must end with the most brutal and violent destruction of all that is human.

So a society which treats individuals as subservient to it, and restricts their freedom of thought and behaviour in the name of some organic ideal, has the makings of a tyranny. Some restrictions on the freedom of behaviour must naturally be enforced, even in an open society, but these should be argued for and motivated by a respect for the rights and freedoms of other individuals, not in order to produce overall social conformity to a blueprint, utopian or otherwise, laid down by rulers claiming uncriticizable insight into the true good for man and society. In the open society, although there are many activities and possibilities open to individuals only because they are members of social institutions or groups (such as voting, defending one's country, getting married, being a member of a team, working in a factory or a university), these larger institutions should be defended and developed to the extent that they further the interests and needs of the individuals who participate in them, and they should be regarded as open to change and reform as a result of criticisms and suggestions from individuals. To regard institutions, or society itself, as having their own existence and rights beyond those of the individuals in them is to prepare the way for totalitarian thinking and tyrannical policies.

In this section I have defended the open society partly by analysing some of its advantages, but principally by pointing to the defects, in human terms, of closed societies. What I would stress is that in most parts of the world now a purely natural or organic closed society (Popper's tribal society) is no longer a real option. Any closing off of thought, discussion and personal liberty in general requires positively repressive measures. When repression is not introduced by a ruling clique for purely cynical and self-interested motives, it is in the name of some theory of society: religious, social or political. It is particularly to the latter type of case that Popper's arguments are directed. Of course, they may fail to convince the committed totalitarian, who can always appeal to his faith in his dogma to justify whatever human suffering results from the repressive imposition of his blueprint. As with my earlier arguments against religious fund- amentalism and Rousseauian intuitionism, one's attitude here will partly depend on one's attitude to the particular dogma in question. Indeed, it may be doubted whether there can be any arguments against dogmatic procedures in politics or education in general, so that what is needed is an examination of the merits and demerits of each dogma individually. Thus, it will be said, we should argue against the Amish or the Ayatollahs by con- sidering the truth or falsity of their beliefs, rather than by adducing general arguments against the suppression and control of learning. I have tried to show, on the other hand, that this is too modest. Apart from the fact that inflexible dogmatists are unlikely to be any more convinced by arguments directed against their specific dogmas than they are by general arguments in favour of the open society, there surely are, as I have tried to show, some considerations arising from the possibility of error in any belief and from the possibility of unsuspected unwelcome consequences of any policy which would apply whatever the dogma or the policy, and which ought to have some weight in favour of an open society even for a committed believer, who might not hitherto have appreciated the full implications of the forcible imposition of his beliefs on others. Moreover, not all believers in religious or political systems are inflexibly dogmatic to the extent of wishing actively to suppress possible opposition. To an extent, some of the considerations I have brought forward here and in Chapter 1 may appeal to them, and serve also to define the extent to which particular groups of believers are inflexible and illiberal concerning their beliefs.

In defending the open society against closed societies I have not said anything in detail about the precise degree to which individuals should be able to do what they want. I have defined it in terms of the respect there is in the society for individual freedom and of the ability of individuals to criticize and change governments. In the sense in which I have defined the notion, an open society could be economically highly laissez-faire, or incorporate a considerable degree of state-directed care and welfare. This is as it should be, for decisions here should be pre-eminently matters of public discussion, in terms of the respective consequences of the various measures introduced. So, consonant with a general respect for individual freedom, members of an open society could argue, say, for a high level of taxation in order to promote wide-ranging programmes of health and education, or for low levels of taxation in the belief that people are better off having to take personal responsibility for such matters. Apart from general considerations, however, such as having laws to prevent individuals from violating the rights of others, there is one important respect in which anyone committed to the values of the open society will want the state to oversee individual activity. We have already touched on it in the previous section: if we are to have individuals involved in making choices, public and private, we will want them sufficiently educated to make reasonable choices. Therefore, we should expect the state to see that all individuals have a reasonable education, and this means a thorough grounding in the areas considered in the previous section. To an extent, then, pluralism in adult life precludes too much choice for children while they are still being educated, for too much choice during one's education may well restrict one's range of choice and perspective later. It is no qualification of one's commitment to an open, pluralist society, then, to insist that education should not be freed from having to come up to standards overseen by the state.

On the other hand, although the state should ensure, as Mill says, that parents give all children an education enabling them to live and to make their choices in life, and this is as much a duty of the state as it is to ensure that parents feed their children, it is important, in view of the truth-seeking and critical role of education and learning, that the education system should preserve a degree of autonomy from the state. This provides a strong argument for ensuring that at least part of the education system is not funded completely by the government. As Mill (1859, pp. 239-40) also pointed out, the danger inherent in an education system directed and monopolized by the state is that it will become 'a mere contrivance for moulding people to be exactly like one another' and that it will open up strong possibilities of a 'despotism over the mind'. The temptation for politicians to interfere with the autonomy of the education system would undoubtedly increase if none of it was financially independent of the state.

## CONCLUSION

In this chapter I have explored possible justifications for education, and developed a scheme of education to fit people for life in an open society. I have also tried to explain why an open society is preferable to a closed society, especially now that tribalism has largely disappeared and any closed society would have to be imposed on people from above. In this defence of the open society, I stressed the importance of a respect for truth and of the critical approach in ensuring that tyranny and exploitation are avoided. This is ultimately why values other than those of immediate individual happiness or self-realization need to be stressed in education, and why those who care about living in an open society should also care about educational standards and achievements.

# 3  LEARNING AND TEACHING

## INTRODUCTION

Discussion in this area is often flawed by superficiality and false
dichotomies. For example we constantly hear that what teachers
should aim to do is produce understanding in their pupils, rather
than merely modify their pupils' behaviour by getting them to
repeat things by rote and so on. Indoctrination is condemned
because it involves the transmission of false beliefs. We are told
to encourage creativity rather than to impose models from outside.
Information is contrasted with imagination. Yet understanding
cannot be separated from what a man does. It is not a mental
accompaniment to behaviour: and speaking of someone understanding something presupposes at bottom the presence of shared
reactions on the parts of those involved. If the transmission of
false beliefs was in itself objectionable then science teaching
would be ruled out, for we have no conclusive proof of scientific
theories (because they have applications beyond anything we have
experienced), and, as history shows us, most of the scientific
theories held as true at any given time are later shown to be
false. Creativity, even in the arts, is hardly possible without
some understanding of the tradition or problems which define the
scope for originality and innovation. Equally, the most valued
imaginative leaps in science were made only by people who had a
profound understanding of the nature of the problem concerned,
and hence of why and how their insight might be a solution to
the problem. Indeed, when a work in art or science is praised as
creative or imaginative, this is normally because of the new light
it throws on old problems or situations, rather than as a remark
about the mental states or feelings of freedom of the author.
Distinctions exist between creativity and fantasy, imagination and
whimsy, and we should surely aim to encourage in our pupils the
former member of each of these pairs, rather than the latter.

In this chapter I will begin by giving a very basic and general
characterization of the notion of understanding. This will be
followed by an attempt to show that this analysis of understanding
does not involve relativism in any objectionable sense. Then
various conclusions about what is and is not desirable in teaching
will be drawn in the light of what has been said here and in
Chapter 2.

UNDERSTANDING

The sort of learning of skills and subjects advocated in Chapter 2 in most cases naturally implies more than automatic or reflex responses on the part of the learner. It involves the ability to make judgments, to apply skills, to weigh up alternatives. It involves an awareness of what one is doing; in short, it implies understanding of what one is confronted with.

A crucial point about notions like understanding, thinking effectively, being able to communicate and so on is that they require some subject matter to be understood, thought about and communicated. You cannot just understand, think or communicate; there has to be something you are understanding, thinking about or communicating. This point has rightly been emphasized by P. H. Hirst (1965), in his criticism of taking a spuriously general mental ability such as the ability to think effectively or to communicate as an aim of education. As Hirst points out, depending on the subject matter of one's thinking, quite different abilities and degrees of success might be at stake. A man who can understand and explain Latin poetry sensitively and intelligently might be a complete duffer when it comes to physics; nor is there any necessary transfer of ability in one area to ability in another. Moreover, in speaking of a man's understanding something, we are speaking of an achievement or success he has with some problem or concept, and the criterion of success here is his ability to come up to some public and previously existing standard of performance. The arguments for this point and its implications are to be found in the account of understanding given by Wittgenstein in his 'Philosophical Investigations' (1953).

Wittgenstein was much exercised by the problems involved in our use of mental concepts. For we speak of other people having thoughts and feelings and mental abilities, without being able to look directly into their minds. How do we know what it is for someone else to be understanding something? What does it mean to speak of someone understanding something? These may seem to be abstract and abstruse questions, but they should be of interest to educators, because educators generally aim to produce understanding in other people. If it is to produce something essentially inside somebody's mind, how can you set about doing it or know that you have succeeded?

One approach to this problem can be mentioned immediately, in order to reject it as beside the point. It might be said that anyone who understands a particular concept, say of a geometrical point, is in a certain brain state, in principle observable and describable, and that our aim in getting someone to understand the concept is to produce that brain state in him. It may well be true that anyone who understands the notion of a point, say, has a particular connection in his brain which people who do not understand this do not have. However, pointing to this connection cannot be the answer to our question about how we know

that he understands it, because we would be able to say that
anyone who understands the concept is in such and such a brain
state only because we had discovered a correlation between the
brain state and the state of understanding what a point is, and
this requires the ability to identify the two independently. In
practice, of course, we can identify the state of understanding,
while we know very little about the specific correlations between
mental states and brain states. If we knew more, and were able
to produce brain states of 'mathematical understanding', say by
electrical or chemical means, this would undoubtedly have a profound effect on our conceptions both of people and of education,
although estimating the success of our work would presumably
still have to be made by checking that people who had been
operated on did manifest their understanding in the old ways.
Indeed, our interest in knowing whether people did understand
things or not would continue to be primarily an interest in their
actual and potential behaviour rather than an interest in their
brains. So we can identify people's understandings of particular
concepts without knowing anything about their brains, and the
need for using our present method will not completely go even if
we knew all that there was to be known about brains. So what is
the method by which we actually judge that someone really
understands something?

Understanding something is an achievement. It does not occur
just because an individual desires it or thinks that it has
occurred, and it can exist even if the individual in question is
doubtful about it (if, for example, he is terrified of a teacher
who is examining him). So a person's understanding is partially
independent of what he himself thinks about it. It is also
independent of what is in his mind or mentally present to him at
any point, because whatever is present to his mind at any point
is consistent with him failing to understand. Let us consider as
an example a person's understanding of the meaning of a word,
say 'uphill'. Now it could be that the dictionary definition might
be passing through his mind at the point in question, yet,
because he did not correctly understand all the words of the
definition, he might still use the word incorrectly, and hence
(we would say) fail to understand it. Even if a mental image of
an old man walking up a hill occurred to him as well, this would
not guarantee a correct understanding of 'uphill', because the
image itself still has to be interpreted and, as Wittgenstein
(1953, p. 54n) says, a Martian might understand the same image
as being a picture of someone sliding downhill. Even if an arrow
was added to the picture pointing in the right direction, that
would not mislead only if you understood that the arrow was to
be read as pointing in the direction of its head, and any clari-
fication of that point could also be misunderstood. Wittgenstein's
conclusion is that the meaning of a word, or of a sentence, or of
a picture, or of a sign is to be analysed in terms of its use, and to
understand any of these things is to be able to use them correctly. But one's use of something like a word or a sign is the

way one employs it in communication or reacts to it, and this is essentially a matter of long-term public activity, rather than of immediate, private mental events.

Wittgenstein's analysis of understanding the meaning of a word can be extended to other types of understanding. Some understanding, like mending a puncture or firing a pot, is directly practical, and involves being able to do something rather than to say anything (or there is no understanding). Other understanding can be regarded as more theoretical, in that it does not involve being able to do or make anything. But even here the criterion for its existence is the ability to manifest it in some way in expression or behaviour, and the extent to which one understands some idea is the extent to which one can speak about it or use it in one's thought or reasoning (again something manifested in practice). Of course, I can understand ideas and even know that I understand them without actually expressing them or manifesting my understanding in any way. I can also think about them privately and have relevant images when I am thinking about them. But Wittgenstein's arguments show that these private thoughts and images get the sense they do from the way they would fit into my behaviour and the way I would express them in my discourse, and it is in terms of the way that this potential behaviour of mine accords with the public understanding and use of the idea that the correctness of my understanding is judged. Wittgenstein's arguments also show that the presence of mental thoughts or images is neither necessary nor sufficient for understanding. Thus my understanding of the theory of relativity is to be assessed according to whether what I would say about it, and the conclusions I would draw from it, correspond to what Einstein said about it; and to say that I do understand the theory is just to say that what I would say does correspond to Einstein's thought. Of course, there might be occasions where someone understands something like a poem idiosyncratically and originally, where there is no hard and fast correct interpretation, but we would still expect some expression or manifestation of this original interpretation. An understanding which makes no difference to a man's words or behaviour (at least potentially) is an understanding in name only, a mere beating of the air. If a man thinks he understands something and tries to express it, but can in no way do so, his struggle against the constriction of his dumbness is painful just because he realizes that what he thought he understood he never had. The manifestation of the understanding, to be recognized as such, has to come up to public standards of appropriateness or we will have no grounds for predicating it of others. This remains true even in cases where someone's original achievement actually changes those standards in some way; in such a case the change will have to be visible as a continuation of and an improvement on what previously existed.

The type of understanding which educators are aiming to produce is most often understanding in areas that have already been

well charted, and what they are interested in doing is bringing
pupils to some proficiency in these areas. I spoke in Chapter 1
of the disadvantages of leaving children to make their own primitive attempts to grasp concepts and theories which it has taken
generations of experts to develop. So we need to see what is
involved in understanding the methods and techniques of a well-
established discipline. Both because it is Wittgenstein's own
example and because it would seem at first sight to be a case
where nothing but the autonomous working of pure reason is
involved, I will consider something involved in elementary mathematics (cf. Wittgenstein, 1953, pp. 74-6). What comes out from
this is a further indication of the insufficiency of an analysis of
understanding in terms of mental contents, together with the
idea that understanding something even as theoretical as a
mathematical rule involves sharing a practical procedure, and
ultimately a form of life.

The example concerns an attempt to teach a pupil how to add,
and how to continue arithmetical series by adding. We begin by
giving him the rule for adding 2 to a given quantity. What we
are doing is to teach the rule which is to be followed when you
see '+2'. The example is intended to bring out what is involved
in the notion of following a rule (which is central to the concept
of understanding, as many important cases of understanding
can usefully be seen in terms of following rules for the use of
words or symbols, or pieces in games). At first, our pupil seems
to grasp the point well, and he continues the series correctly
right up to 994, 996, 998, 1,000. But when he gets to 1,000, he
continues the series 1,004, 1,008, 1,012, 1,016. . . . We say to
him that he is making a mistake, and that he is no longer doing
the same as he was or the same as we told him. He may immediately see this, but Wittgenstein asks us to consider a case where
he replies that (in his opinion) he is doing the same, and our
explanations and examples cannot budge him. He cannot see that
he is not obeying our original instruction and teaching. Wittgenstein says that it comes naturally to this pupil to understand
our instruction 'Add 2' as we would understand 'Add 2 up to
1,000, add 4 up to 2,000, add 6 up to 3,000 and so on.'

What we have here is certainly an example of bizarre behaviour
on the part of the pupil, but it could be that there was nothing
in the instructions and examples we gave him which would have
explicitly ruled out his applying the rule in the way he does. His
mistake is not one that is possible for us, because we know that
the application of rules for addition is not affected by the mere
presence of quantities greater than 1,000. Part of Wittgenstein's
point, though, is to get us to see that in the application of any
rule, there will be a large number of assumptions which are not
made explicit. This is partly because there is no need to make
them explicit - because of the way we are by nature or are
trained in our upbringing, we just do follow them - but also
because all the rules involved in the use of a concept or procedure could not be made explicit, for the words or signs used

in the explanation would themselves have to be explained, and
so on ad infinitum. At a certain point we cease having any
justifications or explanations for our rules, we just act and react;
and communication with people who did not share these reactions
would hardly be possible. Like following the arrow or the pointed
finger in the intended direction, or taking crying as a sign of
pain, or being attracted by and noticing bright colours and the
voices of other human beings, there do seem to be certain primitive and basic human reactions common to all people. Such
reactions cannot in any obvious way be further justified or
explained, but without them and without our noticing certain
features of the world, without any further pointing or gesturing,
it is hard to see how any language-learning or explanations of
rules could begin at all, because there would be no way of
attracting the learner's attention in the right way. (By speaking
here of a primitive and basic human reaction, I do not mean that
a new-born baby or a child exposed to no socialization at all will
necessarily manifest it. What I mean is something that any non-
deficient human being brought up in the company of other human
beings will pick up, without explicit prompting, though some
such reactions, such as noticing the pain of other people, come
fairly late in a child's chronological development.)

It is worth being aware that there are elements in Wittgenstein's
philosophy of mathematics that are wrong, for example, his claim
(1967, p. 77) that each new theorem represents a new decision
on the part of mathematicians: this claim may be part of what is
behind his example of the pupil learning to add. Some sense must
be given to the notion of consistency in mathematics, or it is
hard to see what would be meant by speaking of a theorem or
calculation at all. Similarly, the claim (1953, p. 81) that any
piece of conduct could on some interpretation be made to appear
consistent with any rule appears far-fetched. This may also be
part of what is behind the addition example, but it is hard to see
how, if we had added to our original explanation to our pupil
the explicit instruction that 1,000 + 2 was to yield 1,002, his
conduct in the example could have been made to appear consistent on any interpretation of our new instructions. However,
we do not have to accept these extreme claims in order to
accept as valid the point that in any process of rule-following,
all sorts of assumptions are made and understood which, in the
nature of things, cannot be made fully explicit. Understanding
a rule means that we will know how to react and how to apply it
in many cases for which we have not been given explicit
instruction. What is at issue is not just a response to a set
stimulus, but an awareness of the significance of the response,
so that we can apply it to circumstances quite different from
those in which it was originally taught. A common practice such
as mathematics or speaking a language further requires that
people engaging in it shall, by and large, agree in their
reactions to these new situations. Not every application of a rule
of mathematics or governing the use of a word can be spelled

out in advance, nor can it be present to an individual's consciousness, because there are endless possible new applications of every word. Yet activities like mathematics and speech are successfully carried on. This suggests a large measure of agreement in the reactions of those engaging in them, and also that what their common understanding consists in is just this sharing of reactions.

This is not to deny that reactions may differ, even among those who fully understand the present use of a word, about how it is to be applied in some completely new set of circumstances. Consider, for example, the use of the concept of a person if cloning or brain transplants became common. Many rules and many concepts are not fully determined in all possible applications where new decisions will be needed (here Wittgenstein's conventionalism is correct). But the point remains that for a successful system of communication or calculation, these undetermined applications must be the exceptions rather than the norm. It is possible to think of worlds in which mathematics, say, would be impossible, because people in their calculations rarely agreed with each other as to what followed from what, or because their memories were too short. We can imagine, too, worlds which were physically quite different from ours, which would make calculating difficult or even impossible. For example, there might be nothing that lasted long enough to write numbers with, or quantities of things and marks we made might be continually altering at random. The world might be so different that the deviant pupil's 1,004, 1,008, 1,012 seemed more reasonable and natural than our 1,002, 1,004, 1,006: perhaps the mere presence of quantities of over 1,000 had a doubling effect on things added to them. So all sorts of facts about the world, and about human beings and their capacities, underlie both our choice of rules and the rule-following reactions which make such practices as calculating possible. In this sense, even mathematics rests on an empirical basis, and could imaginably be different. But what needs to be stressed here is not the world-dependent nature of mathematics so much as the way in which the teaching of it assumes certain reactions in learners, and that these reactions are not the only ones possible or the only ones imaginable, given our starting points. Arithmetic presumably requires, as basic on the part of learners, the perception of disparate quantities, separate objects or moments rather than an undifferentiated flux, while the example of the deviant pupil shows that, without any instructions to the contrary, reacting differently than us when dealing with quantities greater than 1,000 may have nothing (absolutely speaking) illogical about it, and might even have seemed more natural had the world been different. Of course, on the whole we are not interested in teaching mathematics with no application to our world. We attempt to instil those practices which we have adopted, but because not everything that the practice implies can be spelled out explicitly this means attempting to get our pupil to internalize our own reactions, so that he will go on as we want. If this internalization of reaction could not be achieved, we could not teach the practice of mathematics, because we would have to teach each new sum or theorem as a new fact unconnected with what had already been learned, and this would be tantamount to losing the notion of a proof.

What I hope has emerged so far from this section is the extent to which a man's understanding, even of a mathematical rule or the meaning of a word, cannot be divorced from his behaviour and reactions, natural and learned. What goes for mathematics and language goes even more for science and the arts, where there is a clearer sense in which one is being introduced to public traditions of thought and practice, and where there is generally less attempt to spell out definitions and concepts in explicit detail. Even where in science there is an attempt to do this, it is frequently only in order to summarize the role the concept plays in certain theories and experiments. The definition then gets its sense from the practice, a point on which Dewey was quite correct. It would be difficult to see how any understanding of a word like 'electron' could be gained independently of some grasp of the theories and experiments in which it features, or how we could understand the concept 'sonata form' independently of some knowledge of the tradition of Haydn, Mozart and Beethoven. To know merely a mechanical paradigm of a sonata movement as involving the exposition, development and recapitulation of two themes, one in the tonic and the other in the dominant, is really to know virtually nothing of classical sonata form. Understanding of the concepts central to science and the arts is essentially an understanding of living traditions of research and creation, and a sharing of them, as Dewey would put it. In the arts there can be all the difference in the world between two performances of the same work, even though from an objective point of view both correctly give the same notes or steps, and these differences are often explained by appeal to the traditions in which the performers have been trained and have learned, or failed to learn, the significance of the steps or notes.

So understanding words or following rules is a matter of learning how to use or apply them. Understanding concepts and theories in science and the arts involves understanding something of the activity of scientists and artists. In all these cases of understanding, what is at issue is a grasp of public knowledge and traditions which is necessarily publicly expressible and assessable. So the understanding we aim at in teaching is indeed an ability to use what is understood, and to that extent may be seen as an awareness of what is learned, but it would be quite wrong to analyse this awareness in terms of private mental accompaniments to the learning process, or to make a sharp distinction between understanding a concept and being able to use or apply it. Thus, if rote learning is to be condemned, it is because learning by rote may not involve any ability to apply what is learned, not because rote learning involves external speech rather than internal thought.

The conclusion that understanding languages, systems of calculation and other disciplines is based in shared reactions, natural and learned, has implications for two opposed views of learning. On the one hand, there is the view often attributed to Locke, according to which the learner is like an empty blackboard (or tabula rasa) on which experiences are written or impressed from without, which the learner then connects and associates with each other according to their similarities and dissimilarities, and so builds up a set of concepts and theories about the world. Against this view, it needs to be emphasized that there are any number of ways in which two or more experiences could be regarded as similar or dissimilar, and from which concepts could be abstracted and predictions made. Without some prior idea on the part of the learner as to which features of his experience to attend to, it is doubtful that there could be any systematic noting and categorizing of features at all, no framework with which to begin to sift and make sense of the flux of experience. No doubt the small-centred picture of experience possessed by a dog is very different from our visually centred one. One could imagine a dog categorizing as similar objects that seemed quite different to us. A set of implicit ideas about what to attend to would be needed even if the learner's experience included someone pointing to certain features of his experience and attempting to teach him the meanings of words by uttering the names of those features. Assuming that the learner understood the pointing gesture (and try teaching that to a fish or even to a dog), whatever is pointed at can be categorized in innumerable ways. Thus in pointing to my pencil I am simultaneously pointing at a pencil, a colour, a shape, something wooden, something sharp, something straight and so on. Unless the learner realized that 'red' was a colour word, and had some notion of what it was to be a colour, there is no guarantee that he would correctly realize the significance of my uttering 'red' while pointing. Even if I then go on to point to a red book, the learner could still misinterpret 'red' as referring to the straight edge common to both, rather than the colour. Such misunderstandings could be systematically and indefinitely multiplied.

The conclusion is that picking features out of experience requires some implicit focus of attention or scheme of classification on the part of the learner: hence learning about the environment cannot consist simply in environmental inputs impressing themselves on a passive receiver of sensations. Although the receiver develops his schemes of classification in the light of his experiences, having any experiences at all presupposes in him a framework for classifying those experiences. Further, the learning of a public language or discipline requires that the learner's focus of attention be in tune with that of the teacher, which brings out again the need for common reactions and interests basic to human life as a presupposition of

successful communication. Indeed, as each person's route into
experience is rather different, it is hard to see how, as a tabula
rasa and without a mental structure and dispositions in tune with
those of his parents and teachers, a new-born child could ever
begin to understand the messages given to him by his parents
or to learn a language at all.

So human beings are not empty tablets, awaiting inscriptions
from experience. They do naturally have basic interests and
inchoate frameworks with which to structure experience. But we
should not regard the learning process as simply the growth and
development of these natural dispositions to react in specific
ways to particular types of experience rather than to others,
nor should we regard the structures underlying these dispositions as knowledge of an innate or instinctive sort. The reason
for this is that a disposition to respond to or recognize particular types of stimuli is not itself knowledge that anything is the
case, or even knowledge of the experiential content of the
stimuli. A dispositional structure needs to be filled out or given
some sensory content by the particular experiences that it
structures, while the actual knowledge that something is the case
requires, in addition to a scheme of classification, the assurance
(usually through sensation) that some item of experience is
really to be categorized in a particular way. Further, any primitive dispositions to structure experience in certain ways can be
refined or even overturned both by the actual experiences we
have and by later, more sophisticated schemes of classification
which are built on our earlier dispositions and experiences.
Natural science can be regarded as the elaboration, refinement
and correction of our primitive picture of the world around us,
but, as Quine (1969, p. 128) has emphasized, many of the
features of importance to our prescientific world picture are
regarded as unimportant in science. Thus colour is a major
element of ordinary experience, a fact reflected in the presence
of colour schemes of some sort in all natural languages. It is
easy to see the value of colour perception in food-gathering and
so on. But physics does without colour, explaining it in terms
of wavelengths and excluding it from any significant role in its
own explanations of phenomena. So physics corrects our natural
disposition to classify in terms of colour; colour is not one of
the basic or structural properties of matter. Similarly, the distinctions between substances that seemed to be of significance to
men in their ordinary lives (wood, coal, gold, silver, iron, oil,
water, etc.) have been much redrawn in chemistry, and shown
to be of only limited explanatory power. So science, although
based in natural and primitive reactions to the external world,
has involved the correction and development of these reactions.
To learn science is not simply to develop one's natural reactions
(if these could even be distinguished in practice), but to enter
a cultural tradition, whose development has been historically
quite unpredictable because of a dual unpredictability: that of
the reactions of nature to our make-up and probings and of the

imaginative leaps of the individuals who probed.

In a similar way, it is possible to think of mathematics and art as being based in natural reactions, but transcending these reactions. Thus, if we did not react to the indefinite flux of experience by individuating what we take to be solid, enduring and (for a time) unchanging objects, it is hard to see how we could ever have come to count or number things. But typical of mathematics is the unpredictable discovery, which can often appear baffling and upsetting; such as the discovery of irrational numbers or of Gödel's incompleteness theorem. Equally, artistic expression is based in the human tendency to symbolize and to express needs and interests imaginatively. Painting, dancing, singing and story-telling, all purposeless from an instrumental point of view, would appear to be found in all cultures, and may therefore be reasonably counted as basic and natural human reactions. But it would be highly implausible to think of developing traditions of art as simply the flowering of these natural reactions, if only because different cultures have developed their art-forms in such different ways. So mathematics and art are, like science, based in natural human reactions; but, like science, they are also cultural artefacts, unpredictable and developing.

When we speak of people understanding things, whether these are theoretical matters or practical, we are speaking of what they can in principle manifest in their behaviour, either verbally or practically. This recognition of the understanding of others implies, on the part of all concerned, a community of reactions, interests and goals; in important cases what is involved is common acceptance of sets of rules, and membership of particular traditions in which primitive and natural reactions have been worked on and developed in new and unexpected ways. In order to bring out just what is being claimed here, this section will be closed with a brief consideration of a thesis of David Hamlyn (1978, pp. 80-7 and 1981), according to which it is not merely mutual communication and the recognition of the understanding of others that requires a common form of life. According to Hamlyn, having any sort of knowledge and experience in itself requires on the part of the knower a conception of himself as a member of a community of other knowers and experiencers who can correct his understanding of the world. Hamlyn is not claiming just that in practice children learn from contact with other people, nor is he pointing to the fact that educators are primarily interested in introducing pupils to public traditions of knowledge and experience. He is claiming that outside the context of public standards of correctness and interpersonal relationships (or animal surrogates for such), there is no such thing as knowledge or experience. His view would thus seem to point to a theoretical inadequacy in accounts of learning (such as those of Skinner, Chomsky and Piaget) which, in one way or another, consider the child or learner in isolation from his or her social environment - as an isolated experiencer, theorizer or

constructor. Whether or not his view actually has this consequence for the views of Skinner and the others (and this is open
to question - cf. D. E. Cooper, 1980b), it is not clear that
Hamlyn's arguments actually establish his central contention,
that any understanding of the world requires that the under-
stander be capable of recognizing that other experiencers might
or might not agree with his view of the world - that, in other
words, he shares in a common form of life with others.

Hamlyn argues that perceptual judgments - for example, I see,
feel, hear such and such - (which are surely basic to any sort
of experiential awareness) involve knowledge, first, of what it
is for something to be what it is experienced as. I am not clear
what knowledge is involved in seeing something as blue, when
this experience does not involve some verbally explicit use or
knowledge of the concept blue, but it is certainly true that any
perceptual judgment raises the possibility of knowledge and hence
of truth and falsity at a second point, for any judgment that
something is such and such will be either true or false. Hamlyn
concludes that such judgments presuppose in the experiencer an
understanding of what it is for them to be either true or false,
and hence a conception of truth. Now truth, according to Hamlyn,
is a 'social concept'. By this he means that to speak of something
being true is to speak of other potential observers agreeing that
it is so and of correcting one if it is not. Only in the context of
other observers correcting according to publicly acceptable
standards of correctness could there be any distinction between
a case in which a subject appeared to change his mind about
something and one in which he recognized that what he had previously held was false. Finally, to see something 'as a correction
implies seeing the source of whatever is done as a corrector,
[and] whatever else that involves, it certainly involves seeing
that something as a thing, with desires, interests, etc. - in
other words as a person or as something person-like' (quoted
from an earlier version of Hamlyn, 1981, by D. E. Cooper, 1980b,
pp. 97-8). So, for Hamlyn, perceptual experience raises the
question of the presence or absence of objective knowledge,
knowledge involves having the concept of truth and having the
concept of truth implies seeing oneself as a member of a community of correctors.

It might be objected that Hamlyn's actual argument from the
non-privacy of truth shows only that potential observers would
agree with one. Certainly, as he admits, there can be things
that no one else in fact knows. What he is at pains to rule out is
any truth that is 'logically impossible for others to know' (1978,
p. 81). However, he would presumably argue at this point that
having the concept of truth involves understanding (in some way)
that truth is logically non-private in this sense, and that a
creature that did not actually see itself as a member of a group
of experiencers could have no conception of the public nature of
truth and standards of truth, or of other experiencers even of
a potential sort. While this move seems reasonable enough, what

is open to question is why some understanding of the possible truth or falsity of experiential judgments on the part of the experiencer requires on the part of the experiencer himself a grasp of the public nature of truth as analysed by Hamlyn. What is true is that any true perceptual judgment, even by an animal, must come up to whatever public standards are appropriate for that judgment: but why should an animal or a child itself have to understand this? What is needed on the part of the experiencer is some sense of objectivity, so that it can in principle distinguish reality from illusion in its perceptions. But it is unclear why this sense could not be provided by things (by their actual hardness, taste, feel and so on, as opposed to their seen or expected hardness, taste or feel) rather than by interpersonal correctors. Indeed, there seems to be no reason why a child or an animal should not be led to change its mind as the result of such correction through further experiences of things, and even have an awareness of this. So Hamlyn does not seem to have made impregnable his case that any understanding of one's environment requires a sense of belonging to a group of experiencers with common reactions and interests.

What I have argued in this section is that understanding is not a purely mental process. It affects behaviour and must be manifestable in behaviour. Further, parents and educators have to communicate with their children and pupils, and this requires on the part of the children reactions in common with their elders. Moreover, much of the business of education will be involved with initiating children into public systems of thought and behaviour. Finally, of course, the recognition of understanding in others (though not necessarily its existence) requires sharing standards of correctness with them. What we now have to examine is whether the need for shared standards and traditions has any relativistic overtones.

## RELATIVISM AND FORMS OF LIFE

> It is what human beings say that is true and false; and they agree in the language they use. That is not agreement in opinions but in form of life. If language is to be a means of communication there must be agreement not only in definitions but also (queer as this may sound) in judgments (Wittgenstein, 1953, p. 88).

In the previous section I argued that we speak of someone understanding something only where he is able to manifest this understanding in some way, in words or actions; and that for this expression to be recognized as a sign of understanding he will have to satisfy publicly intelligible criteria or standards. These standards are public because they are based in traditions of behaviour which in turn are possible because of the fact that sharing a human nature involves a sharing of reactions, natural and learned - what Wittgenstein calls sharing a form of life. It is the fact that communication between people presupposes agreement in this way that enables us to avoid drawing any unacceptably relativistic conclusions from this anthropocentric and tradition-centred account of understanding.

Relativism, in the sense that I am calling unacceptable, is the idea that we are never in a position to give valid reasons for saying that one of two or more theories on a given subject is closer to the truth than another. This is, of course, implied by those writers considered in Chapter 1 who claimed that standards of logic and of truth and falsity were culturally relative, and that there was no justification for claiming that one curriculum content was better than another on the grounds that it was closer to the truth. So what is said here is in part a continuation of the answer given to them. The claim that we are never justified in asserting that one theory is closer to the truth than another is a very strong thesis, for it involves more than asserting that any theory of ours is probably false. Because of our limited perspective on nature and human history, and the anthropocentricity of our concepts, it is in fact highly likely that even the best of our theories about man or the world is only partly true, but, as we have seen in Chapter 1, it would not follow from this that it was impossible to make comparative judgments of the relative success of competing theories. Nor would the strong relativistic thesis be vindicated by the existence of theories which we could not understand or translate; for if we could not understand them, then we would not be able to identify their content or subject-matter, and hence would be unable to know which (if any) of our theories they were in competition with. I am not concerned here to defend the view that systems of value or artistic traditions can be objectively ranked. It might be that the most that can be done in ethics and aesthetics is to point to features of various value systems which enable us to recognize an alien system as a system of morality, and so to discuss it with foreigners, and to notice features in foreign works and traditions of art which appeal to people with particular needs or interests and which may be absent from other traditions, or which would not appeal to people from different backgrounds. All I am interested in doing here is to show that the approach to understanding outlined in the previous section does not make it impossible sometimes to rank competing theories with respect to truth, or undermine the anti-relativistic stance of Chapter 1; in doing this, more will be said of what is involved in sharing a form of life.

Let us imagine that we come across a group of people whose life, behaviour and language is on the surface very different from ours. It would seem possible that their understanding of the world would also be different from ours, so different in fact that any useful comparison between our theories and theirs might appear impossible. Our first problem, though, will be to understand what it is they believe, and to do this we will have to understand what it is they say. The way into an untranslated

language will be through that part of the language that deals
with the world of everyday actions and objects, for this is where,
if anywhere, there is likely to be overlap between what we say
and what the foreigners say. Without overlap of this sort, it is
hard to see how translation could proceed at all, involving, as
it does, mapping of words and concepts from one language on to
those of another. Unless there is at least partial overlap at the
level of the observation of gross everyday objects and behaviour,
it is hard to see how translation could begin at all. Fortunately,
as what we are dealing with is not a theoretical system, but a
language spoken by human beings and used to further their
social activity, we are entitled to the assumption that at a basic
level their concerns, interests and needs – and hence their concepts – are likely to be similar to ours. They, too, have to eat
and shelter, they breed and die, laugh and suffer, are capable
of sympathy and hospitality, enter into social and biological
relations, defend themselves, attack others, farm, keep animals,
paint, dance, express their feelings, investigate and explain
their environment and so on. All these things are likely to be
part of the fabric of any life that can be regarded as human;
part of human nature, so to speak. Understanding another way
of life and even another set of values is possible given such
underlying similarity, and interpreting the ways and customs of
others has much to do with seeing how they treat and develop
these basic human needs and reactions. Failure to find a sense
of humour, hospitality or self-preservation in another race should
be regarded, at least in the first instance, as a criticism of the
work of any traveller or anthropologist, because without these
and the other concerns and attitudes mentioned it is doubtful
that we would have a full description of any recognizably human
society. (If we found creatures on another planet similar to us
in appearance, but lacking a significant number of these attri-
butes and reactions, would we regard them as making up a
human society?)

So the basis for understanding the language of another people,
whether it is dealing with morality, art, history or the everyday
world, is the assumption that similar basic interests and reactions are pervasive throughout humanity. At the level of everyday objects, we should seek to identify in their language words
and phrases that seem to refer to those things they are constantly dealing with, such as pots and pans, huts and furniture,
chickens and rabbits. Because of our assumption that we are
dealing with the talk of beings biologically, culturally and
socially similar to ourselves, we can assume that they will be
interested in these things and want to refer to them in some way
or other. (It is true that Quine, 1960, Ch. 2, has raised the
possibility that the ontology of these speakers might be quite
different from ours, and that they always speak about rabbit
'stages' or separated parts of the Great Platonic Rabbit, for
example, and never about spatio-temporally enduring individual
rabbits, and that these differences might remain undetectable to

translators. However, we can leave this possibility aside here, because so long as such differences remain undetectable they can be ignored for the purposes of devising a practical translation scheme. In any case, Gareth Evans, 1975, has shown that in translating a language of only moderate complexity, the sorts of differences Quine alludes to will show up.) Let us suppose that we do succeed in picking out a native term which for all practical purposes is synonymous with the English word 'rabbit'. The important point here is that the meaning of a word is not simply a matter of its being used to label something which appears to our senses. It also involves a rather (open-ended) set of beliefs about what it is that is appearing. As we have seen, Hamlyn (1978, p. 80) argues that perception 'implies knowledge, at least in the sense that it implies knowledge of what it is for something to be whatever things are seen as'. Although it is unclear what this knowledge might be when what is being perceived is not seen under some verbally explicit concept, Hamlyn's point certainly holds good for understanding the perceptual concepts of a language, which is what is at issue here. Also, making perceptual judgments implies that the judgments are true; that the things perceived are as the concepts used to describe them imply. Thus, to call something a rabbit is to say that it is a creature of flesh and blood, that runs across fields, lives in the ground and so on. All this is involved in identifying something as a rabbit, and so is part of the meaning of 'rabbit'. Translating a native term as 'rabbit' will be correct only if the natives share with us at least some of the basic beliefs involved in identifying anything as a rabbit. In the absence of such agreement in belief we would not be justified in translating their term by 'rabbit', as the assumptions involved in the use of the term would be different. Thus, they might be happy to include in their category not only flesh and blood rabbits, but also stuffed rabbit-skins. In such a case, if we could be sure that what we had here was a divergence of meaning and not just a mistake in thinking that stuffed rabbits were alive, it would be wrong to translate their word by the English 'rabbit'. I do not want to claim here that sharing the meaning of a term always involves agreement on the part of all speakers on all the facts identifying what the term refers to. Particularly in the case of a technical or scientific term (such as 'gold' or 'aluminium'), this would be to claim far too much. Presumably only scientists would know just what something had to be for it to be aluminium. But my example is deliberately that of the use of an everyday term, and my point is that unless some beliefs are shared both by us and by the natives about what rabbits are, it is hard to see how we could defend a translation of one of their terms as 'rabbit'.

Divergences of meaning of this sort can sometimes be discovered and original attempts at translation corrected. But it is hard to see how we could discover that what we had was a genuine divergence of meaning, rather than a mistake about stuffed rabbits, and, further, just what the divergence was and how the translation was to be amended, unless we had some means of discovering just what it was they did or did not believe about the objects they were referring to (and hence what it was that led them to lump together live and stuffed rabbits). Merely observing that native speakers have one word for a given class of objects does not reveal which features - real or imagined - of the members of the class actually underlies the use of the single term. At the same time, we can confidently attribute genuinely divergent beliefs to people from cultures other than our own only on the assumption that we have correctly understood and translated what they are saying. Thus the Nuer apparently believe that human twins are also birds. To be sure that this is a correct ascription of belief we will have to be sure that we have correctly translated their words for 'twin' and 'bird', and hence that they agree with us in those beliefs involved in identifying a pair of twins (that they are children born simultaneously of the same woman) and a bird (that the creature is a flying oviparous biped). Of course, the problems involved in understanding such a belief remain immense, for how could children believed by anyone to be born of a woman also fly and lay eggs? This difficulty tempts one to suppose that what is involved here is either a mistranslation or a non-literal, symbolic statement. Evans-Pritchard (1965, pp. 128-33) apparently opts for the symbolic alternative. He says that the proposition that twins are birds is not taken by the Nuer in any ordinary sense, and that they are aware of miming when, in ritual, they treat human twins as if they were birds. However, he also maintains that the Nuer hold that twins are more than just like birds; but his own explanation of the belief (that in Nuer cosmology, both twins and birds are special revelations of Spirit) seems to reduce to saying just that. The intractability of the problem of explaining such beliefs underlines the fact that what is really at issue in many cases is not so much the acceptability of the beliefs as their intelligibility.

It is sometimes said (e.g. by Quine, 1960, p. 59) that a principle of charity is needed in translation, for understanding a foreign utterance requires that we do not see it as too outlandish and difficult to follow. The phrase 'principle of charity' is perhaps unfortunate here, as it suggests something supererogatory. What is really at issue is something fundamental. Translation is part of the process whereby we come to understand the minds and behaviour of other people. If a translation leads us to attribute to them either beliefs that are completely unreasonable, given their behaviour and the beliefs we think that they have from our attributing certain concepts to them in the first place (beliefs about the identifying properties of birds, twins and rabbits, for example), or beliefs whose implications are quite unclear (if we don't know just what is being implied or excluded when there is a talk of a bird), then our translation is failing in its objective. Translation, if it is successful, implies that there is a large measure of agreement in belief between the translator and his subjects, both to secure translation of the concepts we are attributing to the foreign speakers and to secure a genuine understanding of the beliefs the translation leads us to attribute to them. As Davidson (from whom much of what is said here is drawn) (1975, p. 20) says, error is only identifiable given a basis of agreement in belief, but too much error on the part of the foreigner simply makes understanding him impossible, because he will continually appear to be contradicting himself, ignoring what our previous translations would suggest ought to be obvious to him and so on. But why, it will be asked, speak of native error when we are concerned with mapping a foreign language on to our own? Could the error not be as much on our side as on theirs? The answer is that while too much error on either side would cause a breakdown of translation, we have to look at things from our own point of view. From our point of view, our language is reasonably successful as a means of communication, which suggests that most, though not necessarily all, of our beliefs involved in identifying everyday objects (and the implications of such beliefs) are correct. Of course, many of our more theoretical beliefs could be false (and confrontation with another point of view could lead us to make corrections here and in other places), but speaking a language successfully implies a great deal of truth in our everyday observational beliefs; it implies that the objects observed and spoken about mostly do have the properties involved in their identification.

Let us then assume that we have a workable and working translation of at least the observational component of a foreign language, and that we find that some native theoretical belief disagrees with one of ours. What I want to suggest now is that, in many cases, the earlier measure of agreement in belief presupposed by the working translation will often provide a means for comparing the success of the two. Let us take as an example the beliefs reported by Frazer (1922, pp. 896-8) of many tribes in the south of Nigeria that individual humans have external souls living in wild animals, such as leopards, elephants and crocodiles. When the bearer of one's external soul dies or is injured, the human being will also die or be injured and vice versa. Of course, western scientific biology recognizes no such relationship; its explanations of death are quite different. Now, if the belief about one's bush soul was sufficiently specific, it might be possible to attempt to falsify it by showing that there were deaths of the bush souls of human individuals that were not accompanied by deaths of the humans. Because of our agreements at the observational level, we might all be able to agree on this. This could be contrasted with the greater predictive success of scientific explanations of death. If the bush soul belief was quite unspecific, so that it was impossible for any individual to know which animal had his bush soul, it could be shown that any genuine explanation of a natural event brings with it specific and independently testable predictions. Any other sort of

'explanation' is really no explanation at all, for, to use one of
Popper's examples, if the explanation of a storm is Poseidon's
anger and Poseidon's anger is only evidenced by the storm,
speaking of Poseidon's anger is effectively doing no more than
saying that there is a storm. Using arguments such as these, we
might be able to convince people that there was no special
relationship in nature between animals and men. (To say that
the relationship is a spiritual one is tantamount to admitting
this.)

In fact, what would probably happen is that all sorts of explanations for one's survival after the death of the bearer of one's
bush soul would be advanced. This would be exactly analogous
to a scientist attempting to explain away the failure of some experiment or observation to confirm some theory of his. To be
sure, abandonment of a theory immediately and just because it
is confronted with a piece of counter-evidence would often be
premature and unscientific. There often are explanations for
apparent refutations of theories, explanations which are themselves confirmed. Thus Neptune was discovered because its
existence was put forward as a possible explanation of the apparently un-Newtonian orbit of Uranus. Also, it is difficult to say
in advance exactly how much counter-evidence a theory should
be allowed before it has to be abandoned. However, if we have
on the one hand a theory which involves large amounts of
counter-evidence and attempts to explain this away, and, on the
other, another theory which covers the same subject and is
faced with very little counter-evidence and so needs few saving
explanations, it would seem irrational to hold on to the first
theory. The irrationality would be compounded if the second
theory fitted into a network of largely successful explanations
of nature, while the first was part of a conceptual scheme whose
explanations and predictions were constantly coming unstuck and
having to be explained away.

So, understanding the beliefs and theories of another group
involves translating their language and concepts into ours. Only
thus can we identify the subject matter of their discourse. In
doing this, we will presuppose on their part, and discover to be
the case if we are successful, a large measure of agreement
between us all about everyday factual matters. This agreement
can form the basis for comparison and evaluation of more theoretical beliefs, where these diverge. We can test the observational
implications of the theories, and, in some cases, we will be able
to decide for one set of theories and against another. As we have
also argued in Chapter 1, there is nothing in principle preventing the comparison of competing theories, even where deep-level
assumptions are in conflict. This is all that is needed to show
that extreme relativism about theoretical beliefs does not follow
from the supposition that understanding another person or
language involves the mastery of sets of rules and traditions,
for what I have argued here suggests that someone else's
language and beliefs involve enough agreement with him to make

rational decisions between competing theories sometimes possible.
The fact that such decisions are sometimes possible is, of course,
enough to refute the extreme relativism I am attacking here.

It is important, however, not to try to prove too much in this
area. We should not rule out the possibility of beings who experience and understand the world in quite a different way from
us, even though we would not be able to communicate with them
or understand them. Further, even given the common basic
understanding of the world, it is not in practice always possible
to evaluate competing theories, because relative successes and
failures do not all point in one direction. The bias of this section
has certainly been in favour of modern scientific methods and
against folk beliefs, but it could well be that old wives' tales are
just as good as meteorology when it comes to predicting the
weather. What I am saying should not be taken as any endorsement of the apparatus of technology. In fact, the guarded nature
of this refutation of relativism has an important consequence. As
already mentioned, most scientific theories are false and need
improving. Too quick a decision for one theory and against
another can often mean that the true strengths and weakness of
the theories do not emerge. As Mill's arguments showed, a
pluralism of viewpoint can do only good, even where one particular viewpoint is the whole truth. It is, of course, highly unlikely that any current scientific theory is the whole truth about
anything, beset as each is with problems and difficulties - and
just what these problems are and just what their significance is
often only emerge when theories are faced with competition. So
even though common starting points are required for understanding and communication, and even though in this chapter I
have analysed much of the task of educators as being that of
initiating pupils into traditions of thought and behaviour, this
does not conflict with the advocacy in the previous chapter of
pluralism in thought and behaviour. The traditions in question
characteristically develop through pluralism within them, and
through contact with other traditions (although here successful
communication depends on discovering common starting points).
Any apparent conflict between this chapter and the last can
only be because of a failure to grasp the necessity in any healthy
discipline both for common traditions and for individual diversity.

Understanding the morality, social structures and art of other
cultures involves understanding their traditions, and this can
be done with greater or less success because of our shared
human nature and reactions. My argument in favour of the open
society and against tyrannies and closed societies can be seen
as an attempt to argue in favour of one type of society and
against others. The argument was based on certain beliefs about
the fallible state of our knowledge and about human good and
harm. It is difficult to see how any belief could be called a moral
belief that did not relate ultimately to considerations of human
good and harm, so this provides a basis for moral discussion.
Of course, positions in this area will often be affected by people's

general outlook on religion and the world, but there is no reason
why this, too, should not in principle be discussed and differences pin-pointed and analysed. The mere existence of
different traditions of morality and behaviour, and even of
religion, does not necessarily imply a breakdown of communication about these matters, because there may well be certain
features of the world and human nature which all can agree on
as a starting point for discussion. I am not sure how important
it is to want any sense of ultimate truth in these areas, over and
above the feeling that there will always be certain types of consideration which all involved can agree on as relevant (e.g.
that unnecessary pain is a bad thing, and that any belief in a
future life still has to accept the seriousness of death). Here,
even more than in science, pluralism is likely to be desirable to
counteract the stultifying effects of dogma and custom in closing
off possible perspectives and choices. This goes even more for
the arts. Indeed, it is difficult to see why anyone should even
be interested in asserting any absolute supremacy of one tradition over another, when there is so much to be gained from an
understanding of the insights and emphases of different traditions. The history of art shows continually the enlightening and
enlivening effect of the meetings of different traditions.

## TEACHING

I have argued that learning a subject involves at the outset
mastery of a set of rules or, more broadly, entry into a tradition.
I have also suggested that a plurality of viewpoints within a
subject or a tradition, and even a plurality of traditions, is
intellectually valuable; this is in line with the moral arguments
in Chapter 2 in favour of an open, pluralistic society. I want
now to examine some of the implications that all this has for
teaching.

If understanding involves grasping publicly expressible rules
and manifesting this grasp in one's speech or behaviour (or
both), and if these rules and practices are different in kind and
quality in different areas, it is clear that some unspecific faculty
of understanding cannot be developed. To put this more
directly, you have to teach some subject, or you are not teaching at all. The slogan 'teach children, not subjects' is based on
a false antithesis, for you cannot teach someone without at the
same time teaching them something. This is not to say that any
particular subject divisions are justified (see below, Chapter 4),
but only that teaching, like understanding and thought,
requires an object, something taught. If understanding is different in different subject areas, this is not to rule out the
likely transfer of abilities from some areas to others. Thus someone good at physics may well also be good at biology and mathematics. Nevertheless, different criteria for success and different methods exist even in closely related subjects, and a

grasp of the methods of one will not necessarily be equivalent to a grasp of the methods of another. Subjects that are further removed from each other in method and approach would seem to exclude any direct transfer of ability; witness for example the usually embarrassing results when scientists attempt, as scientists, to discuss matters of religion or art. (It is a sign of the times that while such efforts are frequently listened to with respect, no one would even dream of asking Lord Clark for his views on the neutrino.)

Understanding is not only of subjects; it also involves grasping a rule or a tradition. This enables us to make distinctions between what is desirable in teaching and mere rote learning or some simple forms of conditioning. Exaggerated claims are sometimes made in this area, however. Thus Peters (1966, p. 40) says, 'teaching involves discussion and explanation as methods for bringing about an ability to discuss and explain on the part of the learner'. In the first place, as a matter of linguistic usage, it is not clear that one cannot teach someone to repeat bits of nonsense by heart, however pointless it might be. Second (and more important), though, do we always want children to be able to discuss and explain what we are teaching them? In teaching basic addition and subtraction, what we are primarily after is the ability to add and subtract correctly, rather than any discussion of the nature of the mathematical operations. Indeed, this sort of discussion would normally only make sense once the application of the operations had been grasped.

What we do want in teaching, however, and this follows from our analysis of understanding, is an ability to apply what has been learned in circumstances that are new from the learner's point of view. This is sometimes described as awareness of what is learned, but it would seem better to analyse awareness in terms of this ability to apply in practice, rather than in terms of some purely mental feeling or state which would open oneself once more to problems of verification. The ability to apply what is learned to new situations is what distinguishes understanding from purely reflex conditioning, and this is what enables us to criticize accounts of learning (e.g. Hull, 1951, p. 16) which conflate successful learning by trial and error or association with the conditioning of a reflex response. Pure reflex conditioning, like salivation on the part of Pavlov's dogs, does not involve any ability to generalize the response beyond narrow and defined limits of difference or stimulus, whereas even successful learning by association implies that what is learned can be applied in circumstances quite different from those in which it was learned. If I succeed in learning, from putting my hand in boiling water and on a candle, that heat is painful, I will also refrain from putting my hand on electric stoves or on car radiators that I believe to be hot. In other words, I will be aware of the features of the environment that I am picking out to react to. No such awareness of the cause of a reaction is required in the case of a reflex response. Clearly, the sort of learning that most teachers

are ultimately interested in will involve much more than generalized learning by association; it will involve the ability to understand and solve new problems, and even to approach old problems
in new ways, in which the learner is in control of his subject
matter rather than being controlled or stimulated by it. (All
these abilities, from conditioned reflexes to original research,
provided that they came about as the result of teaching, could be
fairly described as examples of behaviour modification in the
pupil by the teacher, so long as the distinctions between the different types of behaviour and different types of modification
were borne in mind.)

If developing one's understanding in any way involves in the
first instance approaching pre-existing subjects and satisfying
existing standards in them, we have a further reason against
denying the authoritative status of the teacher. Although the
ultimate aim of the type of education I am advocating is general
autonomy on the part of individuals, and original research and
development by at least some individuals in various disciplines,
it would be unlikely that these aims could be achieved if, in the
early stages, pupils were regarded as autonomous and capable
of originality in their work. The autonomy advocated in Chapter
2 is an autonomy based on knowledge and insight, and what has
been said in this chapter on understanding shows that neither
knowledge nor insight in any area could be achieved by a beginner who failed to come to grips with the methods and principles
of the relevant discipline or disciplines. Equally, originality and
creativity in any given area are possible for people who understand the area and can see and exploit the potential of some
insight of theirs in the light of the existing problems and
achievements of that area. Even in painting and writing, the
creative significance of genuinely naive (i.e. uneducated) artists
has to be pointed out for what it is by people who do know the
area, and who are able to understand why what has been naively
achieved is a significant moment in the art.

The encouragement of creativity in the arts is something that
has to be handled with great care, because of the ease of mis-
taking for true imagination mere fantasy and wish-fulfilment. As
Iris Murdoch (1977) has persuasively argued, the springs of
both great art and of self-indulgent fantasy are the unconscious;
in fantasy we remain at the level of dream and gratification and
seduction, whereas in true creation the unconscious material
retains its original strength, but is transformed into something
objective in which the persona of the artist is subordinated to
his work, something to set alongside and illuminate reality.
Plato's ambivalent attitude to art comes from his realization of
the power of the seduction possible in artistic fantasy, and his
belief that true beauty is only to be found in the hardness and
clarity of the Ideal World. Lacking this conviction, we require
of art still that it should not be mere sentimental escapism, but
that it also should mirror the inevitability and complexity of
real life. Even where there is only pure form, as in music, it may

be possible to distinguish the genuine from the counterfeit.
Schoenberg's words, 'The artist attains beauty without willing it,
for he is striving only after truthfulness', do at least suggest a
programme in an extremely difficult and largely uncharted area,
and a corrective to the unfortunately widespread educational
idea that there is something valuable in artistic self-expression
in itself, whether or not any serious grappling with problems of
material or expression is involved. (The opposite danger, of an
art consisting only in artifice, technique, formal games and
parody, is currently less real.)

The lack of final authorities in any area, and the advocacy of
pluralism in theories, beliefs and life-styles, mean that although
we are attempting to teach children existing methods and theories, we should want at least some of those we teach eventually
to criticize what already exists and to improve on it. But, as
with choice, satisfactory and constructive criticism can be made
only on the basis of an understanding of what is being chosen
or criticized. Pluralism does not mean that ignorant negativeness
is to be encouraged. What is wanted is the Spinozan ideal of
conversations between rational and informed men, rather than a
mere Dewey-like multiplicity of viewpoint, regardless of quality.
Of course, there is a problem in trying to teach people to be
genuinely critical and original while at the same time retaining
one's authority and attempting to inculcate respect for the
achievements that already exist. If the teacher himself manifests
a critical attitude to some of his material, pupils can easily mimic
this, in which case they are picking up a mannerism from their
authoritative source, rather than learning to think for themselves. In this context, Popper's (1945, vol. 1, pp. 134-7)
warning against attempting to devise institutions for the selection of the outstanding is apposite. He points out that authorities
by their nature tend to select those who respond to their
influence. This means that they will on the whole select medioc-
rities, those who quickly respond to and see what is wanted
(even if this is a 'critical' attitude). Those who are really original and genuinely critical will tend to be rejected by authorities
and by people acting on behalf of authorities. As George Orwell
once said, whoever heard of an eccentric commissar? Musil (1979,
vol. 1, Ch. 29) is even more depressing, suggesting that only
those ideas which find a resonance in other minds are reinforced
by others and condense in one's own mind, whereas any really
extraordinary ideas one has are scattered in space and are lost.
Popper's conclusion is that schools should not set themselves
the task of selecting outstanding leaders because, on the whole,
they will fail, while at the same time transforming themselves
into race-courses for the ambitious. Schools and universities
should concentrate on pursuing their subjects to the best of the
ability of those in them, teachers and learners. Here is the clue
to the development of the critical approach in learners. For in
mastering a subject, they will master its methods and history,
understand how it has advanced and, with luck and imagination,

begin to see how it might be further advanced.

The need for initiating pupils into existing theories and disciplines, given that none of these theories is certain nor any of the methods guaranteed to produce the truth, means that the question of indoctrination is inevitable. For if we are teaching what, in one sense, we know is probably neither the whole truth nor without elements of falsity, are we not guilty of indoctrinating? Discussion in this area has tended to concentrate on defining 'indoctrination' and distinguishing it from related notions such as brainwashing and conditioning (cf. Snook, 1972). There is a certain futility about this, for suppose we decide on a particular definition of 'indoctrination', for example that it is the deliberate inculcation of false or uncertain doctrines to unwilling subjects by morally objectionable means. Who is going to feel threatened by this? Was even Plato going to have his noble lie taught as the literal truth? In other words, definition of the concept will not provide much guidance to educators, because even people who are attempting to instil what others regard as unproven dogmas will not see their beliefs in that light. Nor can we insist that true teaching, as opposed to indoctrination, implies voluntariness and understanding on the part of the learners, for we can and do quite justifiably insist that sometimes pupils learn something whether or not they want to, and whether or not they fully understand the reasons behind what they are learning. Indeed, there would be something futile about a pupil who was forever demanding the reasons for what he was taught. Often, without a certain amount of information and ability to perform operations he would be in no position to understand the underlying rationale for what he was being taught. One can also question the usefulness of introducing the notion of morally objectionable means into the discussion. It is true that most people would object to imprisoning, starving and drugging someone in order to make him assent to some ideology or other, but it could be argued that the objection is really an objection to imprisoning someone against his will and the automaton-like state in which he emerges from the treatment, rather than the brainwashing techniques as such. For if, by electrical and chemical means it was possible to transform some irrational school dropout so that he emerged thinking and reasoning like Einstein, would there be anything morally objectionable, providing the subject underwent the process willingly? Part of one's natural hesitation here is the extreme unlikeliness of anyone actually becoming really creative and original by such means, but why would it be an affront to the respect educators should have for learners to do this if it were possible and the learner was agreeable? He would appear on any count to come out a better and more enlightened person, and he surely should not be criticized for wanting to achieve this state.

More helpful than defining indoctrination is to show what sort of teaching of doctrine is objectionable and why. If a doctrine is a false theory, then science is full of doctrines. So we can hardly object to teaching doctrines as such. If a doctrine is a false theory which has no supporting reasons or evidence, then Christianity or Islam or even Rastafarianism is not a doctrine. So teaching any of them will not be indoctrination. If indoctrination is teaching a false theory or one not conclusively known to be true as true, then teachers of science and history will be in a quandary, because it seems that they will have to preface many of their expositions with the somewhat paradoxical remark that although they believe some theory to be true, it is actually, in all probability, false (even though their actions may well belie the sincerity of this disclaimer).

In the end, we cannot get away from the fact that any subject will contain many false theories or doctrines, and many theories that cannot be adequately justified, and many presuppositions which are simply assumed. Indeed, the idea that every presupposition should be shown to be true contains within itself the seeds of an unending task, for any justification offered will itself require justification. This suggests that what is objectionable is not teaching false or unprovable doctrines as such, or even in arguing (or presupposing) that they are true, for to say out of epistemological scruple that something I believe and am prepared to act on is probably untrue smacks of insincerity. In any case, we cannot highlight and invite criticism of all our presuppositions in any area, because, as with the constancy of length before Einstein, until they come under fire we may not realize just what our presuppositions are and what it is our pupils have to be warned may be untrue. So the teaching of some false and unproven doctrines as true and as assumed is unavoidable. What is objectionable is to teach in such a way as to attempt to close off rational criticism or to suggest that such criticism is unimportant or unnecessary or immoral (as is often the case with religious education, but may also sometimes be the case with conventional liberal tenets). One way of doing this is to suggest by omission and implication that the results achieved in any subject (including a particular ideology or religion, of course) are the whole truth, and to divorce the results from the problems they were designed to solve and the methods involved in establishing them. In areas such as religion and morality where, in many cases, there is no consensus about particular beliefs, this should obviously be made clear from the start. The dangers of indoctrination are perhaps rather more insidious and subtle in areas where there is a general consensus as to the leading theory or viewpoint at any time, but where the theory or viewpoint is not likely to be regarded as satisfactory for ever. To say all this, though, and to inveigh against indoctrination, is far easier than actually getting impressionable pupils to see that what you are teaching and what you care about is far from being the whole truth, but is an achievement struggled for and impermanent.

# 4 THE CURRICULUM

## INTRODUCTION

In Chapter 2, I considered the main subject areas it is necessary
for people to grasp in order to be in a position to make informed
choices about their lives. I also suggested that a certain amount
of practical knowledge and vocational training could reasonably
be imparted in schools, though the precise nature of this would
tend to be determined by prevailing social circumstances.
Indeed, one of the points to be made about the curriculum is that
we will decide about its overall content in the light of our general educational and social aims. In this chapter, I want to consider some philosophical theses concerning the nature of knowledge, which might appear to have some bearing on the way the
curriculum is organized into distinct subjects. I shall argue that
divisions of this sort are not to be made on purely philosophical
grounds, although I shall suggest that there is an important
distinction of method to be made between the humanities and the
sciences. I shall end the chapter by suggesting where there
should and should not be choice by pupils on curricular matters.

## FORMS OF KNOWLEDGE

As we have already seen, P. H. Hirst (1965) argues strongly and
effectively against the view that mental abilities can be developed
in a general way without it mattering what exactly is taught:
that any subject might, indifferently, produce in pupils the same
ability to think effectively. Hirst shows that there is no reason
why there should be any transfer of ability of this sort, because effective thinking in physics requires the mastery of
skills quite different from effective thinking in, say, ballet or
house buying. Hirst, however, wants to argue for a thesis far
stronger than merely pointing out that there are different types
of understanding, depending on the subject being understood,
its methods and emphases. He wants to show that there are
distinct forms of knowledge, which any intellectually developed
person must have mastered or there will be something missing in
his mental development. This is actually the way in which he
attempts to justify his choice of academic curriculum, but I will
now argue that neither the justification nor the division of
knowledge into distinct forms is adequate.
Indeed, the very notion of forms of knowledge is something of

a misnomer. In addition to attacking the idea that a curriculum
can be organized in order to promote general mental abilities,
Hirst also considers what he says is the Greek attitude to knowledge and mental development. According to this, the mind's
function is to pursue knowledge. Hence mental satisfaction
results from the attainment of knowledge. In addition, knowledge
itself can be attained because the mind, correctly used, is in
harmony with reality, and can discover the essential nature of
things. So education came to be seen as the development of the
mind through its own proper function of disinterestedly perceiving essences and organizing this knowledge in its natural
hierarchical form, according to the hierarchy of nature from
matter to reason. According to Hirst, this view of education has
been influential ever since, implicit in the call to cultivate and
develop one's understanding for its own sake, but its metaphysical underpinnings are no longer available to us. For we no
longer accept the realism of the Greeks:

> A liberal education in the pursuit of knowledge is (for them)
> seeking the development of the mind according to what is
> quite external to it, the structure and pattern of reality.
> But if once there is any serious questioning of this
> relationship between mind, knowledge, and reality, the
> whole harmonious structure is liable to disintegrate (Hirst,
> 1965, p. 90).

The results of such a disintegration for education is the loss of
both its patterning (the fitting of the mind into reality according
to the order of reality itself) and its justification (the way the
mind, through the achievement of true knowledge, is to be
thought of as fulfilling its proper function of correctly perceiving
reality). Hirst now attempts another justification and organization of education which does not depend on any metaphysical
doctrine of reality, given that he is unable to accept what he
calls metaphysical realism. The curious thing is that, although
talking of dividing and justifying the curriculum by appeal to
forms of knowledge, neither does he see his forms in terms of
knowledge (as true belief), nor, as we shall see, can some of his
forms be regarded uncontroversially as knowledge.

What Hirst does is assert that there are a number of distinct
and complex ways of understanding experience which, as a
matter of fact, man has achieved. These will be the specific ways
open to us of developing the mind, and because in the forms of
knowledge there are publicly accessible criteria or standards of
achievement, the individual mind is developed through its
initiation into these public standards. That much is in line with
our earlier treatment of understanding. His justification of anyone seeking to develop his mind in this way is, however, precisely parallel to Peters's justification of the pursuit of rational
knowledge for its own sake (cf. above p. 39), and open to the
same objections.

According to Hirst, human life as a whole is structured through
various conceptual schemes. Without such schemes, emotional

experiences and mental attitudes and beliefs would lack intelligible structure. 'To acquire knowledge is to become aware of
experience as structured, organized, and made meaningful in
some quite specific way, and the varieties of human knowledge
constitute the highly developed forms in which man has found
this possible' (1965, p. 98). In acquiring knowledge, we learn
to experience the world in a new way, and develop the mind 'in
its most fundamental aspect' (1965, p. 97). In fact, to have a
rational mind is just to have one's mind developed through entry
into the forms of knowledge. What the forms of knowledge are is
simply the working out in various systematic ways of those principles which underlie any process of rational justification. So in
asking for a rational justification of the forms of knowledge, one
is in fact committed to them; any justification itself presupposes
the principles which underlie the forms of knowledge, so you
cannot consistently ask for a rational justification of them and
fail to see the justification of their pursuit.

This argument is open to the same objections that we made to
Peters's deployment of his similar argument. Asking for a justification of anything does not presuppose a commitment to
rational knowledge for its own sake, because in asking for a
justification of something, one may be asking for a justification
in terms of its use as a means to some specific goal. So one might,
in asking for a justification of the university curriculum, only be
asking if it helps to produce good citizens. Moreover, examination of rational knowledge, certainly as it is embodied in Hirst's
forms or Peters's university curriculum, may lead one to the
conclusion that its pursuit is somehow self-defeating (because
of one's general scepticism) or stultifying and life-denying (from
the point of view of some religious or life goal). Wrong these
reactions may be, but they are hardly inconsistent. More specifically, examination of Hirst's (1965, p. 100) forms of knowledge
makes it hard to see how they can all be regarded as 'simply the
working out' of principles of justification 'in particular ways', or
how indeed some of them can be regarded, in any sense, as
forms of knowledge. Indeed, he denies that they are forms of
knowledge in the Greek sense of corresponding to reality. Instead he finds a surrogate objectivity in the presence in them of
public criteria for distinguishing the true from the false and the
good from the bad, without any commitment to the absolute correctness of these standards. In fact, in the idea of forms of
knowledge he hopes to find a modern alternative approach to
education which would keep the Greek ideas of natural divisions
of knowledge (though without any sense of hierarchical ordering)
and of objectivity (though without epistemological realism).

Having said that the forms of knowledge are the ways by which
experience is structured round the use of accepted public symbols, Hirst gives four criteria (later reduced to three) by which
a form of knowledge can be picked out. These are, first, the
presence of a group of central concepts peculiar to the form, and
not found in other forms. Thus gravity, acceleration, hydrogen

and photosynthesis are characteristics of the sciences; number, integral and matrix, of mathematics; God, sin and predestination, of religion; and so on. Then, second, each form has its own distinctive logical structure by which its concepts can be related. The statements of mechanics can be related, he says, 'in certain strictly limited ways only, and the same is true of historical explanation' (1965, p. 102). Third, each form has its own distinctive way of being tested against experience. The fourth criterion really amounted to saying that each form had its own techniques for exploring experience and testing its statements, but as this really added little to the other three, Hirst dropped it in subsequent presentations of his thesis. Hirst says that although understanding of any particular discipline is something that requires actual practice in it, and that not everything about it can be made explicit, and, further, that his criteria cannot fully or adequately demarcate the whole of modern knowledge, the central feature to which his criteria point is that each discipline can be distinguished by some particular type of test against experience. The interesting feature here is that he wants to distinguish forms of knowledge by their distinctive language and methodology, rather than through their subject-matter. Indeed, having given a list of the forms consisting of mathematics, physical sciences, human sciences, history, religion, literature and the fine arts, moral knowledge and philosophy (later lists put the human sciences and history together as one form), he distinguishes the linguistically and methodologically differentiable forms from what he calls fields of knowledge differentiated in terms of topics. Thus geography is a field drawing on several forms, likewise politics, law, educational theory and so on. But what Hirst is principally concerned about is the forms that 'basically constitute the range of unique ways we have of understanding experience' (1965, p. 105). In line with his denial of metaphysical and epistemological realism, Hirst denies anything eternal or a priori about the forms; hence even more weight is carried by the criteria for picking them out.

According to Hirst, a liberal education should concentrate on the way the forms of knowledge structure experience. Immersion in the concepts, logic and criteria of a discipline, both through concentration in detailed areas of the discipline and through an idea of its whole range, is required in order that the pupil will be able to structure his own experience in the required way, and to understand the way each discipline's way of approaching experience differs from that of the others and the range of its understanding. Of course, Hirst distinguishes the type of pursuit of a discipline he is interested in from practical applications of the discipline, but what is perhaps more noteworthy in Hirst's proposals is the emphasis on grasping the logic and language of a discipline for its own sake, on grasping the way in which, say, a scientist will look at experience, rather than on grasping information about some subject matter. What Hirst is interested in is forms, rather than knowledge.

On the actual detailed curriculum, what Hirst says can be
dealt with fairly briefly. A liberal education (which he stresses
is not the whole of education) will include paradigm examples of
all the forms, and indications of the relationships between them.
There is no specific commitment to any existing curriculum, nor
is there any reason why there should not be integrated studies,
in which one subject matter is looked at from the point of view of
several forms. What is important is that pupils end up with a
grasp of each form and its bearing on the others, and so long as
this is borne in mind integrated studies can be useful. Hirst
rightly warns against taking talk about a discipline having its
own logic to mean that there is only one psychological route into
it. As he says, the logic provides only the framework of a subject, and there may be many ways of gaining access to the
subject and an understanding of its framework. This is an important point: to say that something is logically or ontologically
more basic than something else – to say, for example, that formal
logic is presupposed by mathematics or that chemistry is reduc-
ible to physics – is not to say that mathematics cannot be understood before one has explicitly mastered logic, or chemistry
before one has done physics. Psychologically the reverse process
may well be more effective. This certainly often goes for the
explicit understanding of those fundamental abstract concepts
philosophers often claim are presupposed in judgments of particular sorts. Thus Kant claims that all empirical judgments presuppose the possession by the subject of categories such as
cause and identity. But here it should be remembered that there
are different levels of grasping concepts, and that a child is
hardly likely to come to an explicit grasp of the notion of
causality or of substance before understanding particular examples of causality or substantiality – even if, given that Kant
is right, there is a sense in which understanding the particular
example presupposes the successful application of the general
concept. In any case, as Hirst says, how best to introduce
pupils to a discipline is an empirical rather than a philosophical
question.

Hirst (1965, p. 110), finally, sees a liberal education as consisting in a grasp of the various forms of knowledge, not as
entirely distinct, but as branching out of 'the common area of
everyday knowledge'. He goes on to modify somewhat further
the original impression given of the radical distinctness of the
forms by speaking of them all dealing with one world, of their
having interrelationships and of their making use of each other's
achievements. Nevertheless he concludes by emphasizing that the
end result of a liberal education ought to be the growth of
'clearer and finer distinctions in our experience', rather than a
'quasi-aesthetic unity of the mind' (1965, p. 111). What we now
need to do is to examine in some detail the status of his forms of
knowledge, and to see if his criteria for distinguishing them are
in fact adequate for his purposes.

When we consider the list of forms of knowledge, we find,

perhaps surprisingly, that literature and the arts as well as religion are included. In what sense are the arts knowledge? Does calling religion a form of knowledge imply that at least some basic religious statements, such as, 'There is a God,' are true? Hirst's (1974, pp. 152-64) later attempt to answer the first question only serves to make the phrase 'form of knowledge' yet more suspect. He says that works of art do make statements which are true or false, and that they communicate by artistic means a special type of artistic or aesthetic knowledge (and he does not mean the sort of thing that is <u>written</u> about in art criticism). As a proof of this, he suggests that any symbol system presupposes the idea of truth and falsity to refer to the occasions when the symbols apply and when they do not, respectively, and that the arts use symbol systems. In the absence of the possibility of truth or falsity he says the symbols will have no meaning. Further, we can see the elements of a work of art standing in specific, quasi-linguistic, formal relationships. Finally, he appeals to the existence of agreed standards of judgment about works of art as implying that they must make true or false statements. Indeed, he seems to identify the two, and appeals to the examples of mathematics and ethics as being further cases where the idea of truth seems to get a hold only through agreement about standards of proof (1974, p. 159).

Against all this, we can urge that the possibility of a symbol system being used to make true or false statements depends not on the ability of people to agree about its correct use, in terms, say, of the formal relationships existing between elements of formulae constructed out of the symbols (or else any uninterpreted calculus would be a statement-making language), but on whether elements in the symbol system are used to refer to things outside themselves in such a way that the system can be used to say things about these extra-symbolic objects. In literature, statement-making language is used, but in such a way as to cancel its referential power. Thus 'Hamlet' does not refer to Hamlet, nor did anyone kill Hamlet's father, not because Claudius was innocent, but because there was no Hamlet and hence no father to be killed (or at least, if in the depths of Danish history there were such figures, that is not what the play is about, nor do we judge its quality in terms of its correspondence to their activities). Hirst's idea that the arts use statement-making symbolism may be given more credit than it deserves because in arts such as ballet and music there are notational systems which refer to the elements of the heard or seen work. There is certainly a sense in which statements made in these systems can be judged for truth and falsity, when they are being used to record living events in static form on paper. But the choreology and the score are not the work (music critics reading scores at concerts miss this simple but essential point), and there is no question of a symphony or a ballet actually referring to and making statements about real events (unless the composer or choreographer tells us through words what these statements are). If Hirst wants to show

that the arts are languages, what he has to do in each case is to
specify the elements of the language which are used to refer,
show what they refer to and, further, show how statements can
be constructed out of the language to say things about what is
being referred to. In the absence of any of this, we have to conclude that the mere fact that there is often agreement between
people on artistic matters shows only that the arts - such things
as composing, painting, dancing, acting, singing - are public
forms of experience, rather than of knowledge, and that it is
misleading to think of them in terms of statement-making languages.
This point will become important later on, when we consider which
activities Hirst's criteria might allow on to the curricula.

When we examine the criteria by which Hirst picks out his forms
of knowledge, we find, in accordance with our suspicion that his
forms might be of experience rather than knowledge, that the
emphasis is on the activity rather than on the subject matter to
which the activity might be about. What he emphasizes is the
logic, language and methods of the activity rather than what (if
anything) it is throwing light on. The three criteria imply that
each form has its own central concepts, its own specific logic and
its own means of testing against experience. It might first be
questioned in what sense each form of knowledge can be said to
have its own logic. As logicians speak of logic, logic is the study
of inference and reasoning in its most general form. The laws and
principles of logic are intended to range over all subjects and over
all areas of experience. It would be regarded as odd and requiring
further explanation if some area of experience were held to use a
different logic from the rest of experience. (This is one of the
question marks that hangs over the proposal to regard quantum
physics as having its own peculiar logic; cf. Putnam, 1969. Even
in an example such as this, however, what is at issue is not a
radically different logic, but only initially the suggestion that in
quantum physics, one classically valid law is to be held as invalid.
While it is hard to see how just one law could be different, without some of the logical connectives taking on a different sense and
hence many other laws being subtly changed, what we have here
is hardly the sort of qualitative difference Hirst must be looking
for, for both classical and quantum logic are recognizably very
close to each other in both method and content.) In fact, spelling
out what he means by a different logic, Hirst (1974, p. 90) says
that the presence of different criteria of truth implies the
presence of a different logical structure and laws. It is hard to
see why this should be so. Different criteria of truth may be
present in mathematics, physics and history - e.g. a mathematical theorem is based on provability, a theory in physics on
repeatable observation and experiment, a statement in history on
non-repeatable historical evidence. But it hardly follows from
this that modus ponens (licensing the move from 'If p then q' and
'p' to 'q') and modus tollens (licensing the move from 'If p then q'
and 'not q' to 'not p'), to take two examples or principles of
inference, are not used in each case, or that forms of statement

that count as contradictory in one are not to count as contradictory in another. Indeed, with possible very minor exceptions (such as the one alluded to in connection with quantum physics), it seems that, in fact, exactly the same logic is used in each.

Perhaps the safest conclusion is that by referring to different logics Hirst is actually referring to what he takes logic to be based on, different criteria for truth. In that case, of course, his second criterion becomes an aspect of the third. So now we have two criteria for distinguishing the forms, concepts and tests. But the problem now is seeing what types of concepts and tests belong together, so as to specify a form. As Mary Warnock (1977, p. 100) puts it, without some prior grasp of the subject matter involved, how would we know that, say, cell and symphony belong to different forms, and which form they belonged to (i.e. which other concepts they were to be grouped with)? And, of course, subject matter is a way for Hirst to distinguish fields rather than forms: as indeed it has to be, because, as he rightly notices, the same subject matter can be dealt with by different methods, and what he is primarily interested in is methods. It might be said that you can identify symphony, violin, minim and so on as belonging together by watching the behaviour of musicians, but this would be illegitimate in this context, because it would presuppose on our part the ability to pick out a musician (someone professionally concerned with music) and the ability to isolate what he does in his musical life, and it is precisely this part of his behaviour that we are seeking to pick out. So it is doubtful that we can pick out groups of central concepts and put them together to specify a form without some illegitimate appeal to subject-matter, and the same will probably hold for types of test. Indeed, here a further problem arises, because many philosophers have questioned whether au fond, and despite initial appearances, radically different methods are involved in the different disciplines.

What we have now is a doubt as to whether, even if, as now appears unlikely, Hirst's criteria on their own enable us to distinguish different forms of knowledge, they actually distinguish separate 'voices in a conversation' (as Hirst speaks of the forms at one point), or they are really pointing to different areas of one unified body of knowledge. I shall have more to say in the next section about the idea that the physical sciences and the humanities all really use the same method, but even though I shall argue against that, the following points can still be made against Hirst, which demonstrate the essentially mixed nature of what he takes to be elements of separate forms. What I have in mind is not only cases of one form using the achievements of another; rather, in each form I consider, methods proper to other forms are used as an essential part of its own methods. Thus physics would be unimaginable without mathematics; take away the mathematics and there would not even be a skeleton left, only an almost empty frame with a few dabs of colour here and there. Then mathematics itself, even if we accept the analytic-synthetic distinction, is still based at a fundamental level on empirical features of the world, as I have suggested above (p. 72). (It is a weakness of Hirst's treatment that he appears nowhere to face up to the consequences for his position of Quine's famous and influential rejection in -Two dogmas of empiricism- of the analytic-synthetic distinction, and his consquent holistic attitude to knowledge; cf. Quine, 1951.) History uses knowledge gained from the physical sciences as part of its method for assessing the plausibility of evidence. Thus a historian would not count as good evidence something that seemed physically impossible. Mathematics, too, plays a considerable role in history in various ways. In the other direction, as physics relies on reports of past observations, it sometimes implicitly uses historical canons. This is so, even though repeatability is a key feature of scientific method, because we still have to judge a present experiment as a replication of something from the past.

So there does appear to be more intermingling of method than Hirst might wish to concede between those forms which might uncontroversially be referred to as forms of knowledge. Of the others, the arts and religion are only dubiously forms of knowledge. In so far as religion purports to be knowledge, it relies on historical and perhaps scientific evidence. This leaves us with morality and philosophy. There may well be an irreducible gap between fact and value, in which case morality will have its own distinctive style of argument, though this is not to suggest that it is cut off from all other areas of knowledge (cf. below, Chapter 5).

On philosophy, there is, of course, a divide between philosophers who see it as the most general kind of physics, ultimately empirical and based on empirical knowledge (e.g. Quine), and those who see it as an essentially second-order activity, with its own peculiar problems and solutions (e.g. Wittgenstein). This is not something that can be settled here, and in a way there is no need to, because Hirst hardly deals with the issues involved. Moreover, even if we were to agree with the rather oversimplified version of Wittgenstein's view according to which philosophical problems are problems of meaning rather than of fact, this would not show that philosophy was really a special form of knowledge; it would show rather that philosophical issues and enquiries inevitably come up in all areas of knowledge, and are necessarily dealt with (for better or worse) by workers in those areas, as well as by professional philosophers.

Part of what I have already said about the term 'form of knowledge' might have been put by pointing out that Hirst speaks of knowledge without speaking of truth. That is to say, it is not clear that his forms of knowledge have to be based on true statements. This is the case in different ways with literature and the arts, on the one hand, and religion on the other. We have already seen that Hirst has problems accounting for the truth component of the arts. With religion, the problem seemed to be that talking of it as a form of knowledge is to pre-empt questions about the truth of fundamental religious propositions. For it surely is important to decide whether statements such as 'God exists' are true; if they are not true, then religious statements will mostly be false and the religious attitude as a whole mistaken, in which case it would be odd to call it a form of knowledge. But for Hirst, such fundamental questions cannot even be raised once he has decided that religion is a form of knowledge. The reason for this is that the standards of truth and falsity for the statements of a form of knowledge are internal to that form, part of it, and it is hard to see that the presuppositions of a form could be undermined or even dispassionately examined from within a form.

The likelihood is that by speaking of a form of knowledge, Hirst is more concerned with some particular way of structuring experience, than with sets of true statements. This would certainly be in line with his assimilation of objective truth within a form to the presence of agreed criteria for success among these working within the form, and with his inclusion of religion and the arts among the forms. His criteria, too, as we have seen, emphasize the language and method rather than subject-matter and truth. If, though, he interprets the notion of a form of knowledge widely enough to include the arts and religion, one wonders why he does not include such activities as gambling, games-playing, crime and witchcraft as forms of knowledge. All have their distinctive central concepts and jargon, all have special criteria for success, not precisely similar to the criteria for success of anything else, and all involved in any of these activities tend to agree on the application of these standards. Certainly each of these activities is a unique way of structuring experience, and anyone who does not engage in them or know about them will be missing some possible development of his mind or personality.

It will be said, of course, that crime, witchcraft and gambling are not desirable on a school curriculum and that minds might be better off not being developed in these ways. This brings me to my final objection to the forms of knowledge thesis. It might be that Hirst can tighten up his criteria so as to include just what he wants, to exclude crime and so on; that he can delimit his forms in such a way that we can be assured that the natural sciences, say, are quite different from mathematics and history, and so with the other forms; that we can see that each form is just one and not several (for it is not clear on Hirst's criteria that physics, biology and chemistry do not each constitute one form, and equally sociology, history and psychology, music, sculpture and ballet); and that, finally, the arts and religion can count as forms of knowledge, rather than of experience taken more broadly. Even if all doubts on all these matters can be settled, we might still want to ask why the study of each of the forms is necessary. Hirst's reply, of course, is that each is necessary as an essential aspect of the development of a rational mind; but, as we have seen, there is nothing inconsistent in thinking that the development of some part of the rational mind may be undesirable, or even that the development of a rational mind for its own sake is not desirable at all. The conclusion is that here, as elsewhere, substantive educational decisions are not to be made on essentialist grounds (by analysing the meaning of words like 'mind' or 'rationality'), but that they can be made only in the light of our general aims and objectives in education. I have already argued for all of Hirst's non-philosophical forms on the curriculum, but this has been because a knowledge of their subject matter is necessary to a well-informed and well-adjusted life, rather than because of something distinctive and specific about their methods and approach to experience. That could surely be said about dozens of things which would better not be on the school curriculum. So Hirst does not give us any reason for studying the various forms, arising from their supposed distinctiveness. Nor in fact does he fully establish radical distinctiveness. On the whole, the moral of our examination of Hirst would appear to be that the question of how to divide the curriculum is a pragmatic one, best left to curriculum planners. However, one exception to this pragmatic approach will emerge from considering the question of whether there is an important division in the curriculum between the humanities and the sciences, and whether saying this gives any grounds for speaking of two cultures and preparing pupils for entry into one culture rather than another.

## TWO METHODS, ONE CULTURE

This section falls into two contrasting but connected halves. In the first half, I will consider and reject the view that there is no essential difference between the study of nature and the study of human life. What I say here may appear to be rather abstract and remote from everyday life. In the second half of the section, however, I will show that this is not so at all, and that in fact a clear grasp of the distinction in kind between reflection on nature and reflection on human life is of the utmost importance morally, culturally, politically and educationally.

In considering Hirst's views on the curriculum, I mentioned that they were implicitly in conflict with those of Quine, as expressed in -Two dogmas of empiricism-. In this paper, Quine argued that there was no real difference between statements of meaning and statements of fact, and that knowledge of all sorts formed a unified system in which adjustments at one point would have ramifications throughout the system as a whole. Thus, for example, a change in our physics might involve a change in our logic (as both Reichenbach and Putnam have in different ways suggested in connection with quantum physics); while mathematical developments in alternative geometries, say, could lead to new theories of perception. Quine's point is that the often-canvassed distinctions between mathematics and logic, on the one hand, and the empirical sciences, on the other, are suspect; first, because the distinction between statements of meaning and

statements of fact (the analytic-synthetic distinction) is itself
suspect; second, because decisions in mathematics and logic are
responsive to empirical facts and influence our attitude to them;
and, third, because there is no theory-free language with which
to describe pure empirical data. On all these points, much can be
said in favour of Quine, but it is not clear that arguing in favour
of Quine entails not treating mathematics as a separate subject
from physics in a school curriculum. Indeed, it is not clear that
Quine's thesis has any specific curricular implications. Even if
knowledge is a unity in the way he suggests, with one part hang-
ing on other parts, it certainly cannot be taught as an undifferentiated whole. Also, nothing Quine says rules out the common-
sense assumption, which I have been making throughout this
book and which will be reflected in school curricula, that, on the
surface at least, recognizably different methods are used in day-
to-day work in at least some different areas of knowledge. After
all, mathematicians do not make physical experiments, even if
what they do is related to physical knowledge, nor do historians
go into laboratories, even when relying on the findings of
physicists. But this is not the place for a full examination of
Quine's holism. Once again a philosophical thesis has little relevance to the details of curricular divisions. What, however, is
important here and does appear from suggestions in 'Word and
Object' to be part of Quine's (1960, p. 221) general ontology, is
the suggestion that at the bottom all the sciences use or should
use essentially the same methods, whether physical nature or
human behaviour is being studied. A detailed exposition and
defence of a version of this thesis (sometimes referred to as the
unity of method thesis) appears in Popper's 'Poverty of Historicism' (1957), and it is in this form that I shall consider it. This
is both because Popper's account of the unity of method is fully
developed, and because it connects with an attitude to social
policy which also appears to be inadequate in a significant way.

Part of the context of Popper's defence of the unity of method
is his hostility to those who want to hold that collectives, such
as nations, states or classes, are greater than the individuals
who go to compose them, and that individuals should see themselves as subservient to these greater wholes. Part of his
defence of individual rights is to assert that a human society has
the same ontological status as any ordinary collection of objects,
and no more. Three apples on a plate have mutual relations, by
virtue of being on the same plate, which they would not have if
they were not in this collective, and which transcend what can
be said of them in isolation from each other. But we cannot conclude from this that the apples are affected in some way which
might change their nature, or the laws governing their behaviour,
by virtue of their membership of this system. In much the same
way, Popper thinks, members of different human societies are
only externally affected by their membership of a particular
society. Inside we are all atoms of the same sort, whether we are
ancient Mycenaeans or modern Americans. The differences between

us are to be explained in terms of our different circumstances. A historian or social scientist should not have to appeal to a radically different mentality, given to us by some intuitively perceived spirit of the age, in order to explain our differences in behaviour, any more than a physicist must appeal to supposed differences of physical laws to explain differences in the behaviour of atoms of the same substance under different conditions. Conditions may differ, but men, like physical atoms, remain the same, subject to the same laws. It is the job of the student of human nature to show how the behaviour of human beings follows from the laws which govern it, just as it is the job of the physicist to show how the behaviour of physical objects follows from the laws governing them. In both cases, the explanatory framework is deductive: the behaviour follows from a combination of statements giving the relevant laws and the initial conditions. Anything else represents a failure to understand the effect. The main difference between physics and the human sciences here is that in the latter case one is principally interested in singular events, so the main burden of explanation will consist in showing how usually rather simple laws are applying in rather complicated sets of circumstances. In this, the historian is more like a practical chemist trying to explain what went wrong when a chemical works blew up, than some theoretical physicist whose interest is more in the laws in a general sense.

Two major gains follow from Popper's account of the unity of method, one methodological and the other ethical. Methodologically, his account gives an objective standard of success in historical explanation. Thus, success for a historian is to be judged in terms of his explanations and their deductive smoothness. He is not required to grasp the spirit of some bygone age in a quasi-intuitive or mystical way, nor are we required to make guesses at his success in doing this. Ethically, people are here considered as individuals leading their own lives. The circumstances in which individuals live may be very different, and hence their behaviour different too, but this can all be seen objectively once the circumstances are fully explained. People are not to be excused their responsibilities as people by talk of their being dominated by the spirit of their age or class; once it is seen that the past can be explained without invoking anything of the sort, this becomes clear for the present too. But in addition to insisting on individual responsibility, if we abandon the mystical spirit of an age or class we also take the ground from under the feet of those who would try to remove or eliminate people whom they regard as not conforming to it.

The laws which Popper sees applying to human behaviour are of two sorts. In the first place there are the often trivial and obvious psychological laws which lead to people behaving in particular ways in particular situations. Thus Caesar could be described as ambitious, energetic and so on, and this explains his underlying motivation. Then, second (and Popper sees this as being of greater interest to the student of human affairs), there are laws governing the unintended consequences of human actions. To take the simple example referred to earlier, a man entering the housing market unintentionally pushes house prices up. Popper sees many of the most important results of human activity as unintended effects of this sort, and he sees one of the most vital tasks of social science as being to explore the laws governing these unintended effects. In proposing this he is, of course, denying that human activity can be fully analysed in terms of individual psychology, for much of what happens in history has little to do with the intentions of the agents involved, and happens in spite of rather than because of them.

There is, however, a third vital element in the analysis of human action, which has to do neither with psychological laws nor with laws governing unintended consequences of actions, and this Popper calls the logic of situations. It is here that even in Popper's own account the unity of method begins to break down, and, as we shall see, Popper's account of the logic of situations is far from adequate. The unity of method implies that both physical events and human activity are to be seen in terms of universal laws applied in different circumstances. But even if human atoms follow the same laws everywhere, there is a sense, which Popper admits, in which they are quite unlike physical atoms. For they can perceive their situations and act in the light of chosen goals. They are, in other words, rational agents. Popper proposes that we deal with this by what he calls the logic of situations, according to which we reconstruct the situation in which the agent finds himself and decide what, given his aims, would be the ideal course of action for him at the time. We construct

> a model on the assumption of complete rationality (and perhaps also on the assumption of the possession of complete information) on the part of all the individuals concerned, and of estimating the deviation of the actual behaviour of people from the model behaviour, using the latter as a kind of zero co-ordinate (Popper, 1957, p. 141).

Thus, in explaining why Caesar crossed the Rubicon, what will be of interest are not underlying generalizations about his ambition and energy so much as the reasons why this was or was not the rational choice for him at the time. A vital element in understanding an action, then, will be understanding it as a more or less rational response to some perceived situation.

What Popper is saying here is that human beings faced with decisions are problem solvers or experimenters. Indeed, at one point he goes so far as to say that any social action, even opening a new shop or reserving a theatre ticket, is a social experiment on the part of the agent - a guess about the future based on past experience of similar experiments. It is as experiments of this sort, and in terms of their bearing on the situation in question, that we are to judge and understand human actions generally. If human agents are more than physical atoms in their rationality, a close parallel exists between human action generally and scientific theorizing in particular. In both cases the activity (the action or the theory) involves a hypothesis about the situation in which the individual finds himself, which is then tested for its success against future experience. We understand the action or the theory when we see just how it is a response to a concrete problem, and doing this involves an application of situational logic.

So for Popper, the unity of method involves in the case of human activity the deductive application of laws (as in scientific explanation), supplemented by situational logic. Unfortunately, however, Popper's account of situational logic is totally inadequate for his purposes. In seeing how and why this is so, the extent of the difference between scientific explanation and understanding human activity will become clear, and we will also come to see why social policy cannot (as Popper proposes) be seen as a straightforward matter of social engineering.

For Popper, situational logic is based on the use of what he calls the zero method: a comparison of the actual response with the ideal response demanded by the problem confronting the people involved. This might work for the history of science, where the overall aims and criteria with respect to which individual actions are to be judged are preordained and generally accepted. In science, we can see and understand the moves made by individual scientists in terms of the objective scientific problem confronting them, and their success or failure in dealing with the problem from a scientific point of view. But in human activity generally, the rational thing to do is not fixed independently of the agent's perception of his situation, and his sense of what in life is vital and significant; this, as will become clear, takes us far beyond what can be uncontroversially taken for granted as commonly held by all human beings as such.

This point can be brought out by considering the case of a young man who finds a baby abandoned on a river bank. Most people reading this would probably feel that the rational and compassionate thing to do is save the child. But the hero of a recent play by Edward Bond decides that this type of humanitarianism is highly irrational, if what you want is a revolution, after which such suffering will be altogether eliminated. By palliating suffering now, you are only preventing a complete and genuine cure of the ills of the present, which requires that their full horror is made manifest to all. Popper and I would reply to this that the living have rights as much as the yet unborn, as well as pointing to the uncertain results of a revolution. While this is a reasonable reply to Bond's hero, it does not show his attitude to be irrational. Relative to his aims, his action may well be rational, however contemptible or misguided it seems to others. This example may be extreme, but it is possible to think of other cases where people from particular religious backgrounds do not think of the removal of suffering as being especially urgent: where, indeed, what counts as suffering is defined only in terms of the form of life adopted. You can think here of people living as contemplative monks in the midst of war-torn societies, and of the attitude of the 'Bhagavadgita' in which not only is physical suffering played down, but it is stressed that some types of mental suffering, such as shame, can be felt only by people from certain social strata. In the light of all this fundamental divergence of attitude, Popper's insistence that social policy should concentrate on the practical relief of obvious suffering in order to maximize consensus on both ends and means seems superficially optimistic. It is abundantly clear that what we might consider urgently needed from humanitarian points of view is, in many parts of the world, not seen even as a minimal requirement, and it would be superficial in the extreme to conclude from this that the reason for this is that there is a greater amount of sheer callousness or irrationality in Africa and Asia than in Europe.

It is true that Popper does, in 'Conjectures and Refutations' (1963, pp. 130-1), speak of social traditions providing a background against which agents can predict the consequences of their actions and the likely responses to them. Certainly without such a background, rational social action would hardly be possible. It would follow from this that the zero method should be relativized to the particular tradition in which a particular agent is acting in order to find out what the most rational thing is for him to do. But social contexts and traditions do not simply form part of the predictive background to action, and this is a point Popper (1957, pp, 135-6) appears to miss completely, when, for example, he speaks of notions like 'war', 'army' and so on as theoretical constructions enabling people to construct theories for the interpretation and prediction of pieces of human behaviour, such as the donning of uniform, the killing of others in an organized way and so on. What Popper misses here, possibly in an attempt to preserve the unity of method by seeing social contexts as merely part of the varying experimental conditions, and concepts of action as merely part of a dispensable and replaceable explanatory framework, is the crucial point that social contexts and concepts do not have a merely external relationship to behaviour. What I mean by this is that, depending on the social context and concepts involved, two physically similar pieces of behaviour can count as very different actions. For the sense of an action and its very nature is given by the context: something that does not happen in the physical sciences. Men might be struck and killed in different circumstances, but, depending on those circumstances, we might have an armed robbery, an incident in a battle or a ritual sacrifice. The essential point is that it is the possession by the agents of the concepts of property, nation, religion and so on that makes it possible for a killing to be each or any of these things. As Winch (1963, pp. 127-8) has put it:

> The idea of war ... was not simply invented by people who wanted to explain what happens when societies come into armed conflict. It is an idea which provides the criteria of what is appropriate in the behaviour of members of the conflicting societies. Because my country is at war there

are certain things which I must and certain things which
I must not do. My behaviour is governed, one could say,
by my concept of myself as a member of a belligerent
country. The concept of war belongs <u>essentially</u> to my
behaviour.

It is here that the unity of method finally breaks down. The
social traditions in which people live have an internal relationship
to their actions, and are not simply the experimental conditions
of independently describable actions, nor are the relevant concepts of action explanatory models of an external sort. Thus, to
adapt one of Winch's examples, an apple does not fall because it
possesses the concept of gravity, but the institution of an army
in a society, and the currency given in that society to the
requisite concepts, make all the difference in the world between
what a soldier does when he kills a man in a battle and what he
does killing someone in a drunken brawl.

It will be clear from what has been said that even when we are
describing the behaviour of an individual we often cannot abstract
him from membership of his social group. For many of the concepts under which people act depend on their seeing themselves
as members of groups, sharing the interests, concerns and values
of groups. In addition to the examples of war and army already
considered, we can think immediately of such things as promising,
contracting, lecturing in a university, marrying, being ordained,
receiving a salary, belonging to a team and so on. Much of the
behaviour of any individual is governed by concepts such as
these, and this means that what is done is done only in so far as
the individuals in question see themselves as members of teams,
universities, businesses, armies, societies, religions and so on.
Many of our aims, too, are given to us only because we belong to
one society or group or another. Thus I could hardly intend to
look for a second wife while remaining married to a first in a
society that did not allow polygamy, nor could I attempt to buy
shares in an industry in a non-capitalist society. What is being
said here does not mean that an individual is forced to act in particular ways by his society or by its spirit (so no objectionable
denial of individual choice or responsibility follows from what has
been said). After all, even in a polygamous society, a man need
not marry one wife, let alone three or four. On the other hand,
being in a particular society or group, with its institutions and
concepts, is rather more than a matter of ideas being transmitted to individuals and 'captivating' them, as Popper (1957,
p. 149) suggests. An individual is not made to act patriotically
because of social influences, but his belonging to a nation does
more than merely give him the idea of patriotic action. What it
does is to make it possible for him to act patriotically or unpat-
riotically. It is in terms of his membership of a nation that his
patriotic or unpatriotic action will be recognisable for what it is -
as patriotic or unpatriotic.

So, because of the intimate relationship between social concepts
and actions, there can be no unity of method between natural

science and explanations of human action. For the natural sciences
are concerned with the explanation and prediction of natural phenomena, and in this there is no reason to examine the mentality of
particles, their purposes or the social contexts which give their
behaviour its significance. Natural phenomena, in their interrelationships, do not achieve anything resembling the social significance human beings attach to their interaction. Above all, in
human action, questions of social significance raise questions of
value, which are significantly absent in the natural world. For
institutions such as property and the family both demonstrate
the type of significance that groups of people attach to what would
otherwise be the purely biological tasks of self-preservation and
procreation, and raise for others the task of assessing these significances. Not only, then, do many of the concepts and institutions relating to human behaviour make that behaviour the behaviour it is (rather than merely being instruments of explanation and prediction); they also determine its significance within
a particular group and immediately raise questions of its value.
Thus, to call an action unpatriotic or shameful is immediately to
suggest that, at least from the point of view of the agent's
society, there is something unworthy in what he is doing. From
this, two consequences follow. In the first place, we will not
understand the nature of a man's action until we understand
something of his society, its traditions and meanings. A Japanese
man may disembowel himself in public, but we cannot understand
this as a ritual suicide rather than a bizarre piece of despairing
self-advertisement without understanding Japanese culture, and
what it is that leads the Japanese to think of situations as potentially suicidal. So, even if the student of human affairs does not
need mystical insight into the spirit of the age in order even to
describe a man's actions, let alone explain them, he does need
knowledge of the cultural context in which the actions take place,
and this, of course, may be extremely hard for an outsider to
attain. Then, second, in any cultural context, in the institutions
and language of a people are expressed that whole range of
values and significances which go to make human social life of
ethical rather than of purely biological significance. It is here
that we see the superficiality of Popper's optimism concerning
what he calls social engineering. His optimism consists in the
view that there will be general agreement on those bits of social
policy needed to relieve obvious suffering (social engineering).
His superficiality consists in the belief that in different societies
the same things will easily be recognized as needing urgent attention or even as being evils. For the recognition of a situation as
evil is again not independent of a general background of ethical
beliefs and practices.

In no important sense can the study of human behaviour satisfactorily use the same methods as those of the natural sciences.
For human behaviour is significant behaviour, seen by its agents
as having particular meanings, against a framework of values and
institutions. There is nothing analogous to this in the natural

world, nor in the explanations given in natural sciences are any
questions of value raised. (If questions of value are raised by the
technological applications of scientific theories, this is because
such applications often impinge on points of significance to the
human world, not because the terms of the explanations are themselves implicitly evaluative.) Much of the dissatisfaction felt with
scientific psychology, and even at times with sociology, arises
from the attempt made there to sever behaviour from its social
signigicance and to treat it as a purely animal function, describable in neutral, biological terms. Durkheim's (1952, pp. 43-4)
bizarre lumping together of cases of maternal and military self-
sacrifice with lovers' suicides is only one of the more famous
instances of what happens when actions are analysed in abstraction from their agent's perceptions of them.

Popper's talk of social engineering, as well as his view that
social traditions merely provide an explanatory framework for the
prediction of human action, inevitably recall themes from the controversy between C. P. Snow and F. R. Leavis which resulted
from Snow's 1959 Rede Lecture on the 'two cultures' (Snow, 1964;
Leavis, 1972). In particular, it is worth glancing at Snow's coin-
age of the term 'two cultures', and his antithesis between what he
calls the individual condition and social hope. Of course, part of
what Snow was doing was deploring the fact that scientists and
non-scientists tend to be mutually ignorant. We can all deplore
this. Indeed, I have already said that some scientific knowledge
is requisite for full self-knowledge (and in this I disagree strongly
with Leavis's tendency to treat science as merely a means to an
end, as if a knowledge of the nature of the universe and of the
physical basis of life was of no more than instrumental value).
But what is unfortunate in Snow, even if he disapproves of the
state of affairs that he is pointing to, is his characterization of
mutual ignorance on the two sides of the scientific divide as a
divorce between two cultures; for the implication here is that
there is a set of human significances to be found within a scientific education alone. But science itself, in its theorizing and
researching, leaves all problems of value and morality untouched,
if only because its methods of classifying and explaining natural
phenomena attempt as far as possible to avoid using the very terms
in which questions of value can be raised. It is quite right that it
should, for natural objects do not act for purposes, with significance and within social or institutional frameworks. The rejection
of teleological (purposive) explanations from physics and biology
has led to great advances in knowledge of the structure of matter.
On the other hand, human meaning is all bound up with individual
purposes and feelings and talk of purposes. So the scientist who
knows all about DNA, but who has no knowledge of D. H. Lawrence, say, is not just ignorant on a point of literature; he is
missing one of the most vital contributions to any serious discussion or consideration of what it is for human beings to have
life and what it means to live it in an industrial society. It is not
that there are two competing sets of values, scientific values and

literary values. It is rather that science in itself (as opposed to scientists) does not touch on values or deal with them, and that people who have a purely scientific education are going to be totally unfitted by their education for a serious consideration of matters of value. And this remains true, even though (as I shall suggest in the next chapter) engaging in scientific research can help to foster strong moral qualities such as respect for truth, impartiality and attention to the facts. The trouble is that these virtues, unless joined to a sensitive understanding of human feelings, can lead to a bluff and dismissive attitude to other people's sense of what is significant, especially when that sense appears to stand in the way of material progress and to run counter to what appears rational from a technological point of view. The study of literature, on the other hand, does not (or should not) lead to an establishment of purely literary values. As Leavis (1972, p. 97) puts it:

> The judgments the literary critic is concerned with are judgments about life. What the critical discipline is concerned with is relevance and precision in making and developing them. To think that to have vital contemporary performance of the critical function matters is to think that creative literature matters; and it matters because to have a living literature, a literary tradition that lives in the present - and nothing lives unless it goes on being creative, is to have, as an informing spirit in civilization, an informed, charged and authoritative awareness of inner human nature and human need.

In his lecture, Snow (1964, pp. 6-7, 44) had claimed that while scientific culture (as he puts it) could do little to alleviate the tragic nature of the individual condition of each of us, it can give us social hope in the form of solving problems of starvation and early death, or, as he puts it, jam (for all, presumably) tomorrow. There are several unfortunate aspects of the cast of mind this way of putting things reveals. In the first place, social hope is an odd sort of hope. As Leavis constantly points out, hope, like life and creativity, resides only in individuals. On the other hand, the individual is

> inescapably social . . . in his very individuality. The poet, for instance, didn't create the language without which he couldn't have begun to be a poet, and a language is more than an instrument of expression. He is - let the fusion of metaphors pass - a focal conduit of the life that is one, though it manifests itself only in the myriad individual beings, and his unique identity is not the less a unique identity because the discovery of what it is and means entails a profoundly inward participation in a cultural continuity (1972, pp. 171-2).

This is part of what I was trying to say in attacking the unity of method thesis, for part of what that entailed was the idea of the social atom being only externally related to his social context. So Snow's simple antithesis between the life of the individual and the progress of his society is in several ways suspect.

But to return to the substance of Snow's thought, most dubious of all is the idea that social hope can be conceived simply in terms of the benefits to be gained by applying science through technology - jam tomorrow. I have already criticized the idea, implicit in the social engineering thesis, that there is no great problem in recognizing social needs, and that all that is needed is a broadly utilitarian glance at material ills; I will end this section by considering the difficulty and danger involved in seeing social engineering (as Snow appears to do, even if Popper does not) principally in terms of the wider distribution of the benefits of technology. The problem here is not that people's lives should not be materially improved or that starvation and infant mortality are not in many parts of the world obvious evils needing urgent remedies. We can agree with Snow that they are. The problem is rather that approaching human problems as problems of technology tends to lead one to see human ends in terms of the smooth running of a machine, human individuals in terms of the elements of such a machine and human lives in terms of units of production and consumption. Such instrumentalist thinking not only tend to view human problems and human ends in quantitative terms, where, as Evelyn Waugh for one so often stressed, quantitative judgments simply do not apply, but it also tends to be destructive of that organic sense of the meaning of life which had often been present in pre-technological cultures. (And not only in pre-technological cultures; in our own society we are still baffled and surprised by the disastrous human effects of many slum clearance programmes, and by the idea that people may prefer squalor to efficiency.) What is at issue here is necessarily and pre-eminently an educational issue. We have already seen Peters rightly attacking the idea that education ought to be viewed in a merely technological and instrumentalist spirit, because this perspective leaves open the whole question of what the better material life is for and how it is to be organized. But politicians, both in the west and in the non-industrialized world, daily call for more and more technological emphasis in education. A technologically based education is bound to be an inadequate one, because it will fail to provide the methods by which human culture and human life can be understood, because it will fail to take into account the ways in which men do not live by jam or by economic rationality alone, and because its ethos is destructive of the basic human need for individual significance and quality which was supplied, however misguidedly and irrationally, in many traditional cultures. To quote Leavis (1972, p. 207), for the last time:

> The barbarity of reformist enlightenment is the deadly enemy that must be defeated - the civilized barbarity, complacent, self-indulgent and ignorant, that can see nothing to be quarrelled with in believing, or wanting to believe, that a computer can write a poem. In the interests of self-congratulation it simplifies social problems by eliminating

the life: the complexities it reduces them to are mechanical,
or treatable mechanically - it hates the organic, and its
simplifications kill.

What Leavis goes on to advocate is an education in which there is
a proper stress on the imaginative responses men have made in
art and literature to human life and its problems, and in which
those responses are subjected to examination and assessment in
the light of the highest intellectual standards. I shall have more
to say in the next chapter about the vital role literary education
should play in moral education. Leavis sees the university as the
place in which the task of examining and assessing literature can
best be undertaken, in which each student comes to see himself
as a member of a 'complex collaborative community' engaged in
the critical-creative conflict through which a civilized approach to
life can be fostered. Leavis has been criticized by Hirst (1974,
p. 166) for giving no account of the basis on which moral judgments in the critical-creative conflict are to be made, and for
tending simply to an intuitive endorsement of previously held
values. Whether this is fair or not as an assessment of Leavis's
own work, there is nothing in his advocacy of a literary education
to preclude a systematic examination of moral values. Indeed, talk
of a critical-creative conflict would appear to require just such
an examination. What is impressive about Leavis is the clarity with
which he sees that moral questions in the broadest sense are
introduced and grappled with in literature in such a way that they
are obviously of vital and living significance. This point has been
well made by G. H. Bantock (1963, p. 176), who insists that even
specialists in other disciplines should acquire a close acquaintance
with literature, 'the one discipline which reflects on and sensi-
tizes to general human behaviour at its most concrete level of
daily intercourse', which yet requires no special vocabulary, and
which, 'even if not read with the deepest understanding, must
yet inevitably extend the range of the non-specialist's awareness
of the human situation.'

Thus the study of literature should not only be what Leavis
calls the 'humane centre' of any satisfactory education, it is also
a necessary preparation for any deep study of moral philosophy,
taking that to be a study of the general principles underlying
moral evaluations. Moreover, it is clear that science, being factual,
value-free and, above all in its repudiation of anthropocentricity,
does not even begin to deal with questions of human significance
from the point of view of what makes them humanly significant.
However, even if the critical-creative conflict itself is seen as
primarily taking place in universities rather than schools, there
is no reason why schools could not introduce their pupils to some
of its aspects.

The stress on high intellectual standards in humanistic areas is,
of course, vital. In a way, we are taken back here to the problem raised by Rousseau and Tolstoy, of how best in the modern
world to retain any sense of human warmth and organicity. But
we have gone beyond the innocence and over simplifications

implicit in their solutions. The same degree of precision and complexity that is necessary for science and technology must be sought in humanistic studies. Naivety and the return to the tribe are not going to help us now. What is wrong is not the complexity of modern industry and modern society, it is the simplicity of so much of the political, administrative and journalistic cliché by which our lives are lived and our problems addressed. It is in this respect that Snow's blandness and optimism is both most marked and most depressing, as when, for example, he talks of the 'scientific culture' taking 'in its stride' the transformations needed to provide 'jam tomorrow' for the poorer countries – a task apparently seen in terms of producing in them enough 'scientists and technicians and engineers' to industrialize them totally. Can anyone who actually looks really be so complacent about the results of industrialization in the Third World, when it so often brings in its wake only cultural destruction and moral deprivation, or indeed about the effects of industrialization on the lives of the majority of consumers in the west?

Many themes from Euripides's 'The Bacchae' are worth reflecting on here. We have presented to us an antithesis between the rational and non-rational parts of man's nature. There is a rational, calculating ruler (Pentheus) and the irrational god of life, creativity, wine, violence and abandon (Dionysus). Pentheus expels Dionysus from the city of Thebes, because he sees him as a danger to the city, but Dionysus has already won over the women of Thebes, and he leads them in rites of frenzied dancing on Mount Parnassus. Pentheus, though, burns with curiosity about what he is missing and spies on the revellers. He is seen and captured and torn to pieces by the followers of Dionysus, among whom is his own mother. We see today an increasing stress on a rationalistic, technological organization of life, a destruction of organic living and significance, and the same separation as in 'The Bacchae' between the artificial controls of day-to-day living and the occasional outbursts of uncontrolled frenzy. We need an education that can help us to make sense of the significances people have given to their lives, and which marks out the differences between studying nature and studying human life. We need to be able to provide for the material conditions of life in as sane and practical a way as possible, but we also need to foster some sense of meaning for our lives. To do this we must above all come to grips with the cultural achievements of the past, and for this an education which presents them and considers them seriously is vital. For these achievements are not just objects in museums; they are the profoundest ways our predecessors have expressed their sense of the significance of life. In seriously considering and criticizing them we can learn much of value for our own lives; and what we learn from them we are hardly likely to discover for ourselves, starting from scratch, any more than any one of us could discover the whole of science from scratch. Naturally, these achievements are not the last word either in science or in the humanities; in both spheres they are to be criticized and developed.

But effective criticism and development must start from a position of understanding.

## CHOICE AND THE CURRICULUM

A constant theme of this book has been the way in which educational decisions are and should be made in the light of overall conceptions of human nature and society. Thus, much of Chapter 2 was an elaboration of the educational implications of autonomous existence in a pluralist society. The ideal curriculum from this point of view, would be one which fulfilled the requirements laid down in Chapter 2; one, in other words, which fitted children for adult life in the relevant respects. In the previous section, we emphasized the importance of an education in both the sciences and the humanities. In some broad areas, then, there would be little room for curricular choice on the part of the pupils. Indeed, a degree of compulsion in childhood would be necessary for a reasonably independent adult life, and schools and parents would be shirking their duties if they did not attempt in some way to ground children in certain disciplines, whether the children particularly liked it at the time or not.

To be more specific, some grounding in the natural sciences, in human studies (from history to psychology), in the humanities (literature and the arts) and in religious knowledge is the essential core of any reasonably adequate education, whatever the individuals in question are likely to do in their future lives. There should be little room for choice in schools on whether to tackle any of these subject areas, although choices of particular topics and emphases within the areas might be made available, particularly at the later stages of education. On vocational training, while some very general and basic technical skills and knowledge might be compulsorily taught to all because of their wide usefulness, in an ideal world a range of choices regarding more specific skills or jobs might be desirable, for what is being aimed at here is not knowledge for its own worth, but more for its instrumental value. Perhaps, for social reasons, like Solon in ancient Athens we might insist that all children emerge from schools with some practical trade; the segregation of societies into blue- and white-collar workers is in many ways thoroughly undesirable. But even if we insist on everyone undergoing training for a practical trade, the good that will result from this does not depend on whether the trade is plumbing, gas fitting, sewing or carpentry, and choice could be offered here.

Here an important point arises. Schools themselves exist for the mutual benefit of those being taught in them and, to a lesser extent, of the society in which they live. They do not exist for their own sake, or for the sake of teachers; so, unless what is being done in them can be shown to be of benefit to the pupils or to society, we will have no justification either for the social expense involved or, more importantly, for the enforced deprivation

of the pupils' liberty. Unfortunately there can often be apparent
tensions between the individual and social ends of schooling. Thus,
although I have argued for the social benefits of particular subjects being carried on at a high intellectual level, I have not said
that any particular individuals should be forced to pursue them at
a high level. All that each pupil, however able, is to be required
to do is have sufficient grounding in a subject to enable him to
make reasonable choices for himself (including whether to pursue
that subject further). Sufficient here might not mean very advanced. In the same way, it is not the business of schools to
force pupils, either by default or more positively, into particular
types of jobs. Even though this might be done because of a supposed social need, a genuinely pluralist society should always
seek to maximize individual freedom, and the onus must always be
on those who seek to restrict choice to show that there is some
vitally pressing reason for such a restriction. Certainly a society
that provided itself with factory fodder through a policy of educational deprivation could hardly claim to be concerned for individual rights or freedoms, and the social goods that accrued from
such a policy would presumably be somewhat unevenly distributed.
Believers in social pluralism must always be prepared to face the
fact that members of a society may prefer to act in socially incon-
venient ways; or, to put this less negatively, they may prefer
other goods than productivity and the material prosperity of their
society as a whole. Naturally, if this other-worldliness began to
endanger life, or security, then there would be grounds for the
use of compulsion, even for a believer in individual freedom,
because all freedoms are threatened by starvation and unmanage-
able debt. Nevertheless, for the pluralist, there is at a higher
level a reconciliation of these tensions between individual freedoms and social goods, because he can always argue that the
social good that overrides all others for him is the existence of
the pluralist society in which people are free to make their own
lives and choices. For this man, then, there is no ultimate conflict between the individual goal of education (enabling a person
to reach social and intellectual maturity) and the social goal of
education (a society of mature people).

So, from a pluralist point of view, we can say that the deprivation of a child's liberty involved in schooling is justified to
the extent that it promotes his own individual liberty and the
respect he has for the liberties of others. The academic core of
the curriculum, some (unspecified) vocational training, and moral
education are justified to that extent, the academic core because
it forms the basis necessary for personal decisions in life, moral
education because it leads to an understanding of the rights of
others and vocational training because it will provide the basis
for self-sufficiency. (We might further defend a Solon-like policy
of insisting on the learning of a practical skill on the grounds
that it will lead to greater mutual respect in society, which is
itself part of what is involved in respecting the rights and liberties of others.) It follows from this analysis that while the whole

of the academic core should be compulsory, because without it the materials for one's own judgments and choices will be missing, there is room for choice in the vocational area of education. One does not need more than one or two vocational subjects, because self-sufficiency does not require that each individual has every skill or trade, and neither does one already need to have a particular skill in order to choose to try to acquire it. At most we would require children to take one or two from a range of available vocational options. On the other hand, one does need some knowledge of science and human beings to be able to form sensible attitudes in one's life.

That there is scope for choice on curricular matters is, from a pluralist point of view, an entirely good thing, because, as J. P. White (1973, p. 71) puts it: 'the child is not simply an adult in the making. He is also a child, with his own life to lead, who should be left free to do what he wants as far as possible.' Thus we should respect, as far as we can, the individuality and personality of the child rather than filling up every moment of his day with compulsory lessons and what we think is good for him. We should also help him to get used to making choices for himself. White further suggests that many 'familiar timetable items', such as foreign languages, painting, games, cookery, handicraft and so on, should not be compulsory. Indeed, as I have suggested in Chapter 2 (p. 55), it may be partly because school timetables are compulsorily filled with subjects that ought to be voluntary that the broad general education advocated there can seem over-ambitious in terms of time. Although White's overall perspective is somewhat different from mine, on my view too, none of the subjects White lists should be compulsory, even though one or other of these topics might be taken as one's compulsory vocational subject or subjects. White is rightly insistent that the onus of proof must always be on those who want activities to be compulsory, and where there is no proof, then there is no justification in ramming them down children's throats. This seems particularly true in the case of games, whose only rationale is enjoyment; otherwise you do not have a game, properly speaking. It is often claimed that games build character, but, as will emerge in the next chapter, what is important in moral education could in no sense be conceived of as being provided either primarily or indeed even very fully in games. There are plenty of other ways in which people can learn to co-operate and to struggle against hardship, and plenty of virtues other than these which we should want to cultivate. It may be that schools should ensure that their pupils have a minimum degree of health and physical fitness, as this is a necessary precondition for efficient learning, but the emphasis should surely be on minima here. After all, some people just don't like physical activity, and there seems no good reason to force them to undertake it: in no way is it obvious that someone who undertakes a little physical activity as is consistent with reasonable health is any less able to exercise his autonomy in a mature or responsible way.

White also makes the interesting suggestion that the school day might be clearly divided into, say, a morning of compulsory activities, and an afternoon of voluntary ones. As he says, the case for running a voluntary system in parallel with the compulsory one is that it underlines the respect in which children are not merely educands, but people leading their own lives (1973, p. 70). If, in my scheme of things, it were possible to place all the academic work in the mornings, then the afternoons could be left free for choices from a range of vocational topics, and perhaps for other activities as well, which some pupils enjoy, such as games or painting or handicrafts. I should emphasize here that the main aspect of artistic education in the academic part of education as I conceive it will be that of the appreciation and understanding of great works and traditions, and, like White (1973, p. 41), I do not see that this type of appreciation necessarily requires much executive knowledge or ability. On the other hand, there are good reasons for the good of both pupils and schools for providing facilities in the school for children voluntarily to develop their own artistic talents. Indeed, being confronted with works of quality may well lead them to want to try for themselves, and so it would be a good thing for guidance and materials to be readily available.

It might be objected that the academic and serious vocational training which is being made compulsory will really only get underway when pupils have reached a certain stage of maturity, say at secondary level, and that most of what is done in primary schools should, on my scheme of things, be voluntary. It is surely an empirical matter to determine just how and at what age a basic academic and vocational education might best be started: it might indeed be that there is very little that can be done in many areas before the age of seven, and that only gradual increases can be made in the amount of, say, science or mathematics that can be taught before the secondary level. If all or any of this is true, then there should be rather less compulsion at the primary school level than at the secondary level; perhaps compulsory schooling should not even be begun until after children are five or even seven years of age. As White (1973, p. 72) remarks, on all these matters, we are at the moment very much in the dark. What is important is that having a clear sense of what is wanted from education will also bring a clear sense of those areas of the curriculum which should be compulsory and those which ought to be voluntary, while to have some areas where choice is possible can only be to the good in an educational system one of whose main aims is to foster autonomy and self-sufficiency.

# 5  MORAL EDUCATION

In Chapter 2, I argued that one of the tasks of education was to impart an understanding of morality. There are obvious reasons why this is desirable. What we want to do in schooling is to prepare pupils for adult life. Therefore it is necessary to give them a good basis for self-sufficiency, both economic and intellectual. Equally, though, as life is not purely economic and intellectual but also emotional and personal, some insight is needed into the way in which one ought to conduct one's personal and social life. This is the place of moral education.

Now, it might be argued that school is not the right place for moral education, on at least two grounds. First, that whatever values are considered desirable and worth teaching, such as honesty or respect for others, are best and most effectively learned in more informal circumstances than in the school, above all in the home, where the child will have his or her original and closest experiences of being treated as a moral being and of seeing moral attitudes in practice. Undoubtedly, this last point is true; indeed, it is hard to see how, in the absence of love and respect and honesty from parents and relatives or substitutes for them, a child could even begin to learn what it is to be a person or to see others as persons at all. For to see oneself or another as a person is to see or be seen as a centre of feeling and consciousness, entitled to care and respect. Without some experience of being treated oneself in this way, and without seeing others being treated like this by those close to one, it is unlikely that one could ever come to know what it is for oneself to be a person, or for others to be any more than objects capable either of furthering or frustrating one's own aims. But the importance of the immediate family in moral education does not mean that the school does not have a genuine role to play. For even if the basic experience necessary for an understanding of what it is to be a moral being (or a person) and the basic moral attitudes themselves cannot be transmitted in school, a more systematic treatment of morality can certainly be undertaken there. Moreover, new applications of morality and further discussion of moral questions will arise necessarily both in school life and in subjects studied at school. This last point means that moral matters cannot be avoided in school, even if it was thought desirable that they should be. Morality is intrinsic both to the conduct of teachers and teaching, and, in various ways, to the content of the various subjects being taught.

This, however, brings us to a second line of doubt about the place of morality in school. In speaking of the teaching of morality is one speaking of teaching a specific subject, like history or physics? To suggest that this was the case would be to imply that there could be experts in morality and that there could be research and discovery in it. Against this idea, it will be said that being moral does not involve cleverness, intellectual expertise or education, and that the prime aim of moral education is to produce habitual moral behaviour. So a good man does not need lessons in morality, any more than a runner needs lessons in physiology. This is not a conclusive reply, however, for two reasons. First, even though cleverness is neither necessary nor sufficient for goodness, a study of moral principles and argument might help people to realize that they would be inconsistent if they did not apply their principles, such as those of justice or fairness, to cases they had not previously thought of as falling under them. Also, there surely is some virtue in getting people to reflect on just what principles they hold and how they might be justified. This brings us on to the second way in which morality might be regarded as a specific study in its own right; for there is room for a systematic analysis of the basis of moral argument. However, moral philosophy – for this is what such an analysis would be – would hardly be in place in school except at the highest level, while what I have been calling the moral aspect of teaching and the various subjects is pervasive throughout schooling. So it is perhaps better not to think of moral education in terms of the teaching of a specific subject, but rather in terms of its implications for schooling as a whole.

It is clear that a teacher dealing with a class of pupils is in an exposed personal position. What he or she does on a personal level will be scrutinized by the pupils, who will obviously pick on such traits as impartiality, fairness, lateness, tidiness, impatience, sobriety, consistency and so on. All this is too obvious to need any further comment, beyond underlining the fact that, whether the teacher likes it or not, he or she is being judged on a moral and personal level by the pupils all the time. Clearly one important part of moral education in the school consists in the training by example given by the teachers.

But there is something else of great moral significance which the teacher can communicate to pupils through his classroom behaviour which is not, perhaps, so obvious, and this is the attitude manifested to the subject in the teaching itself. All along I have stressed the way in which subjects have standards internal to them; what should be emphasized here is that these standards have a moral side to them. Clearly, in any field of study respect for truth and accuracy is of paramount importance, and this should become apparent in teaching. In practice this means that such moral qualities as impartiality, objectivity, willingness to listen to others and to submit to evidence and reason are central to the pursuit and teaching of any subject. That these are moral qualities becomes clear when one reflects that a large part of moral behaviour consists in the readiness to consider one's own desires and opinions in the light of the desires and opinions of others, and to see oneself as only one person among others, who may have equally valid rights and points of view. In the study of science, particularly, the virtues of impartiality and submission to evidence ought to be cultivated, while the study of literature should help to develop a sense of the feelings and humanity of others, without which (as I shall explain further later) the attempt to apply moral principles in one's dealings with others is likely to be ineffectual.

So, both in his attitude to his subject and in his behaviour generally, the teacher will necessarily be communicating certain moral qualities (good or bad) to the pupils. This is one reason why it would be wrong to think of moral education in terms of a special class in 'morality' or moral philosophy. Morality is not, in fact, a body of knowledge in the way physics (for example) is. This is what is right in the claim that there is no special subject here. To speak of a man's moral beliefs or his immoral behaviour is to speak of his attitudes and behaviour in his life as a whole, to those around him and to his work, in so far as those attitudes and the resulting actions can be seen as good or bad, right or wrong, humanly speaking. This involves an assessment of his attitudes and behaviour in the light of the respect he shows or fails to show to others, his concern for their rights, for justice, for truth, for not causing unnecessary pain, for fulfilling the duties he has and so on. Although different people may have different attitudes on these matters, it is the stand that is taken on them that characterizes a man's morality. Hence, as has been said, morality and questions of morality inevitably arise in the very activity of teaching, even if the content of what was being taught was completely abstract and appeared to have no moral implications in itself.

But a great deal of what is taught has a substantive bearing on morality, both in raising moral questions and in providing material relevant to them. This shows again that morality is not something over and above other activities and on a par with them, but rather arises from the human concerns and implications of these other activities, and points to another way in which moral issues inevitably arise throughout schooling. It is obvious that this is the case with literary and historical studies, where a large part of one's attention will constantly be directed to questions of the rightness or wrongness of the behaviour of individuals. Indeed, I shall suggest later that literary studies are an indispensable part of moral education. But even in studying the 'pure' sciences, moral questions can arise, on, for example, the acceptability of certain lines of research, or perhaps, very generally, on the human implications of a scientific or technological attitude to nature and life. Also, scientific knowledge is often necessary for an informed attitude to moral issues, particularly those raised by technology itself, such as the ethics of genetic or nuclear engineering. One of the ethical values of science teaching could well be to show pupils how ethical questions are often very complex and require knowledge and judgment over and above emotion, however deep and well intentioned. As teachers are not just subject experts or teaching machines, but also human beings in a human relationship with their pupils, it would be quite wrong for them not to spend some time exploring the ethical implications of what they are teaching. Some of the left wing strictures on curricular divisions and the examination system will be justified if scholastic divisions and syllabuses lead teachers to approach and present their subjects in a moral and human vacuum, though even to do this will be for teachers to evince a moral attitude by default, so to speak.

What has emerged so far is that teaching is an activity in which moral issues arise inevitably, and in which teachers necessarily manifest some of their moral attitudes and qualities (or lack of them). Given this, the question arises as to the type of attitude to moral issues a teacher should adopt when dealing with them explicitly, as I have argued that he should. There would appear to be a double danger here, arising from the fact that the teacher is in a position of authority over his pupils. This authority itself has two aspects. First, the teacher knows more than the pupils about particular subjects. Second, he has to keep some sort of control within the class, and this will involve, among other things, protecting individual pupils from being bullied, stamping out thieving and so on. In the performance of these duties, teachers cannot necessarily wait for acquiescence and reason from all members of a class. Sometimes moral rules will have to be enforced in much the same way as school rules which may have little or no intrinsic validity outside the school (such as silence at assembly). In other words, pupils may, on occasion, just have to be forced to restrain aggressive or acquisitive impulses. There is the further complication that with young children, at least, moral reasoning may be impossible, in that they are psychologically unable to see or understand appeals to general moral principles such as those of fairness, sympathy and so on. The dangers arising from all this are, first, that pupils may come to see and obey moral rules as stemming largely from the personal authority of educators, and second, that they may fail to distinguish rules of moral importance from those which simply have to do with the good running of a particular institution. If this is what results from schooling, then it is quite likely that the moral rules which have been enforced there will be given up after school, along with the authority of the teacher and the demands of the institution.

The problem of the authoritarian aspects of moral education is exacerbated when we remember that what we want from moral education is not any sort of adherence to moral principles, but an adherence that is fully internalized and does not require policing. Now it may be psychologically possible to internalize external authorities and their edicts (according to Freud we all do this to a greater or lesser extent). But a mere internalization of an authority is not, it will be said, what truly moral behaviour

is based on. Since Kant, it has been customary for moral philosophers to distinguish between autonomous and heteronomous
moralities, the former accepted because the agent himself thinks
on the basis of rational reflection that it is good, and the latter
because he feels forced to obey some authority, human or divine.
Only the former - a morality freely chosen in the light of reason -
is a morality worthy of the name when we are dealing with free,
rational agents. According to Kant, if we follow the words of
Christ, believing him to be the Blessed One of God, we are implicitly judging for ourselves that his words are good, and we
should ideally make and defend this choice in the light of reason.
Autonomy in morals, free rational choice of principles, is then
taken to be the ideal outcome of moral education. For Peters
(1966, p. 197), as for many others who have written on moral
education, being morally autonomous involves regulating one's
life by rules or principles 'which one has accepted for oneself',
and which can be given justification through appeal to higher
order principles, such as 'impartiality, liberty, truth-telling,
and the consideration of interests', which are themselves rationally justifiable (1963, p. 51). Downie, Loudfoot and Telfer (1974,
p. 58) rather grandly follow Kant in seeing the possession of a
rational will as the ability to govern one's conduct by rules which
one sees as binding on oneself and on all rational beings. Hare
(1964, pp. 77-8) sees moral maturity in learning to make decisions
of principle, which we realize can 'only be verified by reference
to a standard or set of principles which we have by our own
decision accepted and made our own'. Anything else will be
objectionably heteronomous, and in any case, it might be added,
who is in a position to tell other people what is really good? Isn't
this pre-eminently a matter which each man has a duty to consider
for himself? So a problem necessarily involved in moral education
is to see how a moral educator can avoid being an authoritarian
indoctrinator, trying to enforce a morality on an agent who
should ideally be freely and rationally deciding for himself.

As the problem has so far been put, it amounts to this. The
child's initiation into morality consists in his being ordered to
obey rules. He obeys only because he sees the rules as upheld
by an authority whom he knows he has to obey and who, in any
case, is giving him other non-moral orders too. Yet moral behaviour is behaviour governed by principles rationally accepted
by a self-determining agent. How can what is originally obeyed
as a heteronomous rule become something genuinely chosen,
freely and rationally? This picture of moral development and the
moral philosophy behind it will be widely familiar from psychological as well as philosophical sources. On reflection, though, it
is difficult to see what special problem this picture presents for
moral education. For surely, in all subjects, we begin by simply
telling children things. Only later do they come to understand
the reasons for what they are told, and to accept or reject things
for themselves on their own merits. In morality, as in other areas,
there is nothing inconsistent or paradoxical in first laying down

things that have to be accepted and later leading pupils to see
and evaluate the reasons for what they have been told. Indeed,
it is hard to see how reasons could be appreciated for what they
are unless they were seen as supporting or justifying propositions that were already understood and (provisionally) accepted.
A teacher or a school would be going against the ideal of moral
autonomy only if he or they laid down moral commands that were
in their eyes unreasonable, or else at a later stage there were no
provision for introducing pupils to the elements involved in moral
reasoning and moral choice. If there is provision for a later
introduction to moral reasoning, there is nothing necessarily
objectionable in a teacher or a school initially simply telling pupils
what they thought was right and making them conform to these
principles, providing the means of enforcement respect the fact
that the subjects involved are children with individual needs and
personalities and capable of feeling, if not mature reasoning.
People have to do the best they can, and in the moral case this
means passing on those principles one sincerely and reasonably
holds. To fail to do this where it is appropriate is to be less than
fully human in one's attitude to others, and, as we have seen,
there are occasions where it is appropriate for a teacher to do
this. The fact that an individual teacher's principles may be misguided or open to criticism does not mean that he is indoctrinating his pupils in an objectionable way, so long as they are later
given the materials necessary for them to evaluate for themselves
what in the first instance they had simply been told.

So the necessarily authoritarian nature of moral education in
the early years need not conflict with ideals of moral autonomy,
providing scope is later given for more mature moral reasoning.
So far, I have been speaking of morality in terms of the acceptance and justification of rules, and the 'paradox' of moral education, as it is sometimes called, is that to start with the child is
simply forced to obey the rules. What has been so far left out of
this picture is the fact, stressed by Aristotle ('Nicomachean
Ethics', Bk. 2, Ch. 4) that being virtuous is not simply a matter
of doing good things on isolated occasions, it is also a matter of
the habitual exercise of the virtues, and that the acquisition of
a virtue depends on the formation of a virtuous habit. The question that now arises is whether seeing moral education as involving
the inculcation and formation of habits, at a time when the child
is unable to reason morally in any way, intensifies the paradox
of moral education. Peters, whose analysis of the paradox in an
article entitled -Reason and habit- (1963) is given in terms of
the rationality or otherwise of inculcating habits, would appear
to answer that this is not necessarily so, for, as he points out,
to speak of an action being habitual does not preclude its being
thought about, or the habit being stopped or justified in terms
of reasons. It is not necessarily to imply that it is automatic or
that it involves merely reflex responses. So far, then, the fact
that virtues involve habits does not appear to add anything to
the paradox of moral education as we have been considering it.

However, Peters goes on to say something about the nature of morality which will ultimately lead us to question the whole analysis of moral behaviour with which we have so far been dealing. In questioning this analysis, new light will also be thrown on moral education and the associated paradox.

Peters points out, first, that moral habits are habits involving actions which require far more understanding on the part of agents than would be required in purely motor skills. Examples of theft or malice, to take Peters's examples, entail that the person doing the action has an understanding of what it is to be another person, to hurt him or her, to deprive him or her of his property, all of which involve a conscious entry into the human world of interpersonal relationships and institutions in a way that understanding how to walk or to feed oneself does not. Peters (1963, pp. 61-2) writes that 'a child, strictly speaking, cannot be guilty of theft, who has not developed the concept of himself as distinct from others, of property, of the granting of permission, etc.', and he goes on to say that all this may take a long time; far longer, in fact, than it may take to get a child not to do certain things of which authority figures disapprove. At this early stage in the child's development we may stop him from taking the toys of his brothers and sisters, but so long as this is seen by the child as a matter of punctilious conformity to the wishes of the authority figures, like toilet training or not bringing dirt into the house, rather than in terms of respect for the property rights of other people, we shall not have taught the child not to steal, properly speaking, but only to inhibit a narrowly conceived range of movements disapproved of by an authority. As Peters (1963, p. 62) says: 'to learn to act on rules forbidding theft, lying, breaking promises, etc., is necessarily an open-ended business requiring intelligence and a high degree of social sophistication.' Acting on such rules, according to Peters, requires considerable intelligence and insight, in order to see particular actions as falling under a rule. This fact points to a further element in the dissolution of the paradox of moral education, for the rules we are trying to teach in moral education themselves involve the exercise of intelligence and sensitivity. They cannot be blindly obeyed, but can only be applied in the light of human and social understanding. Hence, in the paradox, the antithesis between the blind execution of the whims of an authority and the intelligent exercise of one's rational will turns out to falsify the extent to which intelligence, and the possibility of moral reflection, are involved in learning not to steal or be malicious and so on. Acquiring virtuous habits, then, is not possible without the exercise of one's reason, even if one is encouraged to acquire such habits by authorities. There is, therefore, no great jump between acquiring the habit and reflecting about it rationally; indeed the possibility of rational reflection on such habits would appear to be opened precisely because the exercise of the habit requires intelligence on the part of the agent.

Someone reading what Peters says about reason and habit might agree with him that learning not to steal must be a procedure requiring the use of reason, and hence that there is nothing paradoxical about being encouraged by authorities to acquire the habit as part of a rational moral education, but suggest that the paradox simply reappears at an earlier stage, when the child does not have the ability to grasp the concepts involved in learning moral rules. Here, surely, there are just orders and obedience, and this cannot be part of a moral education preparing people for moral autonomy. A quick way with this objection might be simply to deny that moral education, properly speaking, can begin before a child has reached a certain level of conceptual sophistication; but this is perhaps too quick, because it says nothing about how children might acquire the concepts of interpersonal life, which I am suggesting are involved in moral behaviour. What is valuable in Peters's article is the way in which he emphasizes that morality and moral concepts are tied into a whole social and interpersonal context, and that moral habits (virtues and vices) are possible only for people who have entered this context. What I now want to suggest is that this fact about morality puts a considerable strain on the Kantian model of the ideal moralist being a rational autonomous will choosing its principles in the light of abstract rational considerations.

The picture of morality which emerges from an appreciation of the habitual nature of virtue, and the way in which the practice of the virtues demands an intelligent sensitivity to the situations in which one finds oneself, in order to see just how a particular virtue might be applied, is one which will place far more emphasis on learning how to see situations in certain terms than on abstract reasoning about, and justification of, principles. Take, for example, the virtue of kindness. In order to be kind, I will have to see just what the feelings of others might be, and just what their good might consist in. Its application will require much sensitivity, both in discovering these things, and in knowing how best to resolve conflicts between what someone wants and what is good for them, and also in knowing how to reconcile kindness to one person with the demands of fairness and justice that others might have on me. Equally, understanding the claims that others might have on me will require on my part not an abstract, quasi-legalistic grasp of principle so much as the ability to see and understand situations from their point of view, and to understand that these beings surrounding me are also people with their own feelings, goals, plans, reasons and desires for self-determination and control of their own destiny.

One of the worrying aspects of looking at morality in terms of freely and rationally chosen principles is the nagging feeling that a man might accept in an abstract way that society as a whole needed a general adherence to such principles as truth telling, respect for life, respect for individual liberty and so on, and also that it would be good for him if others acted towards him on such principles, while at the same time feeling little or no inclination to act on such principles in his own life, so long as he was strong enough to get away with it. One could easily imagine a man being quite unmoved by philosophical appeals to consistency between the way he treated others and the way he wanted to be treated himself, or by stratagems such as Rawls's thought-experiment, in which everyone is asked to choose for themselves those laws which they would choose if they were legislating for a society in which no one (including they, the legislators) knew anything about their personal strengths, abilities or backgrounds (cf. Rawls, 1972, p. 12). Indeed, it is unclear why exactly a strong and self-sufficient man who acted only for his own good and never in the light of the needs or rights of others, except in so far as such behaviour might benefit him, would be irrational, as opposed to immoral or inhuman. The problem of moral education and moral choice is not to get people to be rational, but to get them to be human, and getting them to be human is not ideally to be analysed in terms of autonomous agents deciding for themselves the type of life they really want to lead. (Nowell-Smith, for example, says the asking of such questions is part of the connotation of the word 'moral'; 1954, pp. 319-20.)

It is true that the behaviour of a moral man will exemplify a degree of consistency, because he will be habitually virtuous. It will thus be possible to analyse his behaviour in terms of his acting on certain general principles. Indeed, he might frequently appeal in his own deliberations to such principles, in part at least to short-circuit the impossible task he would be presented with if he always had to decide what to do in every new situation, with no preconceptions in the form of general principles to guide his actions. But what we are concerned with here is to see how someone might come to adopt in his behaviour a set of principles which are morally acceptable in having some regard to the rights and feelings of others. I have already said that applying moral principles requires a degree of sensitivity to the human nature of other people. What I now want to suggest is that it is a sensitivity to one's own humanity being shared with that of others, and a corresponding sympathy with them, which forms the basis of moral conduct in the first place, and which gives us the initial and indispensable motivation towards moral behaviour. In other words, part of what is involved in learning what it is to live as a person in a community of other persons is to learn what it is to be treated as a person and to treat others as persons. This knowledge is, above all, the knowledge that people have both feelings and wills of their own, and that it would be inappropriate to regard them as objects to be used and manipulated. No doubt this sense is best learned in a loving family. What is learned may then be extended to others outside one's family, and ultimately finds expression in those abstract general principles such as impartiality, fairness and respect for the rights of others which are seen by many writers as characterizing any fully moral system of conduct. What is to be emphasized here is that such principles will not be chosen by lonely, autonomous agents in an

emotionally empty state of rational reflection. They will be chosen
by those who have some feeling of what it is to be a person among
other persons, and only people with this sense will be able fruit-
fully to apply such principles. We hesitate before Kant's claim
that only actions done out of pure duty are truly moral, and that
any motivating feeling of humanity or love or shame underlying
what one does invalidates its moral purity. The deepest reason
for the hesitation is that what gives one the possibility of acting
morally (or immorally) is the sense that one is a person among
others, and that being a person is to be open to possibilities of
hurt, shame, pleasure, self-fulfilment and so on. This sense may
well be based in a primitive human sense of sympathy for the suf-
ferings and feelings of others, referred to by Rousseau, Hume
and many other eighteenth-century moralists. This primitive
sense of sympathy, however, will be developed as one learns to
live a social life, and to understand the various complex ways in
which people can be helped or frustrated. Ultimately, it becomes
more a question of perception and awareness than of animal feeling, a matter of perceiving the needs of others, both in remote
cases, where one can have no personal experience, and also in
cases where a sophisticated sensitivity to the feelings of a difficult, unattractive old person (for example) is required, rather
than any immediate emotion of animal love or sympathy, which
may in any case be impossible.

As we have seen, one of the most difficult problems confronting
both moral philosophers and moral educators is the problem of
motivation: how do you get people to accept that they should
sometimes act not out of self-interest, but out of respect for the
needs and claims of others? From the point of view of education,
this problem is sometimes presented as that of how one might
bring people to move from a theoretical acceptance of the reasonableness of moral principles to an active acceptance of them in
their own behaviour: but this way of posing the problem, as well
as the associated picture of the rational agent deliberating his
choice of principles, are both untrue to actual moral experience,
as well as making the solution of the problem seem more puzzling
than it need be. For the picture of the autonomous rational agent
deliberating on his principles is indeed difficult to reconcile with
the undoubted fact that, on the whole, this is not how people
feel when they are confronted with a moral choice; for example,
whether to help an injured person. On the whole, they feel that
what has to be done has to be done, and there is no feeling of
freedom on that, although, of course, they will be free simply to
walk away. Moreover, it is rather difficult to see a man as being
genuinely fully autonomous over a matter in which he has long
been accustomed to act in a particular way and to feel and see
things in a particular way. The paradox of moral education is
not formally a paradox; there is a solution to it, as it has been
stated along the lines suggested earlier, but there is something
missing in the picture of morality as being a matter of principles
first simply laid down, and later rationally deliberated. What is

missing is that morality is based in a way of perceiving situations and of having feelings in them, and that moral education is above all a matter of training in perception and feeling.

Moral principles are tied up with feeling and perception in two ways. First, it is only when we perceive and feel we are in a community of persons that moral principles can begin to seem binding on us, for only then will appeals to our sense of fairness or sympathy or shame or guilt in our dealings with others be at all relevant. So long as we regard others as objects to manipulate and be manipulated by, there is no reason for us to sympathize with their problems and frustrations, or to be fair in our treatment of them, or to feel ashamed of their scorn, or guilty for letting them down. What is really being suggested here is that although the details of various moral codes may vary, the basic impulses on which all morality and moral justification is based, and which give people the feeling that they ought to behave morally to others, in whatever form this comes out, are basically those involved in seeing others as persons rather than as objects. As has often been pointed out, even slave owners and thieves perceive virtue in seeing their colleagues, if not their victims, as persons. This sense, of course, is not something that is achieved by command or by rational choice, but by being part of a human society. So, seeing others as people in a general sense is what provides the motivational background to moral action and the acceptance of moral principles, without which their adoption would remain a mystery. But, second, those moral principles that one does come to accept have to be applied in particular cases, and here again perception of the needs and wants of others is often crucial to their application. A general injunction to respect the feelings or rights of others is hardly much use if we cannot see what the feelings of others are, or how they perceive their rights. I am not saying that we should always go along with how people feel or what they think is their due, but that without understanding these things, we shall not even begin to know how to respect their personhood.

It might be said that this identification of moral principle with the perceptions of others as persons still leaves open the question as to why we should treat each other as persons. To ask this question, however, is to misunderstand the point being made. The point is that human beings do behave like this, at least to those in their own groups or societies, and that this is what makes life, social and personal, possible. If you like, it is the precondition of any genuine social life. As to whether this attitude is ultimately justifiable, outside the actual context of human life, or whether, if we were creatures with different psychologies and traditions, we would have these attitudes, one must remain agnostic. Where reason does have a role to play is not so much in the fact that human beings characteristically, in their behaviour and traditions, manifest this tendency to treat at least some other human beings as persons, but in working out the implications of this fact, so as to see the existence of persons where one had not seen it before, and to find out what treating others as persons might involve outside the context of face-to-face encounters with them. Thus one can come to realize by rational reflection that slaves, too, are people, not relevantly different from one's own relations, or that part of one's income surplus to one's own needs should be given to support handicapped people in the community, even if one had never actually met any slaves or any of the handicapped people in question. But, as Iris Murdoch (1970, p. 66) says in 'The Sovereignty of the Good':

> the more the separateness and distinctness of other people is realized, and the fact seen that another man has needs and wishes as demanding as one's own, the harder it becomes to treat a person as a thing.

That one does have this feeling does seem to be a fact about human nature, and a fact on which our life together is based. It is, of course, true that with human life as it is now, life throughout the world would become intolerable generally were people not to strive to extend the recognition of others as persons, and life does become intolerable where this recognition is absent or its implications flaunted. Educators should attempt to cultivate this feeling in their pupils (and justifications of the general social and utilitarian sort just suggested can be given for doing this), but what is of paramount importance is the way in which the feeling that other people are not to be treated as things is not only basic to all moral motivations and justifications, but also something that is part of our natural endowment, and without which one could not begin to enter a society of persons.

This point about the naturalness of the sense of others as persons remains true, even if, as some psychologists have suggested, it appears only at a certain stage of maturation. If one originally saw the world around one as consisting entirely of objects to be used as best one could for one's own purposes, it is hard to see what additional data emanating from some of those objects could lead one to suppose that they were in fact people, and hence to be seen and treated as entitled to respect, as centres of will and consciousness and sympathy, as subjects of pain and desire. Indeed, if a man had no sense that there are other people in the world, who therefore should be looked at in these ways, it is hard to see how any moral argument or discussion could appear relevant to him or carry any conviction with him. So moral education must work on the natural sense we have to sympathize and feel with others as people. (One might add here that one's own sense of what it is to be a person is itself logically dependent on the recognition of others as people, for a large part of what it is to be a person is to see oneself as entering into relationships of various sorts with other people.) The paradox of moral education turns out, then, to overemphasize the place of free rational choice in moral behaviour. Moral behaviour is not so much a matter of an isolated rational agent acting on freely chosen principles, as a development of one's sense of a shared humanity. It is true,

as Peters points out, that in acquiring moral habits one is far
from acting irrationally or unintelligently. Also, there will be
cases where it is unclear just what the right course of action is
(e.g. is it showing more or less respect for others to help them
to commit suicide?) and cases where principles conflict (e.g.
where keeping a promise to someone might involve hurting someone else). Here, too, reason and intelligence have a part to play.
But what I am suggesting now is that abstract reason might not
have as central a role to play as the Kantian picture suggests,
and that the basic source of morality is something far more like a
sense of sympathy, without which moral principles would not even
begin to appear rationally compelling. If this is so, then moral
educators should pay at least as much attention to the development of a moral sensibility as to the analysis of principles and
arguments, and the aim of moral education should be to produce
moral insight in people rather than to get them to choose a set of
principles for themselves.

What does it mean to produce moral insight and sensibility? The
sense of sympathy which is at the bottom of moral behaviour is
fundamentally an other-regarding sense, a realization that the
feelings and views of others should be taken into account. When
you are sympathizing with someone else, you cease to be the
centre of your world. In sympathizing, indeed, you begin to feel
bound by factors outside yourself, which is something that
accords badly with the Kantian ideal of moral autonomy. Iris Murdoch (1970, p. 66), whose criticisms of the Kantian picture of
morality have much influenced me, stresses that in our behaviour
there is a constant tension between self-centred action, attach-
ment and motivation and the exercise of what she calls 'realism of
compassion': that 'unsentimental, detached, unselfish, objective
attention' which enables us to see ourselves and others as we
really are. Our first tendency in life, as in art, is to opt for
selfishness and fantasy (even where these take the masochistic
form of self-pity and ineffectual sentimentality), to see things
and people with ourselves at the centre merely as they impinge
on us and our designs. This, of course, involves the reduction
of people to objects of possible manipulation. She argues that the
old unregenerate egocentric self is so strong, and such a source
of psychic energy, that the rational will (where that is not itself
a manifestation of sin) is largely powerless to rid itself of harmful feelings and attachments:

> Where strong emotions of sexual love, or of hatred,
> resentment, or jealousy are concerned, 'pure will' can
> usually achieve little. It is small use telling oneself 'Stop
> being in love, stop feeling resentment, be just.' What is
> needed is a reorientation which will provide an energy of a
> different kind, from a different source (1970, p. 55).

What we should do is learn to train our attention on to new objects of attention, which it is to be hoped will lead us to be less
egotistical.

It is surprising how little discussion there is in most philo-

sophical treatments of moral education of the fact of selfishness.
Perhaps this is because of the stress on moral choice, for, as
Murdoch implies, Kantianism in morality may be the supreme assertion of the self. However this may be, we can all recognize in
ourselves the conflict between selfish and selfless drives. What
we want from moral education is habits of selflessness, and it is
undoubtedly correct that such habits cannot be acquired by a
mere act of will. A habit of this sort is not only continuous; it
needs intelligence and sensitivity in practice, and it also runs
counter to the strongest drives of our psyche. Murdoch is surely
right to see the formation of such habits requiring the systematic
directing of one's attention in particular ways. She distinguishes
between the clear vision which sees people and things as they
really are, with their needs, individuality, strivings and concerns,
from the distorted vision which sees only from the point of view
of the agent, and is characteristically mean, unjust and lacking
in compassion and understanding of others:

> The moral life, on this view, is something that goes on
> continually, not something that is switched off in between
> the occurrence of explicit moral choices. What happens in
> between such choices is indeed what is crucial. I would like
> on the whole to use the word 'attention' as a good word and
> use some more general term like 'looking' as the neutral
> word. Of course, psychic energy flows, and more readily
> flows, into building up convincingly coherent but false
> pictures of the world, complete with systematic vocabulary..
> .. Attention is the effort to counteract such states of
> illusion (1970, p. 37).

So, underlying moral acts are habits of thought and attention,
which can be cultivated, and which it is the job of moral education to cultivate. This can, not implausibly, be seen as another
way of putting what I had described earlier in terms of cultivating
one's primitive sense that one is surrounded by persons as well
as things. Although Murdoch asserts that unselfishness is not
natural to human beings, I have suggested on logical grounds
that some degree of unselfishness, at least in the sense of a natural sympathy to the feelings of others, is a prerequisite of the
recognition that they are persons. On the other hand, and in
line with what Murdoch says, developing what is implicit in this
sense certainly requires the development of one's perceptions and
sensibilities regarding other people away from oneself and towards
how they actually are. This can only be done by a systematic
attempt to see things as detached from one's own desires and
plans, and in the case of other people this detachment will involve
above all a growing recognition of their individuality and personhood.

It is in seeing moral behaviour as behaviour which is freed from
the quagmire of self that we find the connection between morality
and art, and the place of the study of art in moral education. Of
course philosophers in the Kantian tradition are correct to see
morality as a matter of impartiality and of treating others as ends

in themselves, rather than as means to attain our own selfish ends
and obsessions. What they do not tell us is how we might come to
see people and situations objectively, and to see them as making
demands on us rather than as bridges or obstacles for our desires. Art - good art - can free itself from the obsessions of self
and show us

> how differently the world looks to an objective vision. We
> are presented with a truthful image of the human condition
> in a form which can be steadily contemplated; and indeed
> this is the only context in which many of us are capable of
> contemplating it at all. Art transcends selfish and obsessive
> limitations of personality and can enlarge the sensibility of
> its consumer. It is a kind of goodness by proxy. Most of
> all it exhibits to us the connection, in human beings, of
> clear realistic vision with compassion (Murdoch, 1970, pp.
> 86-7).

The connection is presumably because the decentring involved in
art, as in morality, is, at the same time as being a truthful insight into the idiosyncrasies and failures of others, a sympathetic
recognition of them as centres of feeling and consciousness.

Murdoch recognizes the sense alluded to earlier in which all
intellectual disciplines are moral disciplines, in their concern with
concepts such as justice, accuracy, truthfulness, realism, humility and so on. Indeed, she suggests that the moral application
of such concepts can become clearer through seeing their use in
non-moral contexts. However, art and above all literature remain
'the most educational of all human activities' (1970, p. 88) because they are a place in which the nature of morality can be
seen. For not only does good art exemplify the decentring and
submission to necessity which is morality, and bad art the obses-
sion with self and fantasy and false or harmful excitement which
is the basis of so much wickedness, but an education in literature
is above all 'an education in how to picture and understand human
situations.' This must be more crucial than an initiation into
science, and is the reason why it is more important to know about
Shakespeare than about any scientist, for 'we are men and we
are moral agents before we are scientists, and the place of science
in human life must be discussed in words' (1970, p. 34).

Miss Murdoch further explores the connections between art and
morality, and the distinction between the false consolations
offered by fantasy and bad art on the one hand, and the tough-
ness and truthfulness of good art, in 'The Fire and the Sun'
(1977), but one more theme in 'The Sovereignty of the Good' is
worth mentioning here because of its relevance to moral education. It is the way in which moral concepts have what Mark
Platts (1979, p. 261) calls semantic depth. That is to say, we can
understand in a formal way the conditions of their application
without realizing experientially what they mean. There can indeed be a merely formal grasp of what the just or courageous
thing to do is in a given situation, without any corresponding
sense that this is what one should do or what would be admirable

to do. As Platts (1979, p. 262) puts it, we can become like 'a
Martian who translates our dictionary but has had no <u>experience</u>
of our moral world'. What gives moral concepts life is our seeing
the situations to which they apply as compelling a response in a
particular direction, and this involves attention and care on our
part in the way we see things. Murdoch speaks of value concepts
as requiring understanding in depth, that is, through a deepen-
ing awareness of what it is that they involve and what it is that
gives the situations to which they apply their moral character.
This sort of wisdom is no doubt best gained through personal
experience and is, as Murdoch (1970, pp. 28-9) stresses, an endless task; for example, our understanding of what 'love' means
should be an advance at forty on what it was at twenty, and
what it was at twenty was more complicated than that earlier time
when all we knew was that Mary was loved by the little lamb that
followed her. But experience alone may teach us little without
aids in the direction of depth. Here again, literature can be of
the profoundest importance, either as a help or a hindrance. How
many marriages have been doomed to disillusionment by an uncritical exposure to the view that life is or might be as the wish-
fulfilments of romantic novelists would have it? Salvation may not
be found in Tolstoy or Proust, but a degree of realism and complexity is there that may help us to understand and be ready for
what we will have to suffer.

I have concentrated in the closing part of this chapter on the
views of Iris Murdoch, both because they are an important corrective to a highly influential strand in moral philosophy, and
because they are highly relevant to the question of moral education. The so-called paradox of moral education draws heavily
for its force on too rationalistic a conception of morality. This
conception stresses to an unrealistic degree the elements of
autonomy and choice in ethics. By contrast I have tried to show
how morality is founded in certain features of human nature, and
how moral education should lay stress on developing those features and the ways of perceiving human life which will foster
compassion and justice. Of course, there will still be room for
moral dilemmas, and for discussion of the rightness and wrongness of particular acts and types of act. Moral education has
indeed a role to play in introducing people to the principles
underlying moral argument. But moral argument is only a comparatively small part of moral behaviour, just as moral differences
between men are small in comparison with what are generally
regarded, at least within the limits of one's own group, as virtues, such as justice, truthfulness and sympathy, and which are
implicit in the recognition of others as persons. Without a common
acceptance of such qualities as virtues, moral discussion could
hardly begin, while without some predisposition to treat others
as persons, moral education would hardly be possible. Given that
it is possible, I have argued that its primary task should be to
foster the awareness of what is implicit in recognizing others as
persons, and that the study of art and literature is an essential

means to this end. Apart from the ways in which moral questions are inevitably involved in schooling, which I examined at the start of the chapter, it is perhaps in the study of literature and art that school has its greatest contribution to make to the moral education of its pupils.

# 6 EDUCATION AND SOCIETY

## INTRODUCTION

Education does not take place in isolation from more general
social circumstances. Many educational developments have come
about in response to social needs and changes. Indeed, the
development of universal primary education in many countries
has been linked by historians to the need in business and industry for large numbers of people who could read and write. Even
if this were so, and academic education on a wide scale came
about because of social developments, this does not show that
educators ought to see themselves as wholly subservient to immediate economic needs. As I remarked at the beginning of the
book, however, the most pervasive attack on liberal education
comes nowadays not from religious dogmatists or from arcadian
romantics, but from politicians and educational administrators
who see educational priorities in terms of the needs of the economy.

It is true that the educational system outlined in Chapter 2
included vocational training as an important part. To that extent,
educators should not shut their eyes to the short-term practical
needs of the society in which they are working, as reflected in
the types of employment available. But the heart of the education
advocated here is the disinterested study of the natural world, of
human nature and human history and of the arts. I suggested
that everyone would be better able to live and make decisions
about his or her life with a grounding in these areas, and that, to
bear full fruit, each of these areas should be regarded as having
its own criteria of excellence and success. In other words, the
academic core of the education system is or should be essentially
self-regulating, for what is at issue fundamentally is the pursuit
of truth and the development of the human spirit. These things
cannot be made subservient to any actual social set-up. Indeed,
they provide the basis for the informed criticism and development
of existing set-ups. If we are interested in living in a society that
is composed of people who have some genuine insight into the
world, human nature and themselves, we should want both that
everyone should understand something of the areas outlined in
Chapter 2, and that, in our society, disinterested work in these
areas should be carried on at a high level.

Thus, what is proposed in this book is diametrically opposed to
the vice-chancellor or headmaster who speaks of the ethos of his
university or school as being to serve the needs of industry. It is
one thing to say, as has been said in this book, that some

vocational training should be undertaken in a school; quite another to say that this should characterize the ethos of the place. It is one thing to say that schools or universities should be aware of the needs of industry; quite another to direct all one's energies and efforts to turning out people trained for work in industry and nothing else. To attempt to do that is to overlook entirely the higher social functions of the school or university. It is also to see pupils in terms of pre-assigned social roles rather than as individuals to be led to make their own choices. Finally, it is to see a particular state of society as something given, rather than as something genuinely free people might wish, at least within the limits of practicability, to alter and reform.

Enough has been said during the course of this book about the limitations of the purely technological school or university, and the way these limitations would in the long term adversely affect both the individuals being educated and the society which had such institutions. It remains to consider two other ways in which the educational system advocated here might be criticized from a social point of view. In the first place, it is suggested that such a system, by advocating excellence in study, only serves to reinforce social inequalities, and that equality is an overriding social ideal. Then, second, there is the view that the sort of education being proposed here is beyond the capabilities or interest of a large part of the population (say 40 per cent), and should not even be attempted in the case of this 40 per cent.

## EQUALITY

It is not always clear what those who advocate equality are after. Some inequalities between people, indeed, seem ineradicable, such as inequalities of height or weight. Few people, moreover, would want us to be equal in all respects, as this would be to eliminate the variations and differences between people which make life interesting. Equality, in fact, is a purely formal notion, and before any fruitful discussion of equality can begin it must be clear in what respect equality is being spoken of. Thus, two men can be equal in income, but not in intelligence, or the other way round; or they can be equal in schooling, but not in status and so on.

Education itself immediately raises questions of equality, because, as was noted in Chapter 1, assessments (and hence comparisons) are integral to education. Then, educational opportunities, as well as educational achievements, can be unequal, and inequalities of both can be due to inequality of birth and upbringing, as well as to inequalities of ability. Finally, there are inequalities of status and income which may or may not be related to educational achievements.

The first point to notice is that giving every pupil exactly the same schooling will not have the same outcome in each case. If, for example, the level of the schooling was suited to the abilities

of the average pupil, some children would not get anything out
of it, because they would be starting from too far back. So giving
everyone exactly the same education will not help in their case to
compensate for their poor start. Perhaps, though, in order to get
round the problem of some pupils failing to benefit from identical
schooling, it would be urged that everyone should go at the pace
of the least able beginner, in order to ensure that everyone ended
up the same. Now this would obviously hold the majority of pupils
back, and one wonders what possible justification there could be
for doing this. In other spheres of activity, such as running, it
is not thought unfair that some people should just be better than
others, nor that those who are better should be enabled to develop their talents. The fact that human beings differ in abilities
is not a matter of socially remediable policy, but a fact of nature.
Why then, on grounds of fairness, should the academically able
be artificially handicapped in their pursuit of academic success?
To this, two replies might be given by a committed egalitarian.
In the first place, it would be said that difference of academic
ability is not a socially neutral fact, but largely a matter of inequality of birth and upbringing, while, second, it is important
that such differences be eliminated as far as possible, because
social inequalities in later life are closely related to differences
of academic attainment.

The second point has in fact been challenged on empirical
grounds by Christopher Jencks (1972) and his colleagues, in
their study of the relationship of the correlations between scholastic attainment and success in later life. According to Jencks
(1972, p. 11), only 'rather modest relationships' have been found
between 'cognitive skill and schooling on the one hand and status
and income on the other'. Jencks, who professes an overall commitment to equality within the limits necessary to run society
productively and efficiently, considers that this perhaps surprising fact undercuts any argument in favour of equalizing the
distribution of schooling and cognitive skill. He further argues
that 'experience suggests' that people with relatively little schooling do not, on the whole, value additional schooling for its own
sake as much as people who already have a lot of schooling, so
overall happiness will be increased by giving more to those who
already have more, for those who have little will not mind not
getting more (once, presumably, it is generally accepted that
worldly success has little to do with educational outcomes).
Jencks goes on to propose that, as there is no egalitarian point
to attempting to equalize educational outcomes, there should be
much more freedom of choice regarding education. The point
seems to be that as education does not have a great effect on
status or income, it does not really matter what is done in school,
so people might as well be allowed to do what they want, so as to
maximize what Jencks calls consumer satisfaction.

What is striking about Jencks's position is its crudity. His
egalitarianism apparently covers only status and income on the
one hand, or instant gratification on the other, and anything

that does not affect them is irrelevant to the equality that concerns him. But, if education is a good, surely there should be some commitment - at least on the part of an egalitarian - to equalizing its distribution in some sense or other, as far as this is possible. We shall have more to say on what this sense might be later, but what is fundamentally wrong with Jencks's outlook is his thoroughgoing instrumentalism regarding education, for he sees it only in terms of its effect (or lack of effect) on status, income and short-term gratification. Yet this is surely an extraordinarily narrow and misdirected way of judging educational achievement. What has been shown in this book is that there are various goods to be aimed at in education, and although economic self-sufficiency and consumer satisfaction may be two of them, they are by no means the only or the primary goods. Having insight into truth and human nature is a good that is unconnected with one's status or income, and which may require hard work before it is attained. All would profit from this good, and it is a sign of the times that it should be overlooked in a study of equality and education. In reply to Jencks's point that only those who have a degree of education will actually want more for its own sake, one of the main themes of this book has been to stress that the academic core of education should be given to all irrespective of their current feelings about it, because it is only after having made some progress in these areas that one is capable of making reasonable judgments about them, or indeed about many other things. So even if everyone's experience was as conducive to pessimism as Jencks's on the desire for knowledge and understanding, there are still good reasons for trying to lead people to acquire them, even if this involves something of a struggle.

So Jencks's conclusion about the unimportance of equality in education rests on the fallacy of supposing that the only reasons for insisting on it are to equalize status and income on the one hand, or immediate satisfaction on the other, although presumably Jencks's point that there is not much point in tampering with schooling policy on its own, if what you are after is financial equality, would still hold if his research is correct. I say financial equality here, because in one important respect Jencks's general conclusion about the modesty of the relationship between schooling and later-life needs qualification. What the research actually shows is that occupational status does have a strong relationship to educational attainment (Jencks, 1972, p. 191), although educational attainment is by no means the only factor involved. (Many people with high attainment do not get high-status jobs.) That educational attainment is important to occupational status is obvious when one reflects that entry into many high-status professions, such as medicine and the law, is highly competitive and conditional on above-average performance in various examinations. It should be mentioned here that Jencks (1972, pp. 135-6) actually defines educational attainment in terms of the highest grade of school or university an individual reaches, part of the reason for this being the absence of a national certification system in the USA, where the research was done. However, as there is clearly some relationship between attainment more conventionally considered and entry into the higher grades, we can overlook any ambiguity which may arise from this definition, and simply assert here that Jencks's research has not shown that significant social inequalities are unrelated to educational attainment, when we take occupational status into account as well as income.

It is moreover an undoubted fact that despite formally equal educational opportunity, educational attainment at various levels still reflects the background and upbringing of the pupils, which brings us back to the first egalitarian worry. Thus in the UK for example, despite more than thirty years of universal and free state education at all levels, the proportion of university students from the working classes is still far below the proportion of working-class people in the population as a whole. (Eleven times lower on some estimates - cf. 'Observer', 13 January 1980.) Working-class pupils, for whatever reason, either do not want to go to university or are not well qualified enough to do so in the numbers that the middle-classes do. One effect of this is that the professions where entry depends on university education continue to be dominated by those born into middle- and upper-class families, and the same is no doubt even more emphatically the case when we look at the position from the point of view of under-privileged racial minorities. What all this amounts to is that a large measure of equality of educational opportunity across the population in the UK has done very little to compensate for differences of birth and upbringing; those from highly educated backgrounds continue to do better educationally than those from less educated families. (This is true even in the public sector of education, where the vast majority of children from both working- and middle-classes are educated.) Even if we were to grant that certain racial or class groups had lower average IQs than others, the differences in performance revealed in various studies between, say, middle-class and working-class, or black and white students, remain far greater than could be accounted for by any conceivable IQ differences, and this despite reasonable educational provisions for all (universal primary education, universal secondary education, common university entrance examinations and state grants for university courses). The inescapable fact is that birth and upbringing have a significant effect on academic performance, and one must suppose that this would continue to be the case even if private fee-paying schools for the rich were abolished, in view of the fact that middle-class children in public-sector schools do very much better than working-class children in the same schools.

One's first reaction to this is that it is hardly surprising. That children from homes where reading is encouraged and discussion habitual perform on the whole better at school than children from other homes is only to be expected. In Chapter 1, I tried to show that this does not mean that schooling is necessarily a matter of middle-class indoctrination. Although doubtless some schools attempt to instil middle-class attitudes in various ways, the essentially open nature of academic disciplines ought to make their practice independent of the class interests of particular social groups, and this even though some social groups are naturally more attuned to academic work (though the degree of natural attunement can, I feel, from my knowledge of grammar and private schools, be greatly exaggerated).

One's second reaction to the influence of class environment on educational attainment is to ask why this in itself should be regarded as a cause for concern, any more than that there should be a disproportionate number of Jewish violinists or Welsh choristers or great composers who are sons of musicians. It is true that education, unlike violin playing or singing or writing music, is a good which everyone should be enabled to get, and also that there are some things in education that everyone should be exposed to, but this is not at all to require that everyone should end up at the same educational level. Indeed, to insist on that is to blind oneself both to the fact that people and groups of people just do differ in aptitude and motivation (in all fields, as well as academic) and to the way in which what I have been calling the academic disciplines depend for their development on people whose abilities are above the average. That there should be such a thing as excellence in the pursuit of a discipline, and that this should be recognizable, is also part of what its openness consists in, for such an excellence can come from any quarter, regardless of the class or background of the individual from whom it comes.

It is of crucial importance to distinguish here between equality of educational opportunity and equality of outcome. Where excellence is possible or desirable, as it is in educational fields, equality of outcome may well be undesirable as well as impossible. But, given that the fruits of education are an important component of a good life, there is a strong argument in fairness for equalizing access to them as far as is possible. Doing this does not, as has already been pointed out, necessarily mean that everyone should get exactly the same education, regardless of background or ability. I have argued that a certain level of understanding in various areas is desirable for everyone, especially in the sort of pluralist society in which we live, in which people are expected to be competent, self-supporting and responsible for their own attitudes and decisions. So equality of outcome is desirable to this extent. To get some people up to this level may require special provisions to compensate for their underprivileged home background or their lack of ability. Equally, equality of opportunity in respect of higher levels of education may justify further compensatory schemes. Also, beyond the basic curriculum, fairness will not require giving everyone the same education so much as a schooling tailored to the potential of each. On the other hand, there is no point in lavishing resources on people beyond their ability or desire to profit from them. Thus there is no reason to suppose that everyone will profit from a university course. In

this case, equality of opportunity would seem to require only
that people who can profit from higher education should not be
barred from doing so for lack of money or from unavailability of
whatever compensatory education may be practicable.

To regard overall equality of outcome or attainment as desirable
in education (or, even more confusingly, to conflate equality of
opportunity and equality of outcome) leads to the inescapable
conclusion that no educational system is fair which discriminates
between educational attainments, or which produces differences
in attainments. If this is not to involve deception (in hiding
actual recognizable differences between pupils behind bogus certificates, for example), it is going to mean in the first place that
everyone is artificially held in school at the lowest level. Objectionable as this may be, in its suppression of the individuality of
individual pupils and in its detrimental effects on the pursuit of
the various subjects, the pursuit of equality of educational outcome cannot logically stop at what goes on in school, however.
As has already been seen, educational attainments (in the genuine sense) are in practice closely tied to family background; so to
equalize real educational achievements we would have to remove
all children from their parents at birth, to ensure that nothing
was learned in private. Taking children away from their parents
at birth would also be necessary to eliminate the educational
advantages of a middle-class home. This point ties in with one
egalitarian line of criticism of Jencks's findings, to the effect
that Jencks has not shown the absence of a relationship between
education and income and status in later life, because sociologic-
ally education cannot be considered in terms of what happens at
school in isolation from family background. Taking education to
consist in home background and school performance, there is in
fact a strong relationship between education and one's eventual
status and income. But if you still want to use education, now
taken in this broad sense, as a means of securing social equality,
the logical conclusion is that you eliminate as far as possible home
influence on children, and this is tantamount to saying that they
will have to be removed from their parents to avoid being influenced by them in a hundred and one subtle ways. Few egalitarians
would wish to take their egalitarianism as far as this, and most
would probably admit in the end that differences of educational
attainment are not in themselves undesirable so long as a reasonable and appropriate education is made available to everyone (and
this would include making genuine attempts to compensate for very
bad starts).

But for the egalitarian the problem remains that we cannot think
of educational attainments purely in isolation, and that they reflect and reinforce other inequalities. Thus not only do middle-
class children perform better in school but, by doing so, children of middle-class parents continue to dominate the professions.
Life in the professions, it will be said, is better rewarded and
more desirable than life in a factory. It is necessary to be
cautious here, for it is unclear that vast numbers of working-

class people would actually prefer to work at a desk than in a
factory, although there are undoubtedly jobs that are by any
standards unpleasant and often underpaid. It may seem unfair
that people from certain sectors of society should predominate in
these roles, while others hardly perform them at all, but the
temptation the egalitarian is continually exposed to is to think
that by changing the educational system he can remedy the social
inequalities he objects to. Hence his disappointment that equalizing educational opportunities through providing free and universal access to education at all levels has not opened up
universities and the professions to the working class in large
numbers.

Now, it may be that there are grounds for objecting to the
social and racial inequalities that exist in various societies, but
surely what should be argued about and attacked are the economic and social arrangements in question, whereby mechanical
work is ill paid and despised, and professional people do little or
no manual or menial work. In other words, the problem and the
issues are political and social rather than educational. What we
have so far seen is that there need be nothing objectionable about
differences of educational attainment in themselves, even if these
reflect social differences as opposed to gross unfairness, and
that to attempt to eliminate these educational differences will
involve quite unacceptable measures.

I have deliberately said nothing so far on the vexed question
of a private (fee-paying) sector of education. My overall advocacy of pluralism and suspicion of an education system financially
completely dependent on the state provides reasons in favour of
the existence of such a sector. Also, I have argued that educational advantages naturally accrue to middle-class children, but
that this is not necessarily a bad thing; seen in this light,
private schools may be just a continuation of these advantages.
On the other hand, fee-paying schools are in the UK, for example
(and despite Jencks), clearly and blatantly used to further the
interests of the rich in numerous ways. But if society overall was
less dominated by a small section of people, and if society overall was more equal, there could surely be no objection to people
paying for their children to be educated differently from others,
any more than one could object to a man giving his children
better toys or food, provided always that everyone received a
decent educational minimum and that no one was deprived of educational opportunity through personal lack of money. I wonder,
in fact, if either the parents concerned or their egalitarian critics
would be so excited by the question of private schools if the
money paid out in fees was seen as providing only educational
as opposed to social and occupational advantages. In other words,
the so-called public school controversy in the UK is not really an
educational debate at all, but a debate about the class system in
one of its more obvious manifestations; and as the nature of the
British class system is not a subject of this book, no more will be
said about it here.

The latest egalitarian move in the educational field begins by recognizing that it is through their apparently uneliminable educational superiority that the white middle classes maintain their sway in such fields as medicine and the law. This educational superiority cannot, apparently, be eliminated by compensatory schemes - black and working-class candidates continue in a disproportionate way to fail to get the grades required, despite crash programmes designed to improve their schooling. It is assumed by egalitarians that there are good social reasons for having a reasonable proportion of properly qualified doctors and lawyers from all social and racial groups, and so a policy of what is described as reverse discrimination is proposed. According to this, legal and medical schools in universities (and other schools as well, in some instances) are to operate a policy of selecting a set proportion of candidates from specified minority groups. Thus in many state universities in the USA, for example, some black candidates are admitted to courses in law and medicine, even though if they were of Jewish or Anglo-Saxon origin, say, they would not be selected, because their grades would have been too low. In other words, candidates with lower than normally acceptable grades are taken in just because they are black. It is hoped that by operating this policy of reverse discrimination, as it is called, the proportion of professional people from underprivileged minority groups will increase, thus enhancing the status, self-respect and, eventually, standards of the group.

Reverse discrimination, as the name implies, is a bold attempt to compensate for past unfair discrimination to a group. That there may be a case for such redress is not in doubt. What is doubtful, though, is whether reverse discrimination is the right way to tackle the problem. In many ways, it seems to throw up more difficulties and unfairness than it sorts out. Take, for example, the situation of a white man who would have got into a law school on normal admissions criteria, but who is kept out by a less well qualified black because of that school's quota policy. There is a strong prima facie case for saying that he has been unfairly discriminated against, on grounds, it might be added, of race. Indeed, there is something strongly counter-productive about a measure designed to reduce racial differences, which of its nature emphasizes and possibly exacerbates them. The unfairness would be compounded in a case of a poor white man being excluded by a middle-class black; in any case, the white man would have a strong individual case that he had been unfairly treated, whereas the less well qualified black man would have no individual grounds for saying that he had been unfairly treated at that stage if he had been kept out of university by a better qualified white man.

That there is real, as opposed to prima facie, unfairness to individuals who lose university places because of policies of reverse discrimination has been strongly denied by Ronald Dworkin (1977). Dworkin's argument is complex and sophisticated, but in essence it amounts to claiming that even though there might be an absolute right to an elementary education (without which life would be very difficult), this is not the case with a university education. So there is no absolute right to a university place; in cases of scarcity, criteria for the distribution of places are justified in general because they seem to serve useful social policies. It is true that the implementation of useful social policies must not be allowed to lead to unfairnesses to individuals, but Dworkin argues that while infringement of individual rights does occur in the USA when a properly qualified black man is excluded from a university on grounds of race, there is no infringement of the white man's rights when he is excluded by less well qualified blacks under reverse discrimination. In other words, for Dworkin it is not the use of racial criteria as such that is wrong, but only their use in certain circumstances. As, for Dworkin (1977, p. 227), there is no absolute right for anyone to go to university at all, fairness in the distribution of places consists not in giving everyone equal treatment (giving all applicants the same treatment), but in treating them as equals – i.e. treating them 'with the same respect and concern as anyone else'. Treating people as equals, as opposed to treating them equally, is illustrated by means of an example of two children, one of whom is dying from a disease that is merely making the other uncomfortable. I would not be acting fairly if I treated both equally and tossed a coin to decide which should have the one remaining dose of a drug. Treatment of the children as equals in this case demands that I look to the greater need of the dying child. According to Dworkin, the individual's right to be treated as an equal, which is all he has in the case of a university place, is not infringed by a policy designed to create a more equal society overall, or by one that is justified on certain utilitarian grounds (that is, in terms of the benefits resulting from the policy).

Dworkin needs to distinguish the types of utilitarian grounds on which university admissions policies can be justified, because the defender of a policy excluding blacks altogether could in some circumstances quite plausibly claim that certain social benefits would arise from such a policy (e.g. in Texas after the Second World War, many lawyers were needed to cope with the boom in business, but, because of racial prejudice, law firms could not use black lawyers to help out with the boom; so the wealth of the state and ultimately the welfare of all would be increased by law schools putting all their resources into the training of white lawyers). In a utilitarian context, the right of a man to be treated as an equal involves allowing each man's preferences and their comparative intensity to feature in the calculation of the benefits arising from the policy on a one-man-one-preference basis. According to Dworkin any such calculation would be unfair if it included not only each man's personal preferences and their intensity, but also his external preferences. A personal preference is one which a man has for his own enjoyment of some good or opportunity. Thus I could have a personal preference for an education for myself, or for expert legal advice, or for the consequences of segregation, because of the benefits it might bring me personally in reducing competition for a scarce resource. An external preference is one in which a man wants the assignment of goods or opportunities to others. Thus I can have an external preference for segregation because I disapprove of racial mixing, or for wanting limited resources to go to a swimming pool rather than a theatre because I admire swimmers and disapprove of artistic types, or for the promotion of virtuous men because I approve of virtue. External preferences should not be allowed to enter a fair utilitarian assessment of a policy because they result in a 'form of double counting'; thus the swimmers will be benefited not only by their own preferences and their intensity, but also by the preferences of those who take pleasure in their success. What Dworkin concludes is that while the racial prejudice of the Texans, on which the argument for segregation depended, was an external preference, and so is the preference of certain blacks for black lawyers, some of the utilitarian arguments in favour of reverse discrimination rely on personal preferences. Presumably he has in mind the possible results of reverse discrimination he alluded to earlier in his paper, such as the reduction of social tension, the raising of the quality of legal education (by having black participants in class) and the raising of the intellectual quality of the bar (by encouraging more able blacks to apply for law courses), all of which might plausibly be said to benefit me personally.

The distinction between external and personal preferences is not entirely clear, nor is its use altogether satisfactory. Why, in the first place, would a racist's preference for segregation necessarily be an external preference? It is true that a result of his racism is that others will enjoy or be deprived of certain goods, but this is equally true of a man's personal preference for reducing social tension or for wanting segregation to further his own career. The racist may regard the absence of blacks from his environment as itself a vital part of his own enjoyment of some good or opportunity, namely, a racially pure society; in which case, a policy of segregation could apparently be justified by the personal preferences of a majority of the population, where a majority felt very intensely against some racial minority. So Dworkin's appeal to the personal-external preference distinction cannot rule out a utilitarian justification of segregation, particularly if members of the segregated race were given plenty of resources for their own lives. Nor is it clear that we should be ready to rule out the counting of external preferences in assessing which social policies are to be adopted, for, as Dworkin himself admits, such a move would rule out the counting of altruistic feelings in favour of individuals or groups just as much as the counting of prejudices against them.

However, even given the correctness of this criticism of Dworkin's appeal to the personal-external preference distinction in order to show that a utilitarian can discriminate between segregation and reverse discrimination, there remains what Dworkin calls the ideal (non-utilitarian) justification of such discrimination, which would clearly not apply to segregation. For we may, on moral grounds, just want a more equal society. The basic question, then, remains. Does reverse discrimination deny anyone's right to be treated as an equal? We are told by Dworkin that this right amounts to an entitlement to be treated with the same respect and concern as everyone else, and the example given to illustrate what this means is one where we look at the personal needs of the two sick children. What is striking about reverse discrimination (whether we look at it from an ideal or a utilitarian point of view), and what gives it the continued appearance of unfairness, is that as a policy it shows no respect or concern whatever to individuals qua individuals. Neither the white victim of a policy of reverse discrimination nor the man who benefits from it are shown any respect or concern for themselves at all (except in so far as both are treated merely as representatives of particular racial groups). Hence the possibility of a well-educated and lazy black gaining at the expense of a deserving poor white who has had to struggle against considerable odds. It is difficult to see how the appearance of unfairness can ever be eliminated from an educational policy that both treats people from different racial groups differently and at the same time abstracts from the individual needs and interests of those affected by it. For reverse discrimination neither treats everyone in the same way, nor does it treat them like the sick children in Dworkin's example.

The objection just made to reverse discrimination centres on the fact that the most famous cases of it are cases where reverse discrimination is applied to groups of people. There are, indeed, other objections to this. There is the feeling that in a country such as the USA it will be the groups that lobby most strongly or that can stir up the greatest guilt rather than those that most need it, that are most likely to have such a policy applied in their favour. There are also problems in deciding just who is to belong to a particular group, and so benefit from such a policy. It is true that objections of this sort might not apply to attempts to apply reverse discrimination in a country such as South Africa, where the lines of demarcation and identification of the underprivileged do not present such difficulties. However, even here there would be the feeling that those blacks who had been let into universities under a policy of reverse discrimination would probably do worse than the average all through the course. If the policy is to do what was required of it, then not only the proportion of blacks let into a faculty but also the proportion qualifying must be kept up. One suspects that logically the policy will end up by allowing numbers of ill-qualified blacks to be registered as doctors and lawyers. If that happened then there would certainly be more black doctors and lawyers than there would have been, but there will at the same time be a significant decline in standards among them. Giving underprivileged minorities second-class professional people hardly seems a desirable way of

redressing past unfairness. In addition, if this state of affairs
became widely recognized then a stigma would attach to all doctors
or lawyers from those groups that had benefited from policies of
reverse discrimination, whether this was deserved or not in individual cases.

So there may be reasons for thinking that, as a piece of social
engineering, reverse discrimination may do little good, if its
only consequence is to increase the numbers of professional
people from a group identified as underprivileged. One can also
question the assumption that it is necessary in a fair society for
all sections of the community to have the same proportions of
people in all walks of life. After all, no one objects to the high
proportion of six-footers in basketball teams, or of Scotsmen in
English soccer teams. It might just be that some sections of the
community are better in some fields than others, or traditionally
more orientated to particular spheres. If there was no evidence
of discrimination against, say, black people generally, it is hard
to see why their being underrepresented in various fields should
be so objectionable. What is probably at the root of the feeling
that it is objectionable is the snob value placed by society as a
whole on certain professions - a value, in the case of law and
medicine certainly, which has not been accorded at all times and
all places, and which, in many cases, is ill-deserved. Rather than
tampering with educational procedures, a less class-conscious
attitude to white-collar work might well dissolve the problem. More
radically, the problem of unequal status between jobs might be
solved by political measures to reduce inequalities of reward (and
this is indeed happening in some countries), or even by a Solon-
like policy of making everyone undertake some manual work.

The felt unfairness we noted in connection with Dworkin's treatment of reverse discrimination, and the other problems raised by
policies of reverse discrimination, arise at least in part from the
blanket application of the policy to groups as wholes, irrespective
of the needs and concerns of the individuals directly affected by
the policy. Would a policy of reverse discrimination in favour of
deserving underprivileged individuals be open to the same objections? Obviously, such a policy would not lead to cases like that
of a deserving white being nosed out by an undeserving black,
nor would there be problems concerning membership of groups or
stigmas attaching to groups, though there may be parallel problems in identifying truly deserving individuals. However this may
be, reverse discrimination in favour of individuals taken as individuals would appear to eliminate one major source of the feeling of
unfairness that Dworkin's defence of reverse discrimination in
favour of groups left unsatisfied. But, before deciding too quickly
in favour of reverse discrimination applied to individuals, a number of clarifications are needed.

If we are operating a university admissions policy (or any other
educational admissions system) we may stick rigidly to standard
entry requirements, choosing candidates strictly in order of
grades and marks achieved, or we may prefer to judge not on a

candidate's actual achievements, but on what we take to be his potential. If it is possible to operate the latter system, it has certain advantages, particularly where it appears that standards achieved at one level of education are not, in isolation, a reliable guide to a person's potential at the next level. In operating the more flexible policy, social disadvantages will naturally be taken into account. Indeed, we may feel at times that someone from a poorer background socially or educationally, who has done reasonably well despite his handicaps, may do extremely well in the undisturbed environment of a university, and therefore shows far more potential than some moderate performer from a school with a proven record of examination success. We may also feel that in some subjects, a mix of competent people from all backgrounds would be advantageous for everyone on the course. So, for these two reasons, we may on occasions prefer deserving and promising people from difficult backgrounds to some who have had a much better start and who have done only slightly better in qualifying examinations. But the vital point to notice here is that cases such as these are not, strictly speaking, cases of reverse discrimination. We are not letting people in for extraneous social or racial reasons, but for academic reasons, to do with the potential of the students and the success of a course.

It is significant that Dworkin does not explicitly distinguish the two types of case where people with lower grades are let in and people with higher grades excluded. He indeed appears to assimilate the type of case where the reasons are academic (improving classroom discussion) to the type of case where they are social (to make the community more equal overall). Indeed, it is hardly surprising that he should do this, as he says that educational admissions policies are to be justified in terms of their social effects, and this surely is the root of all the difficulties and feelings of unfairness that surround policies of reverse discrimination. For even though we can agree with Dworkin that not everyone has a right to a university place, given that university places are scarce and important and much in demand, fairness and treating people as equals would seem to require that their distribution was regulated on grounds that were strictly relevant to a person's academic potential, rather than on extraneous social grounds. Academic reasons, then, should be given for academic decisions, and that a person should be allowed on an academic course is an academic judgment. What is unfair about both segregation and reverse discrimination is that irrelevant criteria are being used in selection procedures. For a person's worthiness to enter an academic course now cannot be impaired by the fact that he is black, nor can it be improved by the mere fact that in the past he was very deprived. We may regret his past deprivations and want to do something about them, but the right course of action is not to compound unfairness by excluding someone better qualified, any more than it would be fair to deprive a runner of his sprinting prize because in other places there are people unable to run at all because of lack of food. Dworkin's claim that

entry to a course is to be decided on social grounds may seem
more plausible in the case of semi-vocational subjects such as law
and medicine. Perhaps there is an argument for administering
vocational subjects in a utilitarian way, but if this is going to be
done it should be made quite clear, and any pretence that they
are administered on academic grounds or even that they are academic subjects should be dropped. With academic subjects, on the
other hand, such a move would be a most unfortunate attack on
their independence.

There are indeed great dangers inherent in tampering with
academic standards from the outside. Much of my defence of the
bias-free nature of academic study (presumably even in law and
medicine) was based in the self-regulating nature of the various
subjects (or at least on the extent to which they were genuinely
self-regulating). In an educational system largely financed by the
state (as any system nowadays is bound to be), the amount of
resources available to a particular school, educational programme
or university is going to be in the main controlled from outside
and, in part, for social reasons. These reasons would no doubt
include the need to help deprived pupils overcome bad starts;
and quite properly so, as everyone has a right to a certain level
of education. But the direction of effort and resources from outside need not conflict with the self-regulating nature of a subject,
providing that the work and conduct of the subject at the various
levels it is being funded are governed by standards inherent in
the subject itself. Reverse discrimination, on the other hand,
operates in a way that interferes from outside with the internal
standards of a discipline. Part of what is implied in letting someone on an academic course is that he is recognized to have a
certain academic potential, both in relation to his own future
work and in relation to the contribution he might make to his
subject, which is why it is unfair when irrelevant non-academic
criteria are used for selection. As the integrity of academic
standards is the key to the openness of a discipline, any attempt
to subvert them, even for the best of motives, must be suspect.

To sum up these comments on equality and education: in general it is inappropriate and probably unavailing to attempt to
redress social inequalities by educational, as opposed to political,
means. It would be particularly unfortunate if the attempt to produce social equality through educational means involved tampering with educational standards, for the independence of a
discipline and the integrity of its standards are inextricably
linked. Educational achievements may well reflect and reinforce
social differences, but before concluding that this is necessarily
a bad thing we should ask whether the social differences in
question necessarily involve unacceptable inequalities. Even if
they do, the right way to proceed is to move by attacking the
inequalities themselves, rather than by interfering with selection
procedures or removing children from their parents at birth.
Private-sector schools are objectionable to the extent that they
are part of an unfair social system; they need not be objectionable

in a society with a fair distribution of resources and rewards
(including, of course, the general availability of educational resources).

Despite a lack of commitment to overall equality of final educational outcomes, a certain equality of educational achievement
is desirable, in the sense of giving all pupils a grounding in the
basic academic disciplines, because without such a grounding a
person would be significantly disadvantaged in later life. Equality in this grounding may well involve giving children from
deprived backgrounds more in terms of resources and teachers
than are given to children from educationally better backgrounds.
Beyond this basic grounding, however, there is no reason to
suppose that equality of educational outcome is either possible or
desirable. Indeed, a proper concern for academic excellence
would not be consistent with a drive for equality of outcome. At
the same time, it is desirable both for themselves and for society
to give all pupils within the limits of their ability the chance to
fulfil their academic potential, should they wish to do so - here
again a desirable educational equality (this time of opportunity)
could justify compensatory schemes. We should try to ensure that
individual poverty, as opposed to limited national resources, does
not blight anyone's educational chances. While there is no point
in lavishing resources on those who do not wish for more than a
basic schooling merely in order to preserve a purely formal
equality of educational provision, if we believe that education is
an important good, fairness would seem to demand that anyone
who is able to profit from, say, a university education should be
enabled to do so, within the limits of the money nationally available.

## ELITISM

In Chapter 2, I mentioned the possibility that a broad general
education of the sort there proposed might be beyond the abilities of many pupils, and that to get any worthwhile distance in
subjects such as science or history, a child would have to have
above-average aptitude and motivation. The feeling that a high
proportion of the school population is by nature or culture unfitted for an academic education is one that cannot be lightly
dismissed by anyone with actual experience of teaching. We have
already examined one left-wing response to this feeling, according to which academic education is a white middle-class phenom-
enon which should not be foisted on children from other racial or
social groups. We saw, too, how Rousseau and Tolstoy found
academic study unbearably unnatural and corrupting. But there
is yet another perspective from which pessimism about the availability of academic education stems, and this is what might be
called the elitist point of view, according to which many of the
population (some say 40 per cent or more) are socially and intellectually unfitted for an academic education of any sort. The

elitist point of view shares with left-wing criticism the view that
any such education will be alienating and inappropriate for the
40 per cent in question, as well as the conclusion that what is
needed for them is another type of education altogether. Unlike
the left-wing theorists, however, the elitist places a high value
on academic study, and is also motivated by a concern that academic standards should not be diluted because of the influx of
those unsuited to academic study. What I want to show in this
section, through a consideration of some of the writings of G. H.
Bantock, is that insisting on an academic education for all need
not involve a dilution of standards, and that there is something
spurious in the claim, whether it comes from the political left or
right, that academic study is necessarily alien to people from
classes other than the bourgeoisie. As will become apparent, much
of Bantock's worry seems to stem from a feeling that the strain of
civilization is too great to bear, at least for the working classes.
Like some egalitarian left-wing idealists, and like thinkers of the
cast of Rousseau, there is a definite sense in Bantock that organic tribalism was in some ways a state preferable to one in
which everyone has to struggle and make their own decisions and
choices. From Bantock and his intellectual ancestors this stems
from a belief that many people are incapable of doing this sens-
ibly and are unhappy when faced with such responsibility, and
that for them a traditional hierarchical society affords a greater
chance of happiness. From the left, the yearning for the warmth
of a lost tribalism takes the form of a desire to discredit anything that is not available to everyone; we have seen this tendency most markedly in the case of Dewey. From the right, from
Plato on, there is the sense that the masses are incapable not
only of high culture, but also of full responsibility for their
thoughts and actions. From Dewey and egalitarian thinkers generally, there is, in the name of fraternity, a marked suspicion of
individual freedom of thought as such. This suspicion has already
been examined at sufficient length, but it is striking that thinkers of both left and right can share a distrust of the individual
and of a fully pluralistic society, even if the results of the distrust take them in rather different directions.

Bantock is, as has already been noted, committed to the worth
of the works of high culture. He is also clearly committed to the
pursuit of excellence in academic subjects. On both these points,
there is agreement between Bantock and myself. Where I will
disagree with Bantock and those who think like him is in the con-
flation of these two points into a third and clearly distinguishable
thesis, according to which only the minority who are capable of
academic excellence are really capable of benefiting from a study
of the works of high culture, such as great literature, scientific
theories, world history and so on. The third thesis is clearly
distinguishable from the other two because excellence in any area
is necessarily restricted to a minority: excellence is by definition
only by contrast to the norm. But why, it must be asked, should
high culture be available only to the above average? It is obviously

true that excellent work in the fields of high culture (as in any field) is possible only for a few, but not at all obvious that the majority should not be able to appreciate and learn from the excellent work of the few (and even less obvious that those capable of such appreciation must be from the upper strata of society, measured on economic or occupational criteria). There is indeed a tempting slide from the concept of high culture, and the realization that only a few can excel in it, to the conclusion that high culture is only for an elite, whether this elite is academically or socially defined. The temptation perhaps springs from the unfortunate phrase 'high culture', but this phrase should be used only to contrast activities such as philosophy and physics from other activities such as horse-racing or fishing. All these activities may be part of the culture of a society, but some (such as those considered in Chapter 2) are more worthwhile than others in various respects, and so are sometimes referred to as high culture. However, although the activities of high culture have their own standards of excellence, and hence their own elites, there is no a priori reason to suppose that a member of a cultural elite (such as a top physicist) has also to be a member of a social elite, nor that the majority of the population are incapable of deriving any benefit from an acquaintance with at least some of the works of the cultural elite. Bantock, indeed, does not make the mistake of supposing that the majority are by definition incapable of high culture. Instead, he offers a number of apparently empirical arguments to show that the background and traditions of the working class make it impossible for the majority of working-class children to profit from the sort of introduction to high culture an academic education is supposed to be. I say 'apparently' empirical arguments, because what will emerge from an analysis of them is that they are based in the end on value judgments and social attitudes rather than on hard empirical data.

Bantock (1952, pp. 80-1) sees the problem of quality in education as arising directly from the fact of universal education:

> It is realized that, now that for the first time in human
> history a whole population is being educated, and thus
> clamours for attention, a vast majority can find no place
> in the traditional educational system, for their mental
> abilities are inadequate to the discipline exacted.

Elsewhere (1963, p. 101) he pours scorn on the idea that there might be an unlimited supply of individuals who are capable of cultivation in the sense of being able to respond to such figures as Eliot, Pope, Plato, Wittgenstein, Namier, Gibbon, Leavis and Coleridge. In Bantock's writings it is constantly claimed that a common culture is a mirage in an advanced society in which understanding has so increased in breadth and depth. A large proportion of the population (in some places he speaks of the bottom 40 per cent immediately above the educationally subnormal) will just not benefit from an academic education which attempts to make 'the best that has been thought and said' available to them. Indeed, the effects of such an attempt will be on the one hand, to

alienate the less able from learning altogether and to debase culture itself, on the other.

It will be immediately objected to a claim that academic education
is beyond half or more of the population that its spread is by no
means equal, and that there is a far greater number of children
among the working classes who are academically less able than
could be accounted for by any differences of innate mental ability which could plausibly be said to exist between the working
classes and middle classes. Indeed, as we have seen, in 1980, a
working-class child in the UK is eleven times less likely to go to
university than a middle-class child. So, if we are talking about
untapped supplies of talent, it is surely premature to be as dismissive as Bantock is of the possibility of many more people being
able to profit from academic education than actually do. It is,
however, one of the keystones of Bantock's analysis that he does
not see educability solely, or even primarily, in terms of native
ability. For him, it is no accident that there are comparatively
few working-class undergraduates: the reason is that working-
class life is inimical to literary culture.

> The first generation grammar school boy, for instance,
> often encounters a way of speaking and thinking which may
> be quite alien to the practices and prejudices of his home.
> He becomes de-rooted, and the smatterings of culture he
> receives are not supported by his life out of school (Bantock,
> 1967, p. 179).

The gap between the academic and the non-academic mind is, in
Bantock's analysis, not a quantitative difference of intelligence.
It is a difference between types of mind, roughly corresponding
to the difference between the middle-class mind, with its penchant
for intellection, abstraction, categorization and self-consciousness,
and the working-class mind, which is typically practical, concrete,
affective, unreflective and personal. Although Bantock (1963,
p. 204) speaks of the non-academic child as less able, he is at
pains to point out that working class 'narrowness' of mind is not
necessarily a weakness; it can co-exist with 'a morally stern
individuality which represents something finer than, for instance,
Dewey's pressure for like-mindedness in action'. On the other
hand, children from the working classes have often been formed
by 'historical socio-cultural forces' to find 'the segment of "high"
culture put before them pretty meaningless', to such an extent
that even a high IQ will not necessarily indicate ability to benefit
from what is, in effect, 'a foreign cultural experience' (1965,
p. 150). Bantock backs up his claims that the working classes
are unsuited by their background for academic study, and that
academic curricula are socially irrelevant to them, by appealing to
D. H. Lawrence's Tolstoyan view that while the masses are incapable of what Lawrence calls mind-knowledge, they have a
fine sense of community and of what is truly valuable in life, and
that educators forget these facts at their peril. Bantock (1963,
p. 78) quotes from Lawrence's 'Phoenix':

> Drag a lad who has no capacity for true learning or

understanding through the processes of education and
what do you produce in him, in the end? A profound
contempt for education and for all educated people. It
has meant nothing to him but irritation and disgust. And
that which a man finds irritating and disgusting he finds
odious and contemptible.

For Bantock, the aim of educators should not be to foist an alien
culture on those culturally unable to profit from it. The tragedy
for him is that industrialization, with its impersonal mechanization
of work and life, has destroyed the old folk culture, in which a
genuine human significance was given to working-class activity.
The gap left by this process has not been filled by any general
working-class assimilation of high culture through universal education. Rather, the working classes have been an easy prey to
the unthinking warmth and dishonest fantasy purveyed by the
producers of pop culture and the mass media, by Hollywood,
Wardour Street and the advertisers. The challenge to teachers is
to devise a scheme of education culturally adapted to working-
class needs and lives, which respects and builds on the concrete-
ness and immediacy of working-class attitudes. Rather than
attempting to suppress these attitudes and replace them with
watered-down versions of 'high' or 'minority' culture which are
quite foreign to their own lives, we should be concentrating on
helping working-class children to see through the falsity and
passivity of consumer culture by building on their own penchant
for practical activity (cf. Bantock, 1968, passim).

A third element in Bantock's (1952, p. 81) attack on the attempt
to provide a basic academic education for all is an insistence on
the need to preserve cultural standards through the existence of
a cultural elite: 'No society can exist for long that allows itself to
be governed by the values of the mediocre in the manner encouraged by our civilization.' One is inevitably reminded here of the
Platonic prophecy of the disintegration of a society that is run by
men of copper or iron rather than by men of gold. Like Plato,
Bantock sees a need for a special cultural level and a special education for the gold, which is inaccessible to those formed from
baser metals. A diffusion of education, we are told, has had 'a
deleterious effect on the highest cultural standards' (Bantock,
1963, p. 71), and T. S. Eliot is quoted to the effect that an
essential condition of the preservation of the quality of the
minority culture is that it continues to be a minority culture.

Finally, in addition to the idea that more academic education
inevitably means not only a worse education but also a poisoning
of the cultural spring itself, there is the familiar appeal to the
supposed harmfulness of a little knowledge:

A careful appreciation of the dignity inherent in even a
limited undertaking - limitations consciously appreciated -
would be preferable to a system that makes a superficial
know-all of even the commonest of men (Bantock, 1952,
pp. 81-2).

It is, of course, inevitable that even the ablest of people will

nowadays be able to get only a comparatively superficial understanding of areas beyond his own specializations, but it is unclear
that a superficial understanding must inevitably produce the
smugness of the know-all. There is also - which may be worse -
the smugness of the pig ignorant, and surely, when so many
powerful political, social and religious prejudices are founded on
total ignorance, it is something of a luxury for an educated man
such as Bantock to decry the attempt to relieve ignorance in as
many people as possible. Even though most people are never
going to get very far in most disciplines, the very process of
making a properly guided start in an area of knowledge could
just as easily produce humility as the complacency of the know-all.
Indeed, the know-all condemned by Bantock is often the auto-
didact, the public library intellectual, who thinks that he can
discover all for himself, and who lacks that sense of the complexity and depth of a discipline which can be engendered by good
formal teaching even at an elementary level.

It cannot be denied that Bantock's concerns are real and worrying. The problems arising from the education of the less able,
from the unacademic nature of the social background of many
pupils and from the possible dilution of high culture are too pressing, despite so many years of universal education, to allow for
any complacency about the benefits to be derived from education.
Education is clearly not the social panacea it was once expected
to be. Teachers cannot compete on their own against an atmosphere of hostility to culture and an indifference to civilized values
with any real hope of more than limited success with particular
individuals. A degree of pessimism about the possibilities of education is clearly in place. But it is disastrous to overreact to any
of this, as becomes apparent in examining the implications of
Bantock's proposals.

For Bantock is not simply pointing out difficulties or issuing a
jeremiad. His belief is that as, for intellectual and social reasons,
an academic education of any sort is impossible for 40 per cent or
more of the population, something else must be put in its stead
for the less able. This something else is outlined in the closing
chapter of 'Education in an Industrial Society', and it takes the
form of an education in which there is a stress on pupil activity
and which centres around 'symbol and image rather than on intellectual processes'. What are to be studied and practised are such
concrete things as dance, drama, film, television, painting, pot-
tery, weaving, traditional wood and metal crafts. Presumably the
symbols and images in dance, drama, film and so on are looked at
in their immediacy. Any more general ideas that are connected
with the themes of particular dramas or films will be got at indirectly through the work, rather than systematically, as they
would if they were approached through an academic study of
science, history, literature and so on. Attention will also be paid
to the skills needed in domestic life and in dealing with machines,
as well as physical education. It is notable that there is in all
this a Dewey-like stress on communal activity and on real-life

problems, as well as implicit transgression (which Bantock recognizes) of traditional subject barriers. Perhaps more significant than the details of the curriculum for the less able is the underlying premise, which comes out in considering what is omitted from it. Bantock himself points out that formal history and geography will certainly be absent from such a curriculum; to these must be added theoretical science of any sort, mathematics and literature beyond what is related to 'immediacies of feeling and response'. (Bantock suggests that rather than studying prose, in which the logic is linear, that of sense and connectedness, the less able should be given the type of poetry whose ordering principle is emotional, evocative and imagistic, rather than rational.) As I have already suggested, the parallels between much of what Bantock proposes for the working class and what is wanted by Dewey and the deschoolers are striking, but so too are the parallels between Bantock's ideas and what Plato proposes for the lower echelons of society. What Bantock is after for the less able is, like Plato, an education which engages and directs the emotions, but which stops there. For Bantock, as we saw was the case with Plato (p. 43 above), rational reflection is beyond the ordinary man; it would be wrong to introduce him to it. Like Plato, Bantock (1963, pp. 208-9) sees the requirement for rational decision making (and hence democratic society itself) in terms of a strain, which is beyond the capability of many:

> Other strains are introduced by the fact that the basis of
> moral conduct is becoming increasingly a matter of rational
> assessment and less and less a matter of appeal to authority.
> This, to certain classes in the community, may constitute a
> gain; but, to those who find rational analysis difficult, it
> may constitute a considerable loss.

Elsewhere, Bantock (1952, p. 161) quotes Lawrence as saying that

> The secret is, to commit into the hands of the sacred few
> the responsibility which now lies like torture on the mass.
> Let the few, the leaders, be increasingly responsible for
> the whole. And let the mass be free: save for the choice
> of leaders.

It is true that Bantock explicitly disavows agreement with the social systems of Lawrence and Plato (1963, p. 224n.), but it is hard to see that his educational proposals do not lead inexorably to them. For is he not, in effect, saying that since the masses find thinking difficult, only the academic elite are to be taught to think? This elite will then do their thinking for them. In such a situation, it is clear that some form of benevolent dictatorship would be preferable to Plato's nightmare of a tyranny composed of men from the uneducated masses.

Earlier I said that Bantock's ideas were based on attitudes and prejudices rather than on empirical data. This emerges most clearly when we consider the reason why he thinks that only a sophisticated minority is really capable of intellectual and moral maturity. It is undoubtedly significant that although he refers to

intellectual impoverishment on the part of the less able, he also
says that people from the wrong background will not be able to
grasp 'high' culture, even if they are natively highly intelligent.
The bar to intellectual maturity is above all the social one of
coming from a class to which mind-consciousness is a foreign cultural experience. Now it is striking, in the first place, that many
people from working-class origins have, like Lawrence himself,
achieved greatness in the realms of the mind. So some not only
overcome the supposed barrier of a working-class background,
but, again like Lawrence, are able, precisely because of their
origins, to bring a life and freshness to aspects of high culture
that the middle classes are unable to do, just because they have
been brought up to take it all for granted. One does not have to
concede anything to Dewey's populism to insist that it is often the
outsider who is able, because of his unorthodox viewpoint, and
the struggle he has in coming to it, both to see what is really
vital in works that others hardly notice except as routine, and to
make contributions to a discipline that its traditional inheritors
would be incapable of. More radically, however, one must ask
just what it is that distinguishes the working-class mind from the
middle-class conscious mind. We are told that the working-class
mind is tied up with immediate experience; it is happy with the
specific, but not with the general or the abstract. Now while it
may be true that a manual worker will deal far more in his life
and work with practical than with theoretical questions, this does
not show that he is incapable of generalization and abstraction,
for human beings operate with general terms and abstract concepts all the time. Although bricks and mortar are concrete things,
the concepts of brick and mortar are general ideas, and, in the
case of builders, for example, may be highly refined and clearly
distinguished concepts. Equally, the notions of a fair wage or of
a good boss, or of a good fit between a nut and a bolt, are highly
abstract ones, but ones well within the experience of most workers.
It is only a romanticizing attitude to the warmth of working-class
solidarity that can lead one to think that mental abstraction and
generalization play no part in working-class life. They play a
part in any life in which there is language and discussion. So, at
that level, there is no qualitative difference between the working-
class and the middle-class mind, and, hence, no insuperable barrier of language and culture. To think that there is is to overlook
the way in which abstraction and generalization are central to any
linguistic activity. It is worth recalling here our agreement with
R. S. Peters's claim that the human life is a context in which the
demands of reason are inescapable (see p. 39 above).

There may indeed be a preference among working-class people
for the practical over the theoretical, but this does not show that
they are mentally incapable of theoretical study or reflection, or
of making original contributions to such study (where practical
directness may well be a great asset). The question Bantock is
really asking is whether it is worth trying to introduce large
numbers of people to theoretical study who may not easily take to

it in any form, given that many may not get very far in it, and
this is pre-eminently a question of value. Bantock is presumably
not going to deny that some working-class people are capable of
excelling in academic study. What he is concerned with is the vast
mass, who will achieve little. We have to ask ourselves whether a
man who has even a limited grasp of theoretical matters is better
off than one without such a grasp. There is, of course, the familiar academic distaste for a little knowledge, but then it is certainly arguable that a little soundly based knowledge is better
than a lot of ignorance. Aside from this, however, there are two
more substantial considerations which have not yet been raised.
In the first place, the decision not to allow a pupil any access to
theoretical or academic study, and so to cut him off from the
basis on which the maturity of his decision-making processes
depends, is one that will have to be taken for him by other people.
The problem of deciding who is gold and who silver or copper is
not easy, given the falsity of Plato's magnificent myth; equally,
given that there is no qualitative difference as regards powers
of abstraction and generalization between middle-class and
working-class minds, the decision not to attempt to develop, in a
high proportion of pupils, their latent powers of rational reflection is bound to seem highly arbitrary. Bantock's proposals are
for a totally different approach to the education for the able
(predominantly middle-class) from that for the less able (predominantly working-class). This would make sense only given a
qualitative difference between the mentality of the two classes,
but Bantock does not show such a difference in the relevant
respect. A working-class preference for the practical and the
immediate does not show any inbuilt obstacle to theoretical reflection, given that the powers of abstraction and generalization
which are the basis of theoretical reflection are also involved in
the type of practical activity and discussion in which the working-
classes, even on Bantock's admission, characteristically and fruit-
fully engage. It may be true that many working-class people are
less happy with theoretical reflection, or even have a distaste for
decision making, but the reason may be a combination of lack of
interest and constant indoctrination, in which case the teacher's
role should be one of stimulation and enlightenment, rather than
of acquiescence or postulation of foreign social worlds. At any
rate, it is not a matter of attempting to develop mental processes
for which the necessary powers are totally absent. Then, second,
Bantock often writes as though an academic education were narrowly intellectual and somehow at odds with a development of the
emotions and fails to satisfy the needs of the affective life. He
correctly points out (1963, p. 171) that progress in an academic
discipline involves an acceptance of loneliness and solitariness,
which people from working-class backgrounds may find particularly hard to bear because of the way going to a university, say,
takes them out of their natural environment of warmth and solidarity. But not only am I not suggesting that everyone, even
everyone of ability, should be made to go as far as university,

but an integral part of the academic education I am recommending
for all is a study of literature and the arts, which is directly concerned with the humane centre of life. So academic education is
not intellectual to the exclusion of the engagement of the emotions.

It is far from clear that Bantock has pointed to anything in
working-class life which makes the attempt to give all children a
grounding in science, history and social studies, and in literature
and the arts, utterly pointless. I have argued all along that such
a grounding would be necessary for anyone to be able to face the
strain of civilization with equanimity. It remains a matter of value
to decide whether to give everyone such a grounding, even given
the undoubted fact that this will involve a struggle in many cases
and bear little obvious fruit in many others. I believe that some
such grounding for all, however basic it might be in many cases,
is better than giving half the population no chance in these areas
at all. There are supplementary reasons for this, to do with the
difficulties inherent in drawing as sharp a line between the able
and the less able as Bantock's proposals would require, and the
human cost of error here, but my main reason in favour of my
proposal is that the opposite proposal involves an unacceptably
dismissive attitude to the less able. In effect they are being told,
'You are incapable of understanding what the world is really like,
so you are better off staying within the narrowness of your work
and your social group - at any rate, we shan't do anything to
broaden your horizons.' Bantock's proposals would have many of
the same results as the left-wing demand for curricula confined
to what is relevant to real-life experience, and are open to the
criticisms I made of the demands for relevance in teaching
(Chapter 1, pp. 29-31). But there is more to Bantock's elitism
than purely academic consequences. If the less able are predominantly working class, and if one reason why they are less
able is because of 'socio-historical forces' (i.e. working-class
origins), then his proposals for an education for the less able in
terms of what he takes to be the values of working-class life
begin to have dangerously repressive implications. For not only
are the working classes to be given what is in effect a qualita-
tively inferior education, which will clearly tend to make them
unsuited for professional or administrative posts, but a whole
hereditary cycle of class-based inferiority is to be sustained
through the education system. In other words, Bantock's academic
elite is likely to become a hereditary social elite, and his education system would appear to be inimical to the ideals of openness and maximization of individual freedom and choice defended
in this book. For although, as I argued strongly in the last
section, there is nothing inherently unfair or objectionable about
an education system which honestly recognizes differences of
ability and which allows the excellent to excel, even when these
differences reflect differences of home background, what Bantock
is proposing is a system that effectively cuts the less able off
from any participation at all in the understanding and insight
that is available in high culture. In other words, his academic

elitism is likely to be socially divisive and discriminatory, because of its refusal to admit any possibility of a commonly shared cultural and intellectual basis, and its embedding of this refusal in the education system. His world will be very much one of one type of culture for the educated and another for the workers, and in such a world it would be almost impossible to discern any real distinction between academic success and social success.

From the perspective of what has been said in the last paragraph, Bantock's no doubt genuine concern for the preservation of high cultural values begins to look like a disguised plea for cultural and social privilege. For there is nothing in the demand for a common basic academic education which is inconsistent with the disinterested pursuit of excellence in the various disciplines, nor is there anything in the ideal that everyone shares a basic grounding in several subjects which implies acceptance of Dewey-like universal mediocrity or the absence of distinctions of excellence within those subjects. My quarrel with Dewey was over his claim that what is not fully communicable to all is not worthwhile. Not everything that is valuable in high culture will be fully communicable to anyone (let alone everyone), but this is no reason for despairing of all attempts to communicate something of it to everyone, or for thinking that what is thus communicated will necessarily be too diluted to be of any value. In other words, high cultural standards surely do not rule out a common culture or a common basic curriculum, so long as there is scope for the best to develop beyond the norm. Indeed the sort of respect for learning and high cultural achievement which presumably both Bantock and I would wish to exist in the community as a whole is surely best fostered, not by a superstitious ignorance of culture on the part of the many, but by a personal acquaintance on the part of each member of the community with the standards and values of the various disciplines. It is far from clear that this sort of diffusion of high culture must inevitably mean a dilution of it; how are the standards weakened or even affected by the whole population being introduced to them and to the great achievements that embody them? Moreover, effective participation of the whole society in the democratic process surely presupposes that everyone is recognizably educated to some degree in the way suggested in Chapter 2, which would certainly not be the case if half the population knew only about practical skills and mechanics. It would surely be no argument in favour of Bantock if someone were to point out that this is largely true of England now, that many people prominent in public life show very little sign of a good general education and that people are divided by education and class in the way Bantock proposes. What we have to do is to create a situation in which, although the achievements of the scientist, the philosopher, the civil servant, the manager, the miner, the builder and the farm worker may all be different, in various areas and in various respects, they all have enough knowledge and competence to be able to use the basic achievements of theoretical science, of history and the social sciences and of literature and the arts, to find some sort of personal orientation for themselves in the world (or, as Eliot would put it, to be able to bear the strain of being conscious about everything).

To argue in favour of a basic academic education for all is not to say in any detail how far one can or should go in the disciplines concerned. These are practical questions, largely to be determined by teachers and planners of curricula. What can be argued for on philosophical grounds, however, is that the attempt must be made for social and personal reasons. The reasons Bantock gives for the inability of the working classes to think are spurious, and his proposals are far more likely to lead to repression and false enlightenment, and to be destructive of civilization, than the attempt to provide a universal education in mind consciousness. While in traditional hierarchical societies, it may have been possible to give the masses only limited education without too much damage to the cultural fabric, the structures that made rigid class divisions bearable have largely gone. Either they will have to be artificially imposed or, if power does go to the people we are likely to have a tyranny of the uneducated. Neither prospect is pleasing. The best hope for peaceful development, and for constructive as opposed to destructive conflict in society, is the common basis of a reasoned and informed approach to life and problems, which it is to be hoped an academic education will bring.

It is important to realize that a common basic education does not mean an absence of conflict or disagreement, even on academic matters. As was pointed out in Chapter 2, disagreement and conflict is highly fruitful, even in academic study. But what such study should do is to instil into people the values of reasonableness and of openness in argument. This is hardly likely to emerge from a policy which assumes that the mass of the people are incapable of reasoning and of disinterested study, and which deliberately deprives them of chances in it.

Naturally, as has been pointed out already, the academic core of education is not directly relevant to work outside academic circles, nor should it be expected to have any direct practical bearing on life. It is, therefore, imperative to emphasize as far as possible the inappropriateness of the use of academic examinations as job qualifications. Only by emphasizing this will pupils and students begin to see academic disciplines as means of understanding the world, rather than as bodies of knowledge to be learned in order to get a certificate or degree and relevant to their own experience only in terms of getting a job. (On these problems see Bantock, 1967, pp. 191-2.) On the other hand, there is a great deal to be said for having properly conducted and understood academic examinations. Objective tests of ability not only help people to focus their minds and efforts, but they are also highly effective in bringing about a realization of the existence and nature of the standards of a discipline.

It cannot be pretended that academic work is easy, nor should academic disciplines be sold either as stepping stones to jobs or as instantly gratifying. To adopt these strategies is dishonest

and ultimately self-defeating. But to fail to give all children a
reasonable chance of academic study during their schooldays, or
to reserve such study to the elite who take to it easily, is surely
to deprive the less able of what they are entitled to and what the
school exists pre-eminently to provide. It is because intellectual
and moral maturity are essential to a person's self-respect in a
pluralistic society that Bantock's elitism is to be resisted. To fail
to provide the necessary basis for independence of judgment is
to leave a child open to all sorts of insidious persuaders and pur-
veyors of false enlightenment. Bantock, to be fair, wants his
curriculum for the less able to lead children to unlearn 'the
emotional falseness of popular culture' (1968, p. 83) and to ask
'qualitative questions in relation to the concrete things they all
see and use' (1963, p. 216), but a full independence of judgment,
as well as the critical approach he wants to foster towards works
of dance, drama, film and television, surely require at least some
formal grounding in many areas excluded from Bantock's curriculum.

Independence and maturity of judgment is, in the end, what is
required of a man in a pluralistic society; this is the task teachers
are set - to bring their pupils to a state in which they are informed and disciplined enough to exercise their choice to the best
effect. The task is hard and the problems can seem overwhelming,
especially with the less able, but to call it impossible is tantamount
to admitting that all schools can really do is mind children and
keep them occupied with concrete tasks until they reach the age
at which they can enter the factory. We should indeed be sensitive to the intellectual and cultural difficulties faced by children
embarking on academic work, but we should not give in to the
children or the problems. Here, indeed, we can agree with Lawrence (quoted by Bantock, 1952, p. 177) that we should not stand
for the

> nervous, twisting, wistful, pathetic, centreless children we
> are cursed with: or the fat and self-satisfied, sheep-in-the-
> pasture children who are becoming more common: or the
> impudent, I'm-as-good-as-anybody smirking children who
> are far too numerous.

If we really love children, rather than giving in to them, and to
the difficulties they present, we must be prepared to stimulate
them, to be angry with them, to rouse them, to discipline them,
in order to bring them to freedom and self-respect - and all this
in an intellectual as well as in a moral way.

# CONCLUSION:
## Education and philosophy

In the Introduction to this book I stated that one's educational
aims would reflect one's general ideas about the way people should
live in the world. We saw in the early chapters how various concepts of education depend on various systems of value, and how a
full discussion of educational aims leads one naturally to tackle
substantive questions of value. In later chapters it was suggested
that basic curricular decisions could not be taken in isolation from
one's general view of society, and shown how one particular view
of man and society led to certain conclusions about what should be
taught and to whom. We also saw how any form of teaching and
learning requires on the part of teachers and learners a common
starting point in language and tradition, and ultimately in a
shared human nature. This became important in considering moral
education, which could only begin given primitive reactions of
sympathy on the part of the learner.

Thus it became clear that many educational questions lead to a
discussion of difficult philosophical issues. This book, then, can
be seen not merely as a set of chapters on educational issues, but
also as an introduction to some central philosophical problems,
such as the nature of knowledge and understanding, the distinction between different types of knowledge, relativism, the
basis of morality and the nature of moral choice, the desirability
(or otherwise) of democracy and equality and the status of religious claims. I hope that I have not merely shown the way in
which these and other philosophical questions naturally arise from
many educational debates, but that I have also suggested how a
deeper study of philosophy is required for those who would like
to take the debates further.

# BIBLIOGRAPHY

Althusser, L. (1971), Ideology and ideological state apparatuses, in his 'Lenin and Philosophy and Other Essays', New Left Books, London, pp. 121-73.
Aristotle, 'Nicomachaean Ethics'.
Babs Fafunwa, A. (1967), 'New Perspectives in African Education', George Allen & Unwin, London.
Bantock, G.H. (1952), 'Freedom and Authority in Education', Faber & Faber, London, 1970.
— (1963), 'Education in an Industrial Society', Faber & Faber, London.
— (1965), 'Education and Values', Faber & Faber, London.
— (1967), 'Education, Culture and the Emotions', Faber & Faber, London.
— (1968), 'Culture, Industrialisation and Education', Routledge & Kegan Paul, London.
— (1970), 'T. S. Eliot and Education', Faber & Faber, London.
Barrow, R. (1975), 'Plato, Utilitarianism and Education', Routledge & Kegan Paul, London.
— (1978), 'Radical Education', Martin Robertson, London.
Berlin, I. (1969), 'Four Essays on Liberty', Oxford University Press.
— (1978), 'Russian Thinkers', The Hogarth Press, London.
Bernstein, B. (1971), On the classification and framing of educational knowledge, in Young (1971), pp. 47-69.
Bourdillon, B. (1945), 'The Future of the Colonial Empire', SCM Press, London.
Brown, G. and Hiskett, M. (1975), 'Conflict and Harmony in Education in Tropical Africa', George Allen & Unwin, London.
Cooper, D. (1980a), 'Illusions of Equality', Routledge & Kegan Paul, London.
— (1980b), Experience and the growth of understanding, 'Journal of Philosophy of Education', Vol. 14, no. 1, pp. 97-103.
Davidson, D. (1975), Belief and meaning, in Guttenplan (1975), pp. 7-23.
Dearden, R. (1968), 'The Philosophy of Primary Education', Routledge & Kegan Paul, London.
— (1972), Happiness and education, in Dearden, Hirst and Peters (1972), pp. 95-112.
Dearden, R., Hirst, P. and Peters, R. (editors) (1972), 'Education and the Development of Reason', Routledge & Kegan Paul, London.
Dewey, J. (1916), 'Democracy and Education', Macmillan, New York, 1961.
— (1938), 'Experience and Education', Macmillan, New York.
Downie, R., Loudfoot, E. and Telfer, E. (1974), 'Education and Personal Relationships', Methuen & Co., London.
Durkheim, E. (1952), 'Suicide', Routledge & Kegan Paul, London.
Dworkin, R. (1977), Reverse discrimination, in his 'Taking Rights Seriously', Duckworth, London, pp. 223-39.
Esland, G. (1971), Teaching and learning as the organization of knowledge, in Young (1971), pp. 70-115.
Evans, G. (1975), Identity and predication, 'Journal of Philosophy', Vol. 72, pp. 343-63.
Evans-Pritchard, E. (1956), 'Nuer Religion', Clarendon Press, Oxford.
Frazer, J. (1922), 'The Golden Bough', Macmillan, London, abridged edition, 1957.
Freire, P. (1972), 'Pedagogy of the Oppressed', Penguin Books, Harmondsworth.
Guttenplan, S. (editor) (1975), 'Mind and Language', Oxford University Press.
Hamlyn, D. (1978), 'Experience and the Growth of Understanding', Routledge & Kegan Paul, London.

Hamlyn, D. (1981), What exactly is social about the origins of understanding?, in P. Light and G. Butterworth (editors), 'The Individual and the Social in Cognitive Development', Harvester Press, Brighton.
Hare, R. (1964), 'The Language of Morals', Oxford University Press.
Hirst, P.H. (1965), Liberal education and the nature of knowledge, in Peters (1973d), pp. 87-111.
—— (1974), 'Knowledge and the Curriculum', Routledge & Kegan Paul, London.
Hull, C. (1951), 'Essentials of Behaviour', Yale University Press, New Haven.
Illich, I. (1971), 'Deschooling Society', Calder & Boyars, London.
Jencks, C. (1972), 'Inequality', Penguin Books, Harmondsworth, 1975.
Keddie, N. (1971), Classroom knowledge, in Young (1971), pp. 133-60.
King, E. (1962), 'World Perspectives in Education', Methuen & Co., London.
Kuhn, T. (1962), 'The Structure of Scientific Revolutions', Chicago University Press.
Leavis, F. (1972), 'Nor Shall My Sword', Chatto & Windus, London.
Lévi-Strauss, C. (1966), 'The Savage Mind', Weidenfeld & Nicolson, London.
Mann, T. (1947), 'Doctor Faustus', Penguin Books, Harmondsworth, 1968.
Mao Tse-Tung (1937), Combat liberalism, in Mao Tse-Tung 'Selected Works', Vol. 2, Pergamon Press, Oxford, 1965, pp. 31-3.
Marx, K. and Engels, F. (1845), 'The German Ideology', Collected Works, Vol. 5, Lawrence & Wishart, London, 1976.
Mill, J.S. (1859), 'On Liberty', Fontana Collins, London, (1962).
Murdoch, I. (1970), 'The Sovereignty of the Good', Routledge & Kegan Paul, London.
—— (1977), 'The Fire and the Sun', Oxford University Press.
Musil, R. (1906), 'Young Törless', Granada Publishing, London, 1971.
—— (1979), 'The Man Without Qualities', Picador, London.
Niblett, W. (editor) (1963), 'Moral Education in a Changing Society', Faber & Faber, London.
Nietzsche, F. (1872), 'The Birth of Tragedy'.
—— (1881), 'The Dawn of Day' ('Morgenröte').
Nowell-Smith, P. (1954), 'Ethics', Penguin Books, Harmondsworth.
Peters, R. (1963), Reason and habit: the paradox of moral education, in Niblett (1963), pp. 46-65.
—— (1966), 'Ethics and Education', George Allen & Unwin, London.
—— (1973a), 'Authority, Responsibility and Education', George Allen & Unwin, London, third edition.
—— (1973b), Aims of education: a conceptual enquiry, in Peters (1973d), pp. 11-57.
—— (1973c), The justification of education, in Peters (1973d), pp. 239-67.
—— (1973d), 'The Philosophy of Education', Oxford University Press.
—— (1979), Democratic values and educational aims, 'Teachers College Record', Vol. 80(3), pp. 463-82.
Plato, 'Apology'.
—— 'The Republic'.
Platts, M. (1979), 'Ways of Meaning', Routledge & Kegan Paul, London.
Popper, K. (1945), 'The Open Society and Its Enemies', Routledge & Kegan Paul, London, (1964).
—— (1957), 'The Poverty of Historicism', Routledge & Kegan Paul, London.
—— (1963), 'Conjectures and Refutations', Routledge & Kegan Paul, London.
Postman, N. and Weingartner, C. (1971), 'Teaching as a Subversive Activity', Penguin Books, Harmondsworth.
Prance, N. (1971), The Amish and compulsory school attendance: recent developments, 'Wisconsin Law Review', Vol. 3, pp. 832-53.
Putnam, H. (1969), Is logic empirical?, 'Boston Studies in the Philosophy of Science', Vol. 5, Reidel, Dordrecht, pp. 216-41.
Quine, W. (1951), Two dogmas of empiricism, in his 'From a Logical Point of View', Harper Torchbooks, New York, 1963, pp. 20-46.
—— (1960), 'Word and Object', MIT Press, Cambridge, Massachusetts.
—— (1969), 'Ontological Relativity', Columbia University Press, New York and London.

Rawls, J. (1972), 'A Theory of Justice', Clarendon Press, Oxford.

Reimer, E. (1971), 'School is Dead', Penguin Books, Harmondsworth.

Rosen, C. and Rosen, H. (1973), 'The Language of Primary School Children', Penguin Books, Harmondsworth.

Rousseau, J.J. (1762), 'Emile', J. M. Dent, London, Everyman edition, 1911.

Sarup, M. (1978), 'Marxism and Education', Routledge & Kegan Paul, London.

Scheffler, I. (1973), 'Reason and Teaching', Routledge & Kegan Paul, London.

Snook, I. (1972), 'Concepts of Indoctrination', Routledge & Kegan Paul, London.

Snow, C. (1964), 'The Two Cultures and A Second Look', Cambridge University Press.

Tolstoy, L. (1882), 'A Confession', Oxford University Press, London, 1940.

Warnock, M. (1977), 'Schools of Thought', Faber & Faber, London.

White, J.P. (1973), 'Towards a Compulsory Curriculum', Routledge & Kegan Paul, London.

Winch, P. (1963), 'The Idea of a Social Science', Routledge & Kegan Paul, London.

Wittgenstein, L. (1953), 'Philosophical Investigations', Basil Blackwell, Oxford.

—— (1967), 'Remarks on the Foundations of Mathematics', Basil Blackwell, Oxford.

Wright Mills, C. (1939), Language, logic and culture, 'American Sociological Review', Vol. 4, pp. 670-80.

Young, M. (1977), Curriculum change: limits and possibilities, in Young and Whitty (1977), pp. 236-52.

—— (editor) (1971), 'Knowledge and Control', Collier-Macmillan, London.

Young, M. and Whitty, G. (editors) (1977), 'Society, State and Schooling', Falmer Press, Ringmer.

# INDEX